HARRY POTTER
BAKING
BOOK

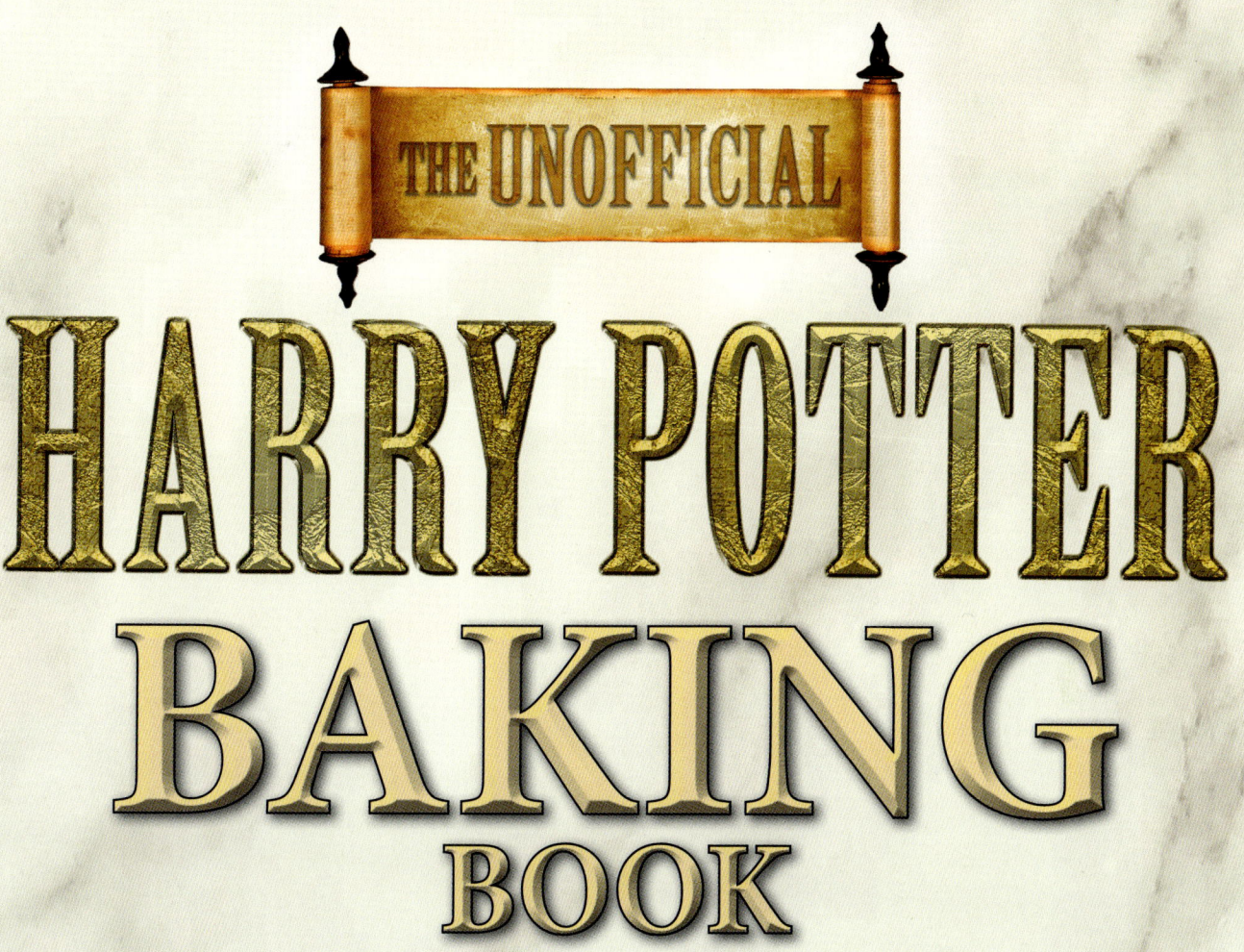

THE UNOFFICIAL HARRY POTTER BAKING BOOK

By Katja Böhm & Tom Grimm

With Photos by Tom Grimm & Dimitrie Harder

For Hannah,

she knows why.

Moseley Road Inc.

Originally published in German by HEEL Verlag GmbH,
under the title: Das inoffizielle Backbuch für Harry Potter Fans
All rights reserved.

HEEL Verlag GmbH,
Pottscheidt Estate
53639 Königswinter, Germany.
Tel.: 02223 9230-0
Fax: 02223 9230-13
E-Mail: info@heel-verlag.de
Web: www.heel-verlag.de

PROJECT MANAGEMENT: Hannah Kwella
PROJECT EDITOR: Tom Grimm, Grinning Cat Productions
RECIPES: Katja Böhm, Tom Grimm
FOOD PHOTOGRAPHY: Dimitrie Harder & Tom Grimm
GRAPHIC DESIGN, TYPESETTING & LAYOUT: Roberts Urlovskis
COPYWRITING: Roberts Urlovskis & Tom Grimm
ENDPAPER ILLUSTRATION & GOLD DOBBY: Angelos Tsirigotis
EDITOR: Andreas Kasprzak

US Editor: Finn Moore
US Production: Adam Moore
Cover Design: Adam Moore
US Publisher: Sean Moore

Translated from the German by Finn Moore

DISCLAIMER
Some words are trademarked and are the property of the trademark holder. They have been used for identification purposes only with no intention of infringement of the trademark. The book is not authorized or endorsed by J.K. Rowling, Pottermore Ltd., Wizarding World Digital LLC., Warner Bros. Entertainment Inc. or any other Harry Potter rights holder. All texts, graphic elements, and properties in this book are used exclusively within the framework of the right of quotation according the German Copyright Act (Urhebergesetz §5) and the Berne Convention; any aforementioned copyright holders and / or other Harry Potter Rights holders remain unaffected.

The recipes in this book are tried and tasted by the author. Every effort has been taken to review each recipe carefully. You may not always achieve the results desired due to various reasons like quality of products, variations in ingredients, individual cooking ability etc. The reader assumes full responsibility for using their best judgment when cooking with raw ingredients such as eggs, and seeking information from an official food safety authority if they are unsure. Readers should review all listed ingredients in a recipe before cooking to ensure that none of the ingredients may cause a potential adverse reaction to anyone eating the food based on recipes featured this book. This includes allergies, pregnancy-related diet restrictions, etc. This book and the recipes contained in it have been written to the best of our knowledge and belief. Neither the publisher nor the author bear responsibility for unintended reactions or adverse affects.

ISBN: 978-1-62669-199-5
Printed in China
10 9 8 7 6 5 4 3 2 1

Index

SWEETS FOR THE SWEET!	10
BUTTERBEER COOKIES	12
FIZZING WHIZZBEES	14
HOGWARTS CRESTS	16
HARRY'S BIRTHDAY CAKE	18
OWL NUTS	20
BUTTERBEER	22
SHORTBREAD HOWLERS	24
BERTIE BOTT'S EVERY FLAVOR BEANS	26
POLYJUICE JELLO	28
DUDLEY DURSLEY'S DONUTS	30
LIQUID APPLE PIE	32
WAFFLES WITH BUTTERBEER SYRUP	34
BUTTERBEER POPCORN	36
BUTTERBEER PUDDING	38
MELT-IN-YOUR-MOUTH SNOWFLAKES	40
BUTTERBEER ICE CREAM	42
AUNT PETUNIA'S CHOCOLATE CAKE	44
JAM DOUGHNUTS	46
HEDWIG THE MUFFIN OWL	48
PEPPERMINT CANDIES	50
BUTTERBEER FUDGE	52
DUMBLEDORE'S FAVORITE TEA	54
PUMPKIN JUICE	56
OWL POPS	58
BUTTERBEER MACARONS	60
AUNT PETUNIA'S WINDTORTE	63
MAGIC BUBBLE BREAD	66
TON-TONGUE TOFFEES	68
MRS. WEASLEY'S CARROT CAKE	70
DROOBLE'S BEST BLOWING GUM	72
DUMBLEDORE'S FAVORITE LEMON DROPS	74
GINGER COOKIES	76
CANARY CREAM PUFFS	78
GOLDEN SNITCH	80
TREACLE TART	82
CANDIED PINEAPPLE	85

ROCK CAKES	88
HICCUP DROPS	90
MINCE PIES	92
FEVER FUDGE	94
GRINGOTTS GOLD COINS	96
RED CURRANT RUM	98
FLOREAN FORTESCUE'S CHILI ICE CREAM	100
FIVE-LAYER TRIFLE	102
PLUM PUDDING	104
MANDRAKE	106
LUNA'S LOVELY FRUIT PUDDING	108
CHRISTMAS CAKE	110
MAGIC CAULDRON	112
SOUR DROPS	114
COTTON CANDY	116
EGGNOG	118
WOLFSBANE POTION	120
CHOCOLATE GATEAU	122
AMORTENTIA	124
BUTTERBEER SHORTBREAD	126
CINNAMON-CARAMEL MAGIC	128
LICORICE WANDS	130
CHOCOLATE ACROMANTULAS	132
ANIMAGUS CAKE	134
BUTTERBEER CHEESECAKE	136
SLUG CLUB PROFITEROLES	138
CRUMPETS	140
PUKING PASTILLES	142
FELIX FELICIS	144
CHOCOLATE STRAWBERRIES	146
PROF. SLUGHORN'S POPCORN BALLS	148
APPLE CAKE	150
PEPPER IMPS	152
BLANCMANGE	154
CROSS BUNS	156
MAGIC BEANS	158
TRIPLE TARTLETS	160
LEMON-CURD ECLAIRS	163

RED CURRANT SYRUP	166
SQUEAKING SUGAR MICE	168
MAGIC POTION	170
STICKY TOFFEE PUDDING	172
SKIVING SNACKS	174
HAGRID'S GRYFFINDOR HOUSE CAKE	176
BRANDY BALLS	178
RASPBERRY JAM	180
FAINTING FANCIES	182
NOSEBLEED NOUGAT	184
LEMON ICE POP	186
CHOCOLATE FROGS	188
GHOST PRETZELS	190
ACKNOWLEDGEMENTS	192

Sweets for the Sweet!

Food and drink play a major role in the magical world of Harry Potter. The wizarding world's sweet tooth is particularly fond of desserts. Whether it's pies, cakes, muffins, cookies, waffles, donuts, candies, chocolates, ice cream, or puddings, when Hagrid proudly serves up his latest baking creations, Mrs. Weasley sends one of her famous "survival packages" full of delicious treats to Hogwarts, or Aunt Petunia surprises the neighbors with impressive baked goods, even the battle against you-know-who is forgotten in one fell swoop!

Enchantment in baking - the title of one of the most famous cookbooks of the wizarding world - is the program for Harry & Co. The book catches Harry's eye on his very first visit to the Burrow, the cozy ancestral home of the Weasley family. The most famous wizard student of all time is particularly taken with Mrs. Weasley's grandiose chocolate cake made for his birthday, as well as the annual Christmas cookies. Yet the preparation of these delights has nothing whatsoever to do with Molly Weasley's wizardry, for, as we know, conjuring food is one of the five "Essential Exceptions" to "Gamp's Law of Elemental Transfiguration," which means that it is impossible to make good food out of nothing. You can conjure it if you know where some is, you can transform it into something else, you can make more of what you already have, but you cannot make a feast out of empty air. In other words, you conjure up already existing food and drink from somewhere else, like a school kitchen, a restaurant, or a pantry. Someone must have already prepared them, with the necessary skill, according to a recipe and using the necessary ingredients - just like in real life!

Which, by the way, is one of the secrets of Harry Potter's phenomenal success. For as fantastic as the wizarding world may seem, it is ultimately only superficially about magic. In fact, on closer inspection, the Potter universe proves to be downright sobering. Apart from their magical powers, Harry and his friends are ultimately ordinary teenagers with the same worries and hardships as all other teenagers: they have to cram for school, are bullied by classmates, experience their first great love and their first bitter disappointment - all things that any of us can identify with.

What's more, in the end it's neither spells nor potions nor any magical gimmicks that make "Dumbledore's Army" triumph over evil, but friendship, courage, loyalty, and a willingness to make sacrifices - basic human virtues that we Muggles possess to the same extent as the wizards in Harry's world. In other words, apart from talking hats, friendly giants with pink umbrellas, motorcycles that rattle through the air, and all that other wizarding stuff, Harry & Co. live in exactly the same realms as we do, in familiar surroundings with familiar problems - and with familiar food and drink, at least for the most part.

Accordingly, you, gentle readers, don't need a wand or any other quirky magical paraphernalia to "summon" the food and drink presented here. All it takes is a visit to the local supermarket, where you can get all the things you need. All you need is a few simple kitchen tools and a little creativity to create tasty delicacies from such mundane ingredients as flour, yeast, and water. After all, the greatest thing about baking is experimenting! That's why these recipes are all just starting points for your own sweet journey.

Just like in the world of Harry Potter, the only limits imposed on you in the kitchen are those of your own imagination. Besides, the greatest magic we Muggles are capable of is making other people happy. What better way to do that than with a legendarily delicious slice of treacle tart?

With this in mind, enjoy your magic!

Katja Böhm & Tom Grimm

BUTTERBEER COOKIES

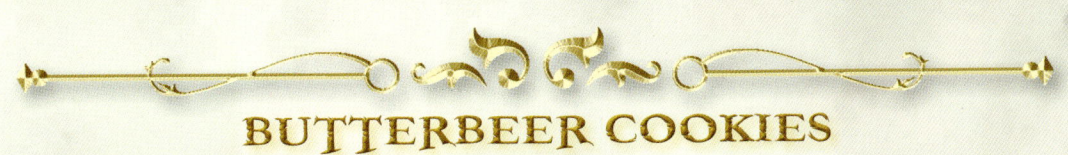

INGREDIENTS FOR APPROX. 25 COOKIES

10 oz soft butter
6 oz cane sugar
1 pinch salt
1 tsp vanilla extract
1 egg
11 oz flour
1 tsp baking powder
5 oz macadamia nuts, coarsely chopped
7 oz butterbeer fudge (see p. 52), coarsely chopped
4 oz dark chocolate, coarsely chopped

1. Preheat the oven to 340 °F heat. Line a baking tray with baking paper.

2. Beat the softened butter in the bowl of a food processor until fluffy. Add the cane sugar, salt and vanilla extract and continue to beat. Add the egg and beat until incorporated

3. In a separate bowl, combine the flour and baking powder. Add to the remaining ingredients in the food processor and mix thoroughly. Finally, add the coarsely-chopped macadamia nuts, butterbeer fudge, and chocolate and stir to combine.

4. Ladle one tablespoon at a time onto a baking sheet with enough space between them. Bake in the preheated oven for about 12-14 minutes. Then remove and let cool completely on the baking sheet.

FIZZING WHIZZBEES

INGREDIENTS FOR APPROX. 20-25 WHIZZBEES
3 fl. oz cherry juice
8 oz sugar
2 oz dextrose
½ tsp citric acid powder (food grade)
2 packets of sherbet powder

Also needed: sugar thermometer, lollipop sticks, lollipop silicone mold (optional).

1. Prepare the silicone mold and the lollipop sticks.
2. Place the cherry juice, sugar, and dextrose in a small saucepan and bring to a boil over medium heat, stirring constantly until the sugar is completely dissolved. Increase the temperature and from now on do not stir! Use the sugar thermometer to check the temperature. When the syrup reaches 310 °F, remove from heat and place on a heat-resistant surface.
3. Quickly stir in the citric acid.
4. Gently pour the mixture into the silicone mold, add the lollipop sticks and leave to harden in the open. Be careful: the sugar mixture is very hot!
5. Once the lollipops have hardened, pour the sherbet powder into a small bowl and roll the Fizzing Whizzbees in it so that they are coated all around. Store in an airtight container.

If you don't have a silicone mold handy, simply line a baking sheet with parchment paper instead, position the lollipop sticks on the sheet, and spoon a blob of sugar syrup onto the top of each stick. Roughly shape the syrup, gently twist the stem to get it right, and then let the whole thing set at your leisure. Then roll in sherbet powder as described above.

HOGWARTS CRESTS

INGREDIENTS FOR APPROX. 8 HOGWARTS CRESTS

For the dough:
9 oz flour
1 packet of baking powder
1 packet of caramel-flavored pudding powder
4 oz butter
4 oz sugar
1 pinch of salt
Some vanilla extract
2 eggs
2 fl. oz milk

For the decoration:
7 oz powdered sugar
3 tbsp lemon juice
Different colored fondant (red, green, yellow, blue)

Also needed: silicone stamps of the different Hogwarts houses, piping bag

1. Preheat the oven to 390 °F heat. Line a baking tray with baking paper.

2. Mix the flour with the baking powder and the pudding powder in a bowl.

3. In a separate bowl, beat the butter with the sugar, salt, and vanilla extract with a hand mixer until fluffy. One at a time, beat in the two eggs. Gradually sift the flour-pudding powder mixture into the butter mixture, stir in the milk, and mix thoroughly.

4. Pour the dough into a piping bag and pipe eight equal-sized blobs onto the baking sheet. (If you don't have a piping bag handy, just cut a small corner off a freezer bag.) Leave enough space between the blobs, as the dough will still run a bit! Bake in the preheated oven for about 10-15 minutes. Remove and let cool completely.

5. Roll out the colored fondant thinly, cut out circular pieces of each with a glass a bit larger than the Hogwarts silicone stamps, and emboss the fondant in each house color with the corresponding crest. As a reminder, Gryffindor is red, Hufflepuff is yellow, Ravenclaw is blue, and Slytherin is green.

6. In a small bowl, mix the powdered sugar with the lemon juice to make a thick cream. Spread the icing evenly over the dough. Then place the fondant crests on top of the still warm, sticky icing, press down lightly, and wait a few minutes for them to stick.

HARRY'S BIRTHDAY CAKE

INGREDIENTS FOR 1 CAKE

For the chocolate cake:
7 oz dark chocolate, coarsely chopped
11oz butter
8 eggs
9 oz sugar
1 tsp vanilla extract
1 pinch of salt
1 oz baking cocoa
2 level tsp baking powder
8 oz flour
For the buttercream:
1 packet vanilla pudding powder
14 fl. oz milk
1 oz sugar
8 oz butter at room temperature
2 oz powdered sugar
Green food coloring
Red food coloring
Also required: springform pan (approx. 10" in diameter), piping bag with fine nozzle

1. Preheat the oven to 320 °F heat. Line the bottom of a springform pan with baking paper.

2. Melt the butter in a saucepan at low temperature. Add the chocolate and melt. Then let the chocolate mixture cool for a few minutes. Meanwhile, in a bowl, whisk together the eggs, sugar, vanilla extract, and salt. Add the cooled chocolate mixture and continue to stir vigorously.

3. In a separate bowl, mix the baking cocoa and baking powder with the flour, add to the wet ingredients, and mix until smooth. Pour into the springform pan and bake in the preheated oven for about 30-35 minutes. Turn the cake out onto a plate and let it cool completely. Remove the baking parchment and cut the cake horizontally once in the middle.

4. Prepare the vanilla pudding according to the package instructions, but only use 13.5 fl. oz of milk and 2 tbsp of sugar. Cover with plastic wrap and let cool to room temperature. Meanwhile, place the room-temperature butter and sifted powdered sugar in a bowl and beat with a mixer until fluffy. Then add the pudding by the tablespoon and continue to beat on high speed. Set aside ¼ of the cream for the filling. Take some of the remaining cream for the writing and color it with green food coloring. Color the rest pink with red food coloring.

5. Place the bottom cake layer on a cake plate and spread evenly with the uncolored buttercream. Place the second cake layer on top, press down lightly and spread the entire cake evenly with the pink cream. Place the green buttercream in a piping bag with a fine nozzle and pipe a birthday greeting onto the cake as desired. Let dry for a few minutes before serving.

OWL NUTS

INGREDIENTS FOR APPROX. 50 OWL NUTS

For the pastry:
5 oz flour
4 oz butter
2 oz sugar
1 egg yolk
1 pinch of salt
1 tbsp water

For the filling:
2 egg whites
1 pinch of salt
1 tsp lemon juice
6 oz sugar
Approx. 50 Toffee candies

Also required: round cookie cutter (approx. 3" in diameter), piping bag with fine nozzle

1. In a large mixing bowl, mix all the ingredients for the dough and place loosely covered with plastic wrap in the refrigerator for one hour.

2. Meanwhile, in an ungreased bowl, beat the egg whites with a pinch of salt and the lemon juice using a hand mixer. Slowly, little by little, add the sugar and continue beating until firm peaks are formed. Chill in the refrigerator.

3. Preheat the oven to 320 °F heat. Line a baking tray with baking paper.

4. Remove the dough from the refrigerator after chilling and roll out on a lightly-floured work surface with a rolling pin until approx. ¼ inch thick. Then, using a round cookie cutter that should be slightly larger than a Toffifee, cut out small circles from the dough and place them on the prepared baking sheet, spacing them slightly apart. Place a Toffifee on each circle of dough, with the "flat" side down.

5. Pour the stiffly-beaten egg whites into a piping bag fitted with a fine nozzle and pipe the meringue onto the Toffifees in a spiral from the bottom to the top. Bake in the oven for about 18 minutes. Remove and let cool on the tray for a few minutes. Best enjoyed still warm while the Toffifee filling is nice and soft and creamy!

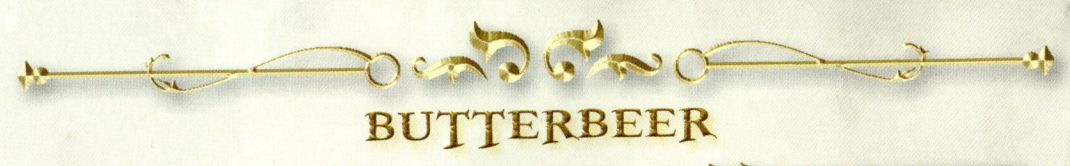

BUTTERBEER

**INGREDIENTS FOR
4 BUTTERBEERS**
1 tsp butter
2 tbsp cane sugar
1 vanilla pod
17 fl. oz milk
4 fl. oz cream
1 tbsp cinnamon
½ tbsp cocoa powder
½ packet vanilla sugar
9 fl. oz malt beer

1. In a saucepan over low heat, melt the butter. Add the cane sugar and stir until lightly caramelized.

2. Cut the vanilla pod lengthwise with a sharp knife and scrape out the pulp. Add the scraped-out pod and the vanilla pulp to the saucepan with the milk, half of the cream, the cinnamon, the cocoa powder and the vanilla sugar. Mix everything thoroughly and simmer briefly. Then remove the saucepan from the heat and stir in the malt beer.

3. Heat the butterbeer again briefly, but never boil it, otherwise flakes will form! Remove from heat and allow to cool slightly.

4. Meanwhile, whip the remaining cream until stiff.

5. Pour the warm butterbeer into heatproof glasses and top each with a spoonful of whipped cream. Serve immediately.

SHORTCRUST HOWLERS

INGREDIENTS FOR APPROX. 5 HOWLERS

For the dough:
7 oz cold butter, in small pieces
4 oz sugar
1 squeeze of lemon
1 pinch of salt
1 egg
11 oz flour
½ packet vanilla sugar
2 oz sour cherry jam

For the decoration:
1 oz chocolate coating
Some baking cocoa
5 black Smarties
1 oz red fondant

Also needed: a C6 envelope as a template, completely unfolded.

To do this, loosen all the corners and glue. Then place it on a piece of cardboard, trace the outline with a felttip pen, and cut it out to make a solid template for the cookie envelopes.

1. Place the butter, sugar, lemon, salt, egg, and vanilla sugar in a bowl and work through using a hand mixer with a dough hook attachment. Add the flour through a sieve and work into a smooth dough. Divide into four equal pieces, shape into flat "bricks," wrap individually in plastic wrap, and refrigerate for at least 3 hours. In the meantime, heat the oven to 340 °F heat and line a baking tray with baking paper.

2. Remove the dough from the refrigerator 10 minutes before you start working with it. Sprinkle the work surface with a little flour and roll out the dough as thinly as possible into a square. Place the template in the center of the dough and trace the outlines. Using the back of a large knife or a pastry card, press the edges of the envelope in a little to reveal a postcard-sized rectangle. Evenly spread 1 tsp of sour cherry jam in the center of this rectangle, then carefully "fold" the envelope. For a guide, consult a pre-folded envelope if necessary.

3. Carefully place the envelope on a lightly-floured work surface and smooth with an angled palette. Fold the remaining envelopes in the same manner, spacing them sufficiently apart on the prepared baking sheet, and bake for about 15-20 minutes. Remove from oven and allow to cool completely.

4. Once the envelopes are completely cool, use black fondant to form the eyes and red fondant to form the mouths of the howlers. Attach to the letters with a little melted chocolate. Finally, using a small brush and some baking cocoa, powder the edges to further accentuate the outline of the howlers.

BERTIE BOTT'S EVERY FLAVOR BEANS

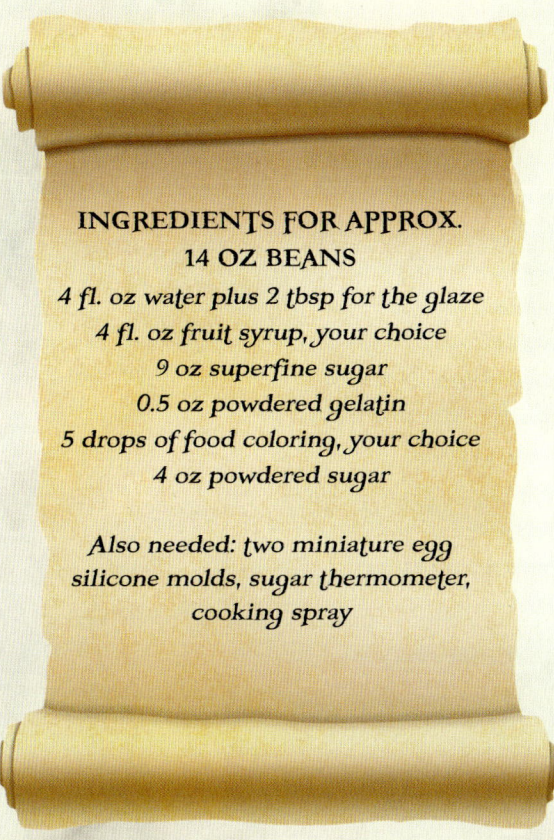

INGREDIENTS FOR APPROX. 14 OZ BEANS

4 fl. oz water plus 2 tbsp for the glaze
4 fl. oz fruit syrup, your choice
9 oz superfine sugar
0.5 oz powdered gelatin
5 drops of food coloring, your choice
4 oz powdered sugar

Also needed: two miniature egg silicone molds, sugar thermometer, cooking spray

1. Put 4 fl. oz of water, the fruit syrup, and the sugar in a saucepan and heat over low heat, stirring gently, until the sugar has completely dissolved. Then stir in the powdered gelatin.

2. Heat, stirring constantly, until the sugar syrup reaches a temperature of 225 °F (approx. 20 minutes). Take great care here, as the syrup is very hot and splashes on the skin can cause severe burns! Check the temperature regularly with a sugar thermometer!

3. Spray the silicone molds generously with the cooking spray.

4. As soon as the syrup has reached the necessary temperature, stir in the food coloring of your desired color and pour the sugar syrup evenly into the wells of the silicone molds. Smooth the tops with a spatula, wrap the molds with plastic wrap, and let them dry overnight.

5. In a small bowl, mix the powdered sugar with 2 tbsp water until smooth. Remove the "egg halves" from the molds. Brush the "cut" sides of the "egg halves" with the icing, glue two together at a time, and let dry for 30 minutes. Store in an airtight container.

With this recipe, you can make Bertie Bott's beans in any color and flavor you like! All you need to change for this is the fruit syrup and food coloring used!

POLYJUICE JELLO

INGREDIENTS FOR 4 SERVINGS
9 sheets gelatin
25 fl. oz clear apple juice
7 stems fresh woodruff, finely chopped
Green food coloring

1. Soak the gelatin leaves in a small bowl of cold water.

2. Put the apple juice and the finely chopped woodruff in a saucepan and heat a little over low heat. Caution: Do not bring to the boil! Allow to infuse for a few minutes and drain through a kitchen sieve.

3. Pour the warm apple juice back into the pot. Squeeze the gelatin, add it to the pot and whisk until it is completely dissolved. Now color the polyjuice with green food coloring, pour into small glasses or bowls, and chill in the refrigerator for at least six hours.

4. Immediately before serving, gently invert onto shallow plates.

DUDLEY DURSLEYS DONUTS

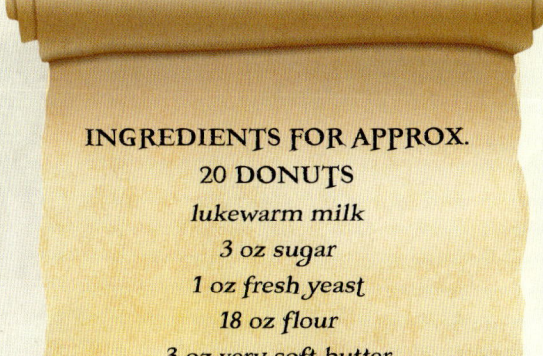

INGREDIENTS FOR APPROX. 20 DONUTS

lukewarm milk
3 oz sugar
1 oz fresh yeast
18 oz flour
3 oz very soft butter
1 egg
1 egg yolk
¼ tsp salt
9 cups frying oil
18 oz pink sugar glaze
4 oz decorating sugar

Also required: donut cutter (approx. 3-4" in diameter).

1. Pour half of the milk into a small bowl. Add 1 tsp of the sugar, crumble the yeast, add to the milk, and stir constantly to dissolve.

2. Put the flour in a mixing bowl and make a well. Pour the milk mixture into this well and mix with a little flour from the sides. Cover with a clean tea towel and let rest in a warm place for ten minutes.

3. Add the butter, egg, egg yolk, and salt and knead for five minutes to form a smooth, soft dough. Cover and leave in a warm place and let rise for 50 minutes.

4. Line two baking sheets with baking paper.

5. Sprinkle the work surface with a little flour and roll out the dough with a rolling pin to a thickness of about inch. Use a donut cutter to cut out circles from the dough. If you don't have a cookie cutter at hand, you can simply use a drinking glass and a slightly smaller shot glass to cut out the dough circle and then the hole inside the donut.

6. Place the doughnuts on the prepared baking sheets with enough space between them, cover them, and let them rest for another 30 minutes.

7. Meanwhile, heat the frying oil in a large saucepan to 320 °F and line a large, flat plate with paper towels. Then fry the donuts a few at a time (not too many at a time!) for 1-2 minutes per side until golden brown, remove from the oil with a slotted spoon, and drain on the paper towel.

8. Let the donuts cool for a few minutes, coat with the icing, and decorate with the decorating sugar as desired.

LIQUID APPLE PIE

INGREDIENTS FOR 10 SHOTS

2 oz whipped cream
Some ice
4 fl. oz vodka
7 fl. oz apple juice
4 fl. oz Licor 43 (vanilla liqueur)
2 tbsp lime juice
Cinnamon powder, to taste
Edible gold dust, to taste

Also required:
10 large shot glasses
(1.5 fl. oz capacity each)

1. Whip the cream in a small bowl with a hand mixer fitted with a whisk until stiff.

2. Fill a cocktail shaker full of ice. Add the vodka, apple juice, vanilla liqueur, and lime juice and shake vigorously for 5-10 seconds.

3. Strain the liquid apple pie evenly into the shot glasses. Leave about ½ inch of space at the top of each one.

4. Place the whipped cream in a freezer bag with the corner cut off and pipe a little of it onto each shot at a time. Decorate with cinnamon and edible gold dust as desired. The shots should be enjoyed promptly, so bottoms up!

If you want to make it easier, you can also use ready-made spray cream. However, it will collapse much faster than fresh whipped cream.

WAFFLES WITH BUTTERBEER SYRUP

INGREDIENTS FOR APPROX. 10 WAFFLES

5 oz soft butter (alternatively margarine) plus a little more, to grease the waffle iron.
3 oz sugar
1 packet vanilla sugar
3 eggs
1 pinch of salt
12.oz flour
1 packet baking powder
9 fl. oz milk
For the butterbeer syrup:
7 oz sugar
2 fl. oz malt beer
7 oz cream
¼ teaspoon butter vanilla extract
Some vanilla pulp (optional)

Also required: Waffle iron

Prepare the waffles:

1. Combine the butter with the sugar, vanilla sugar, eggs, and salt in a mixing bowl and beat with an electric hand mixer until fluffy.

2. In a bowl, mix the flour with the baking powder and gradually stir in the milk, a little at a time.

3. Grease the top and bottom of the waffle iron lightly with butter and preheat.

4. Using a ladle, pour in the appropriate amount batter, spread evenly, close the waffle iron, and bake the waffles according to the manufacturer's instructions until they are nice and golden brown and crispy. Then carefully remove and serve as soon as possible together with the butter beer syrup (see below).

5. Prepare the butter beer syrup:

6. Place the sugar and malt beer in a saucepan and bring to a boil over medium heat, stirring constantly. Simmer until the sugar has completely dissolved, the liquid has completely evaporated, and you have a viscous caramel.

7. Remove from heat and stir in the cream, stirring constantly. Add the butter vanilla extract and a bit of scraped vanilla pulp if desired, mix everything together thoroughly and let cool for a few minutes before using.

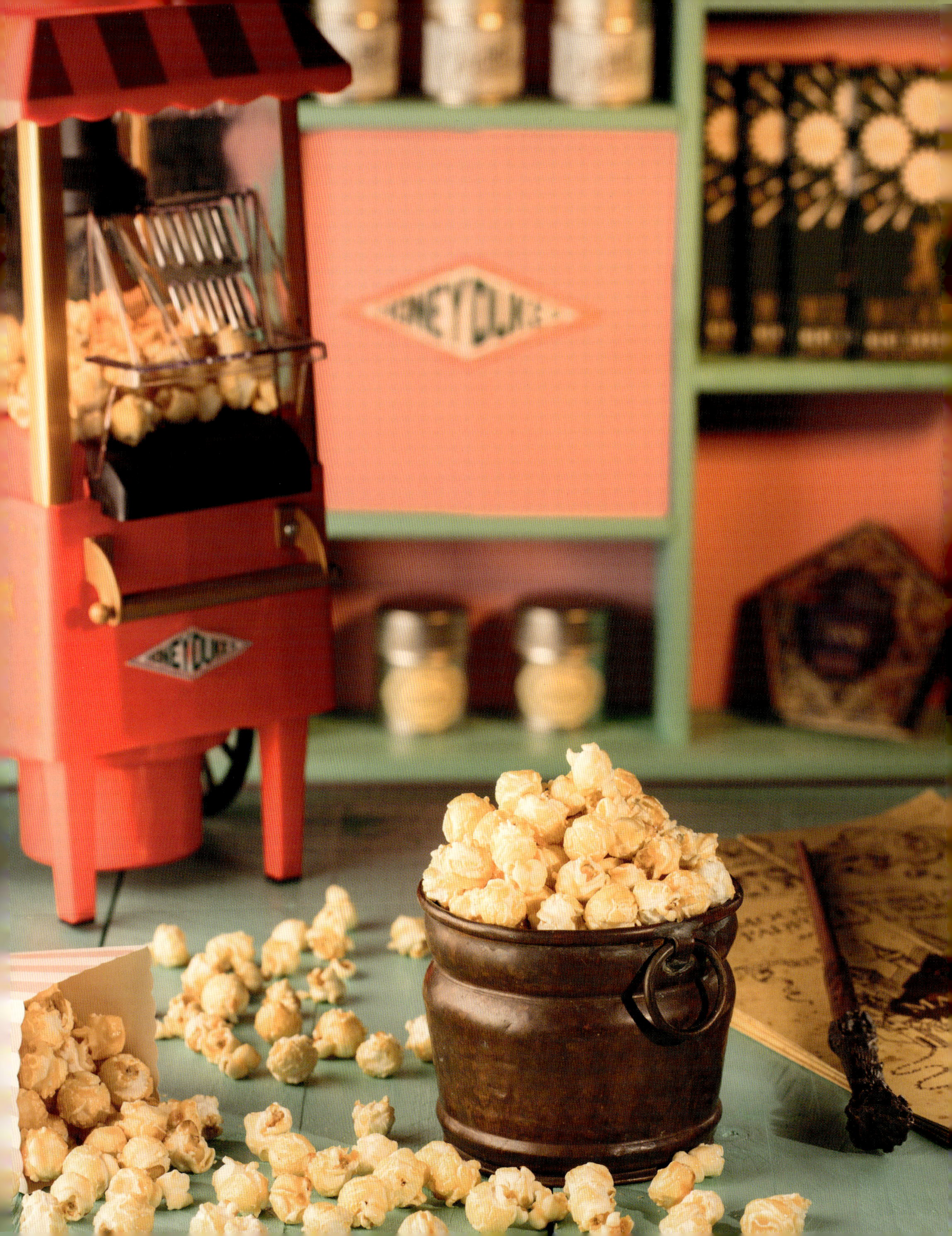

BUTTERBEER POPCORN

INGREDIENTS FOR 4 SERVINGS
1 tbsp canola oil
4 oz popcorn corn
4 oz sugar
2 tbsp butter
tsp butter vanilla extract

1. Heat the canola oil together with the corn in a shallow saucepan over medium heat, stirring constantly. Once the corn begins to pop, place the lid on the pot and reduce the heat to low. Lift the pot occasionally by the handles and swirl the popcorn.

2. When the popcorn has popped completely, remove from the heat and lift off the lid. Transfer the popcorn to a large bowl to cool.

3. Meanwhile, place the sugar in a small saucepan and cook over medium heat until caramelized, stirring occasionally. Once the sugar is brown, add the butter and butter vanilla extract and stir until well combined. Reduce the heat to low, add the cooled popcorn to the butterbeer caramel, and toss to coat the popcorn evenly.

4. Spread on a baking sheet lined with parchment paper and let cool slightly before eating.

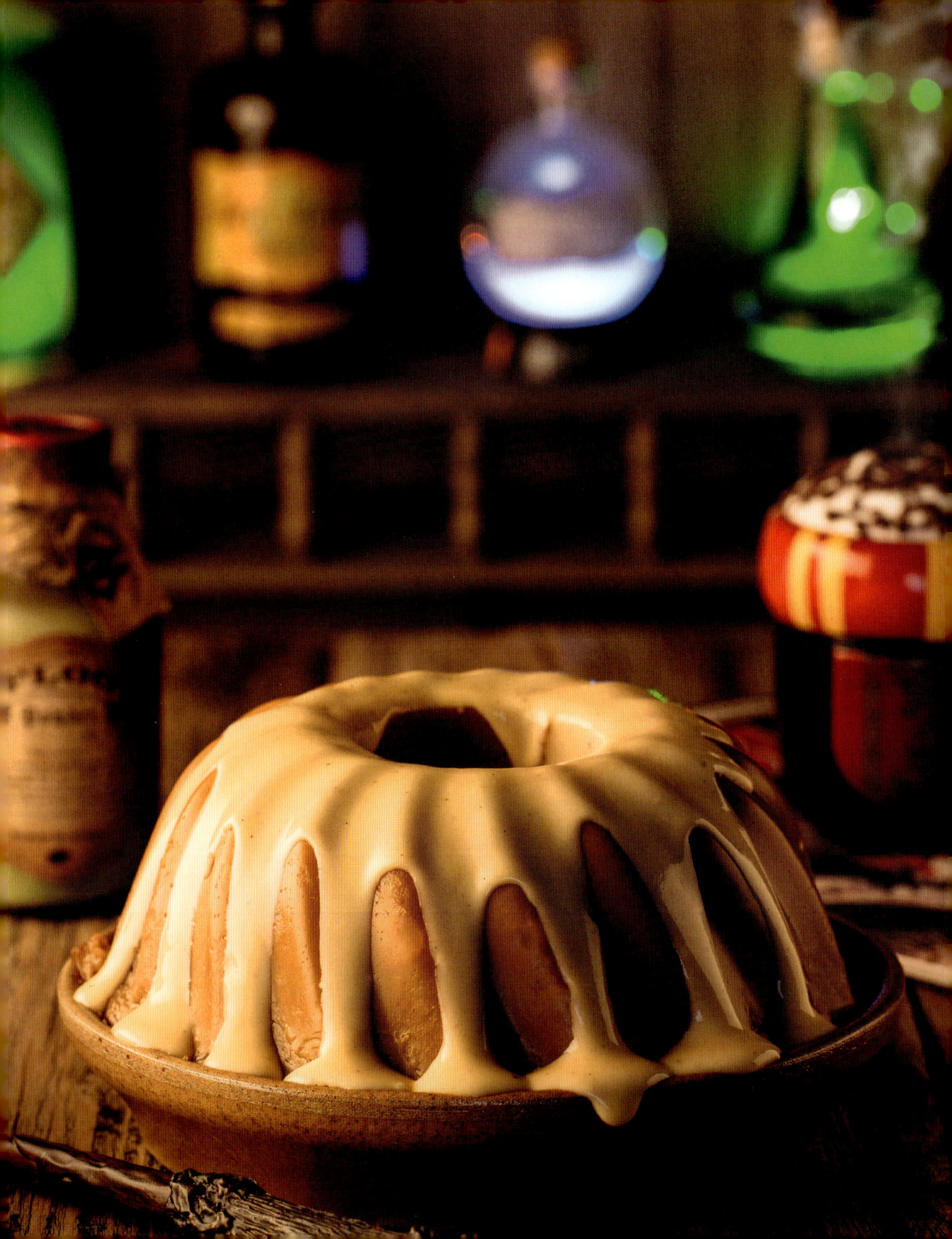

BUTTERBEER PUDDING

INGREDIENTS FOR APPROX. 8 PORTIONS

For the butterbeer pudding:
2 packets of caramel pudding powder
4 oz sugar
27 fl. oz milk
7 oz whipped cream
tsp butter vanilla extract

For the vanilla sauce:
2 eggs
1 heaped tsp cornstarch
7 fl. oz cream
14 fl. oz milk
3 tbsp sugar
1 vanilla bean, scraped out

Also needed: large pudding mold (1 qt capacity)

Prepare the butterbeer pudding:

1. In a bowl, mix the pudding powder with the sugar.
2. In a separate bowl, mix the milk with the cream. Gradually add at least 6 tbsp of the mixture to the pudding powder and stir until smooth.
3. Bring the remaining milk-cream mixture together with the butter-vanilla extract to a boil in a saucepan over medium heat, stirring regularly. Then remove from heat, add the pudding powder and cook, stirring constantly, for at least one minute.
4. Pour the pudding into a cold-rinsed mold and chill in the refrigerator for at least 4 hours.
5. To serve, gently turn the butterbeer pudding out of the mold onto a serving plate. Serve with warm or cold custard (see below).
6. Prepare the custard:
7. Beat the eggs briefly with an electric hand mixer. Add the cornstarch and cream and whisk again until fluffy.
8. In a small saucepan, bring the milk, sugar, and vanilla pulp to a boil over medium heat, stirring regularly. Then whisk the cream-egg mixture into the milk and bring everything to a boil briefly.
9. Remove from heat and let cool for a few minutes before serving. If you want to enjoy the custard cold, refrigerate for at least an hour before serving.

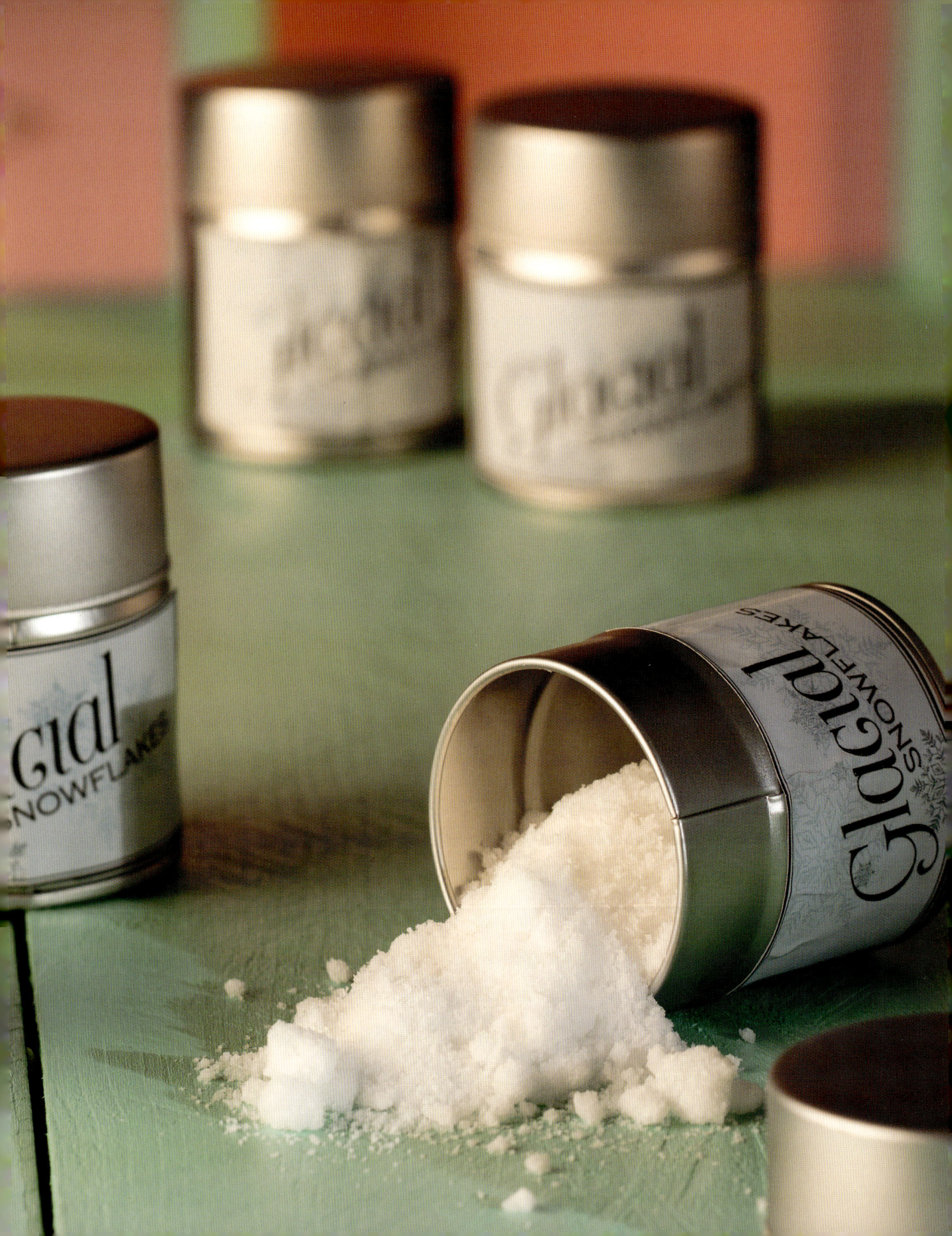
Glacial
SNOWFLAKES

MELT-IN-YOUR-MOUTH SNOWFLAKES

INGREDIENTS FOR APPROX. 2 OZ SNOWFLAKES

1 tsp coconut oil
4 drops peppermint oil (food grade)
2 oz dextrose

1. Warm the coconut oil a little in a small bowl in the microwave so that it becomes liquid.
2. Add the peppermint oil to the coconut oil and mix.
3. Put the dextrose in a separate small bowl and gradually add the coconut peppermint oil. Mix thoroughly to form a consistent, slightly lumpy "snow." Allow to dry for a few minutes.
4. Store in an airtight container.

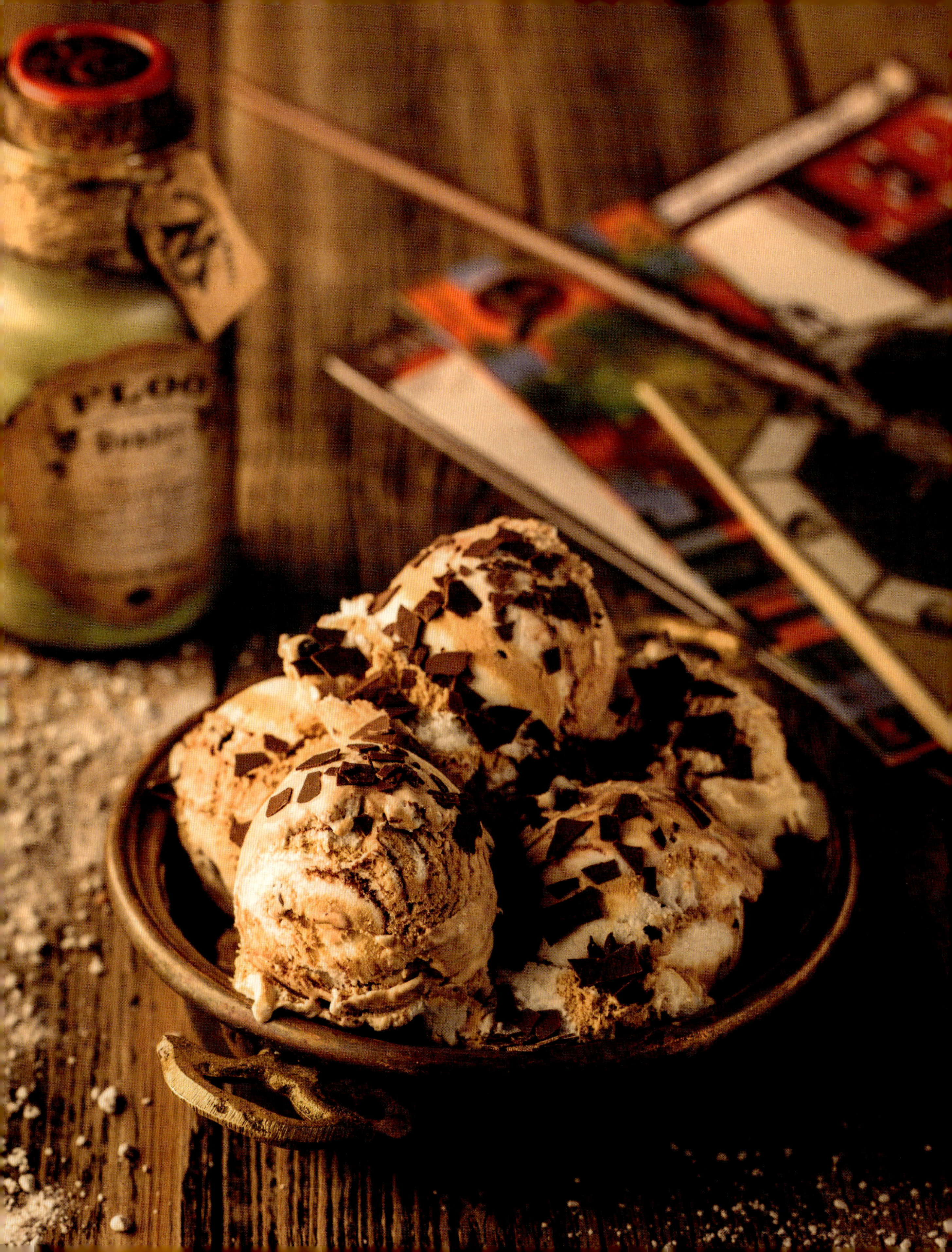

BUTTERBEER ICE CREAM

INGREDIENTS FOR 2-3 SERVINGS

7 oz sugar
2 fl. oz malt beer
6 oz whipped cream
½ tsp butter vanilla extract
Some vanilla pulp, as desired
Chocolate shavings, as garnish
Butter beer syrup, as garnish
(see p. 34)

Also required: Ice cream maker

1. Put the sugar and malt beer in a saucepan and bring to a boil over medium heat, stirring constantly. Simmer until the sugar has completely dissolved, the liquid has completely evaporated, and you have a viscous caramel.

2. Remove from heat and stir in the cream, stirring constantly. Add the butter, vanilla extract, and some scraped out vanilla pulp. Mix everything together thoroughly until you have a smooth cream. Allow to cool for a few minutes and then place in the refrigerator to chill completely (about 2-3 hours).

3. Stir the cold butterbeer mixture well, place in an ice cream maker and process according to manufacturer's instructions. Store in an airtight container in the freezer until ready to use.

4. Serve garnished with chocolate shavings and/or butterbeer sauce as desired.

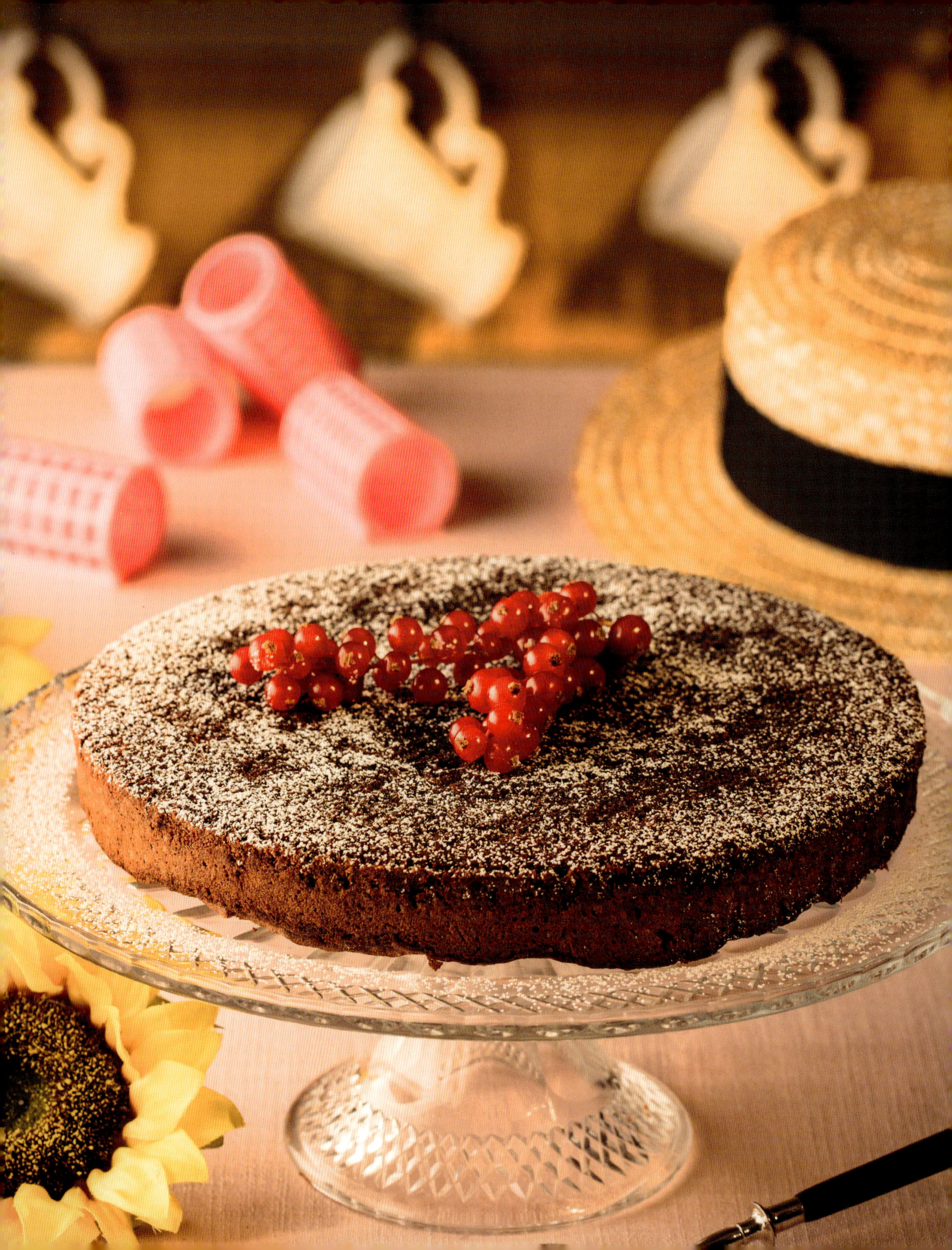

AUNT PETUNIA'S CHOCOLATE CAKE

AUNT PETUNIA'S CHOCOLATE CAKE
INGREDIENTS FOR 1 CAKE

Butter, for greasing the baking dish.
7 oz wheat flour
2 tbsp cocoa powder
1 packet baking powder
7 oz soft butter
6 oz sugar
1 pinch of salt
4 eggs, warm
21 oz sour cherries (from the jar), drained
4 oz chocolate shavings
Powdered sugar
Fresh currants, as garnish
Also required: springform pan (approx. 10" in diameter)

1. Preheat the oven to 350 °F heat. Line the bottom of a springform pan with baking paper and grease the sides well with butter.

2. In a bowl, mix together the wheat flour, cocoa powder, and baking powder.

3. In a separate bowl, using an electric hand mixer, beat the butter with the sugar and salt until white. Then, one at a time, beat in the room temperature eggs and beat until fluffy. Add the cocoa-flour mixture and mix on the lowest speed until a homogeneous mixture is obtained. Add the drained cherries and the chocolate shavings to the batter and fold in. Pour into the prepared springform pan, smooth the top, and bake in the preheated oven for about 50 minutes, or until nothing sticks to a toothpick inserted into the center of the cake when you pull it out. Then remove the cake from the oven and let it cool completely in the pan.

4. Finally, gently remove from the mold, sprinkle with powdered sugar, and serve garnished with fresh currants.

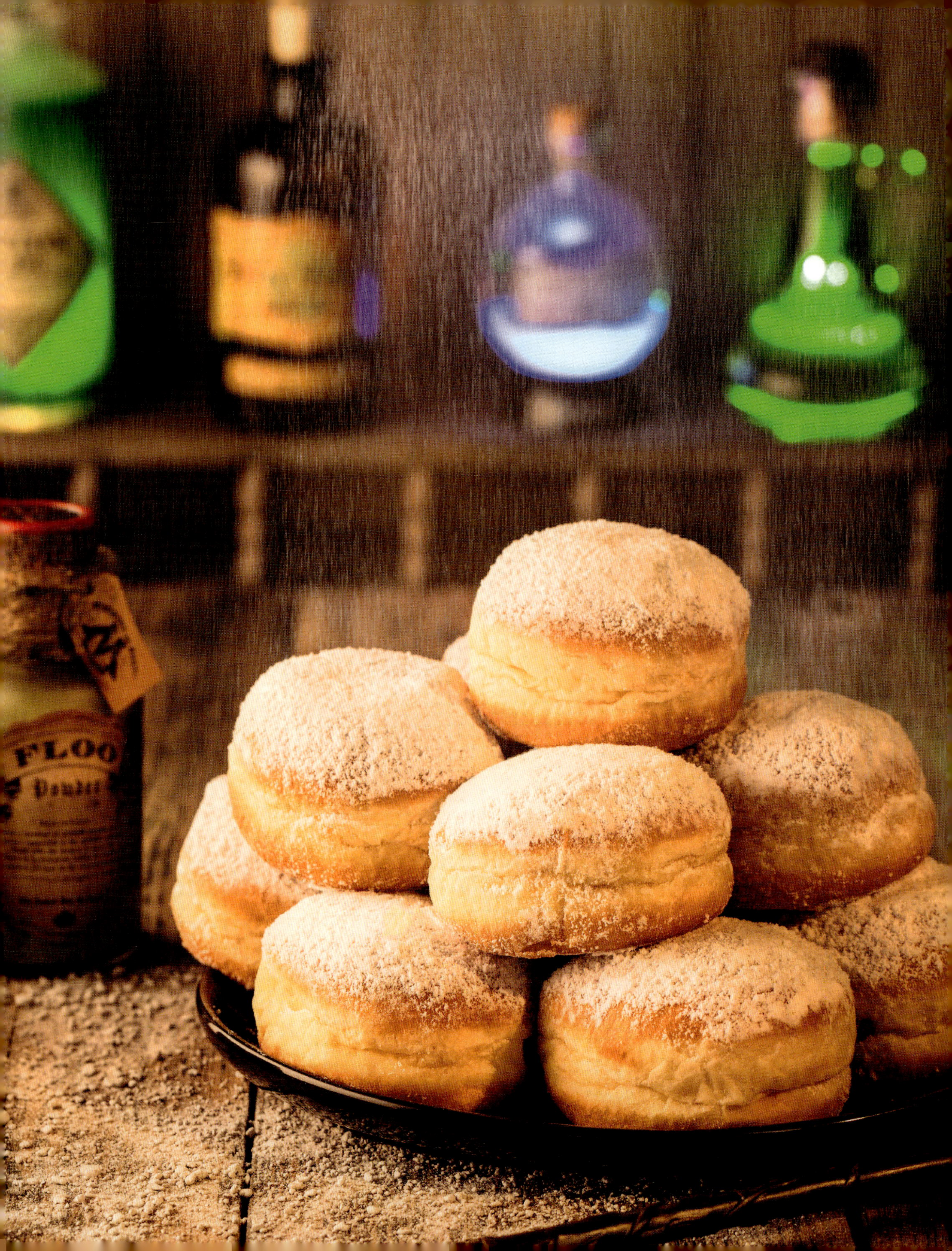
FLOO

JAM DOUGHNUTS

INGREDIENTS FOR APPROX. 12 DOUGHNUTS

For the dough:
1 cube yeast
6 fl. oz lukewarm milk
2 oz sugar plus 3 oz more, for rolling the doughnuts after baking
0.5 oz salt
18 oz flour plus a little more, for sprinkling on the work surface
2 oz butter, at room temperature
2 eggs, at room temperature
Some grated lemon peel

For the filling:
2 oz blueberry jam
2 oz cherry jam
4 oz apricot jam
Green food coloring

Also needed: frying oil, piping bag with long, thin nozzle

Prepare the dough:

1. Dissolve the yeast in the lukewarm milk in a bowl and mix with a little sugar. Leave to stand for ten minutes until the yeast starts to ferment.

2. Now mix all ingredients for the dough into the mixture and knead vigorously to form a smooth dough that no longer sticks to the sides of the bowl. Add a little more flour if necessary. Form the dough into a ball and let it rise in a warm place, covered with a clean tea towel, until it has doubled in volume (about 1 hour).

3. Knead the dough again on a floured work surface and shape it into a dozen balls, each weighing approx. 2 oz. Place the dough balls on a flat plate and let them rise in a warm place, covered, for about 30 minutes.

4. Meanwhile, heat a deep fryer to 320 °F, or alternatively, pour three finger widths of frying oil into a large pot and heat until the oil boils. Using a slotted spoon, carefully place the doughnuts into the hot oil, spacing each one sufficiently apart. Bake a maximum of three doughnuts at a time so that the temperature of the oil does not drop too much. Bake until golden brown on both sides and remove. Briefly dab off excess fat with paper towels and roll the doughnuts in sugar while still hot on a flat plate. Let cool on a cooling rack; only then pipe in the filling (see below).

Prepare the filling:

5. Strain the various jams through a sieve into separate small bowls. Take half of the apricot jam and color it with the green food coloring. Then place each of the different colored jams into a piping bag with a long, thin hole nozzle and pipe some filling into the side of each of the cooled doughnuts so that you end up with jam doughnuts with fillings in the colors of the four houses of Hogwarts.

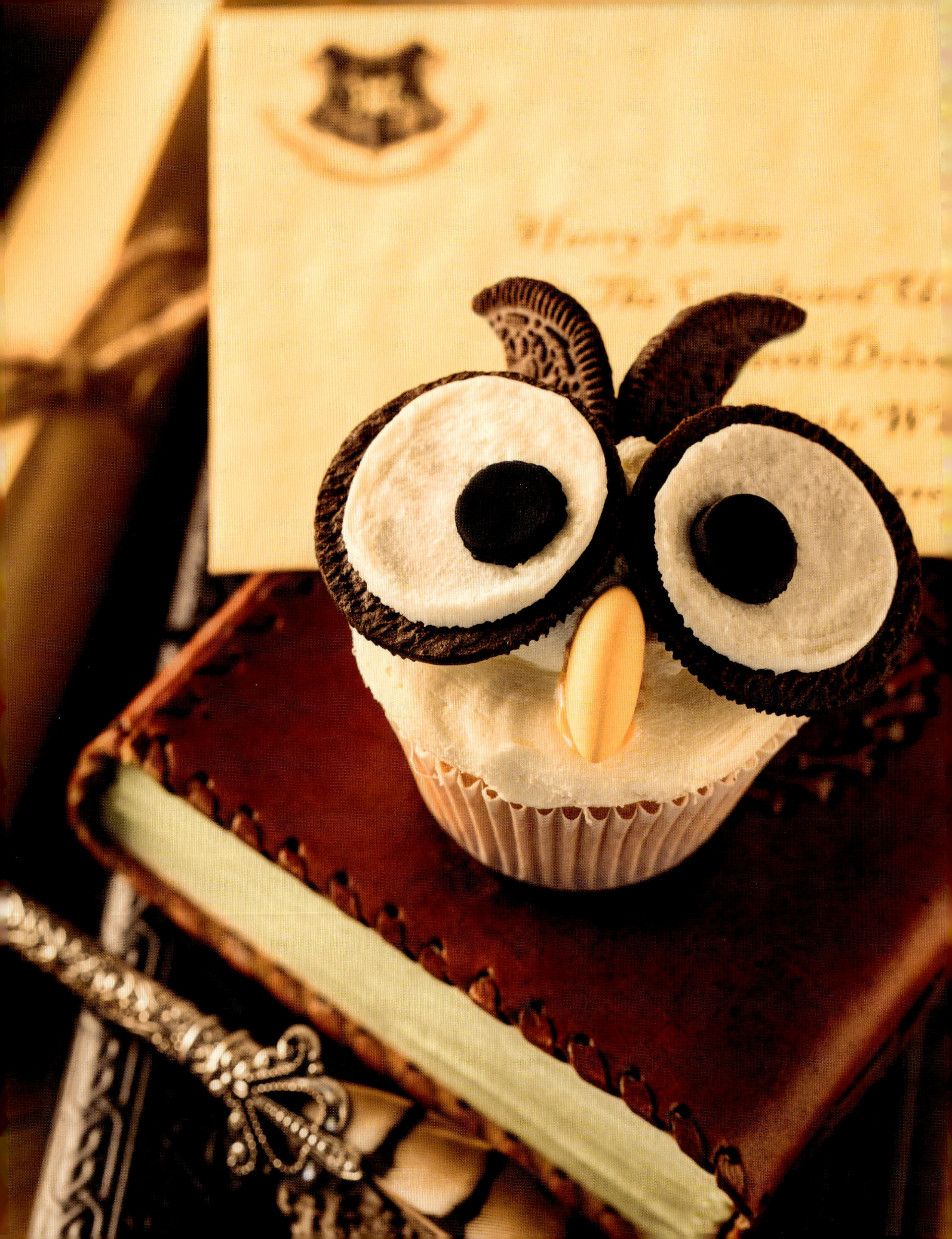

HEDWIG THE MUFFIN OWL

INGREDIENTS FOR 12 MUFFIN OWLS

For the dough:
1 oz soft butter
4 oz peanut butter
1 packet vanilla sugar
5 oz cane sugar
2 eggs
1 pinch of salt
1 tsp baking powder
5 oz flour
3 fl. oz milk

For the cream:
5 oz butter, at room temperature
5 oz powdered sugar
5 oz cream cheese, at room temperature

For the decoration
24 Oreo cookies (or other chocolate cookies with vanilla filling)
24 black M&M's (or other candy-coated chocolate)
12 orange M&M's

Also needed:
12 muffin tray, twelve muffin paper cups.

1. Preheat the oven to 350 °F heat. Fill a 12-muffin tray with paper cups.

2. Beat the butter, peanut butter, vanilla sugar, and cane sugar in a bowl until fluffy. One at a time, beat in the eggs, add the salt, and mix thoroughly.

3. In a separate bowl, mix the baking powder with the flour and sift. Then alternately add the flour/baking powder mixture and the milk, continuing to stir steadily until a creamy batter forms. Divide evenly among the muffin tins and bake in the oven on the middle rack for 20 minutes. Remove and let cool completely in the pan.

4. Meanwhile, beat the butter and powdered sugar until light and fluffy. Stir in the cream cheese and refrigerate for 30 minutes to chill.

5. Gently remove the muffins from the baking tray.

6. Place the cooled cream in a piping bag and pipe evenly over the top of the muffins.

7. Carefully separate the cookie halves so that the vanilla filling "sticks" to one half. Cut the other half in half. Gently dip the "whole" cookie halves into the warm cream with the filling facing up as eyes. Then attach a black M&M to each as an "eye". Press the half cookies into the cream as "eyebrows." Place an orange M&M diagonally in the cream as a beak for each. Let set for a few minutes.

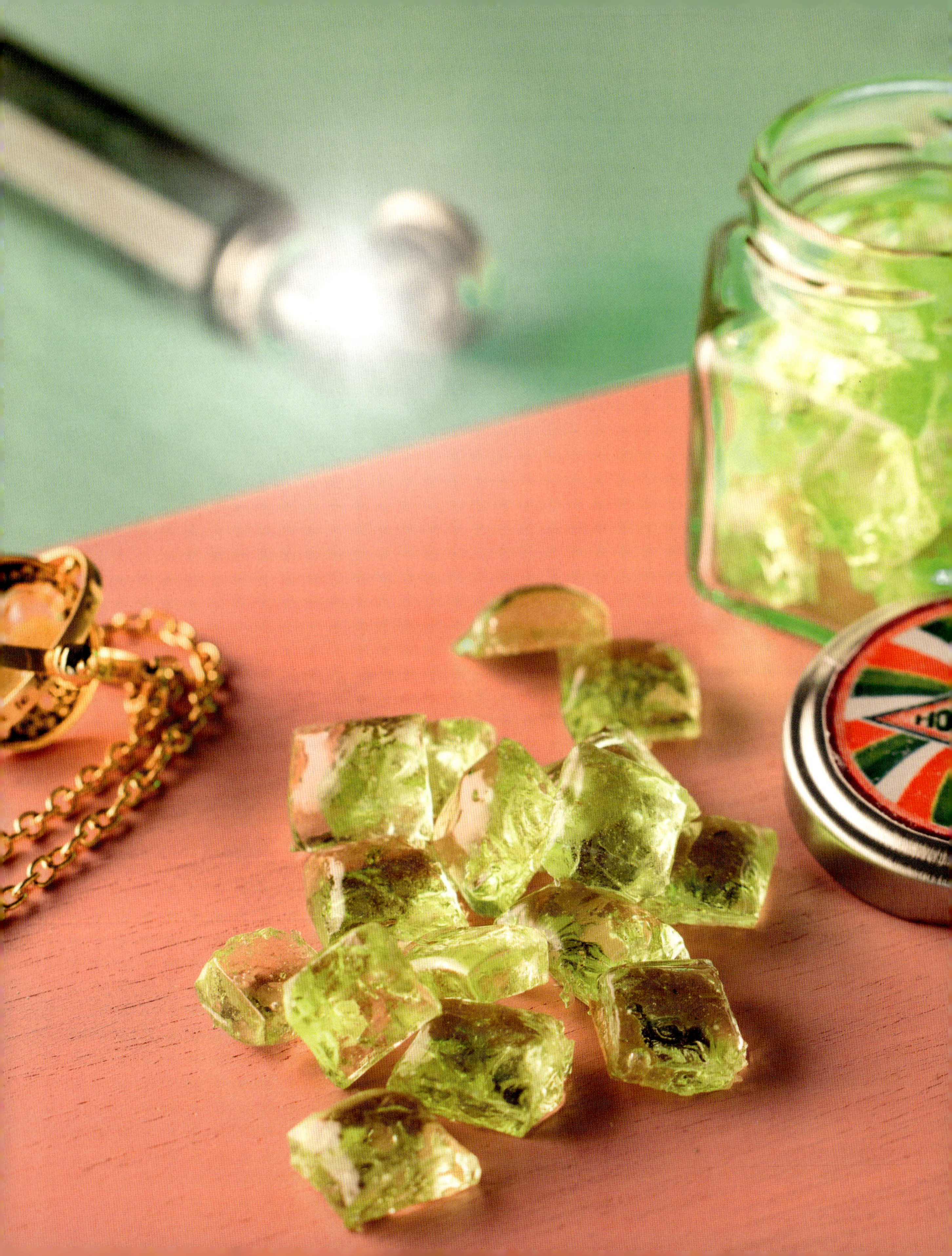

PEPPERMINT CANDIES

INGREDIENTS FOR APPROX. 50-80 CANDIES (DEPENDING ON SIZE)

5 fl. oz water
16 oz sugar
3 oz dextrose
3-4 drops of peppermint oil
Green food coloring
Powdered sugar
Also needed: sugar thermometer, silicone mat

1. Mix the water, sugar and dextrose in a small saucepan and stir over medium heat until the sugar is completely dissolved. Then increase the heat and stop stirring from now on! Use a sugar thermometer to check the temperature until the whole thing measures exactly 310 °F. Remove from the heat and place on a heat-resistant surface.

2. Quickly stir in the peppermint oil and (depending on the desired color intensity) the food coloring.

3. Pour the mixture carefully onto the silicone mat. Caution: Very hot! Let sit for 1-2 minutes to firm up a bit. Then, using a pastry scraper or a lightly greased knife, press the later breaking points into the candy mixture.

4. Allow to dry completely, uncovered. Then break up into individual candies with your hands.

5. Put the powdered sugar in a bowl and roll the peppermint candies in it so that they are covered all over. Store in an airtight container.

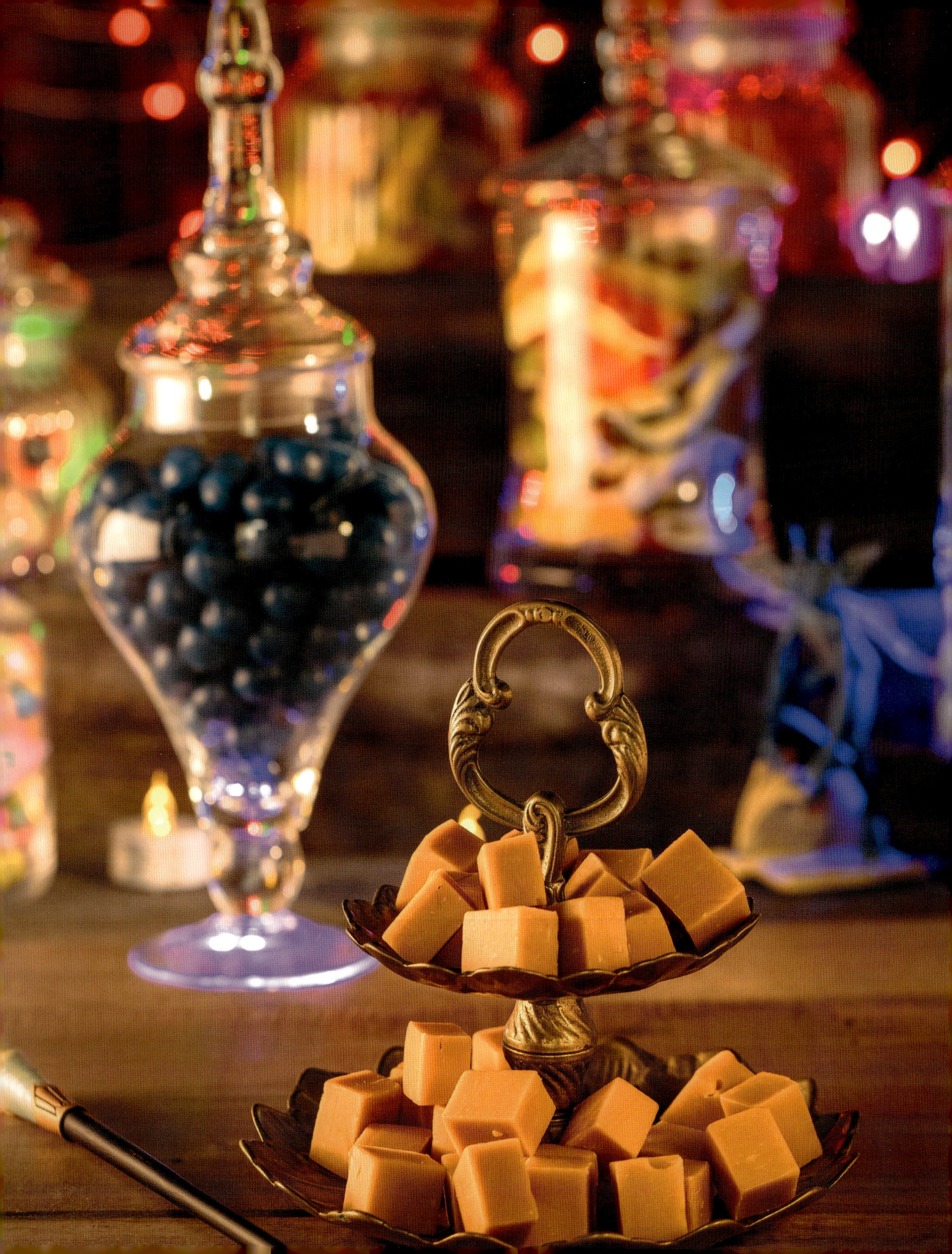

BUTTERBEER FUDGE

INGREDIENTS FOR APPROX. 12 PORTIONS
1 oz butter
4 fl. oz malt beer
5 oz sugar
14 oz condensed milk, sweetened
1 strong pinch of salt

You will also need: a rectangular baking dish (approx. 9" x 11.5") that is as shallow as possible.

1. Line a baking dish with baking paper so that the paper hangs over the sides. Grease with some of the butter.

2. Bring the remaining butter, malt beer, and sugar to a boil in a saucepan over medium heat, stirring constantly. Whisk in the condensed milk and salt. Simmer gently for at least 20 minutes, stirring periodically to make sure nothing burns.

3. Simmer until the mixture becomes visibly thicker and takes on a caramel color. When the mixture has the consistency of creamy, solid honey, carefully pour it into the baking dish, smooth the top and let it cool completely at room temperature (approx. 3-4 hours).

4. Place in the freezer for about 20 minutes before slicing to prevent the fudge from sticking when touched. Then carefully turn out of the mold onto a board and cut into bite-sized pieces with a large, sharp knife. Store in an airtight container.

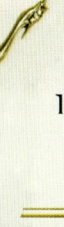

If you want to "spice up" your Butterbeer Fudge a bit more, just add a good shot of rum to the batter!

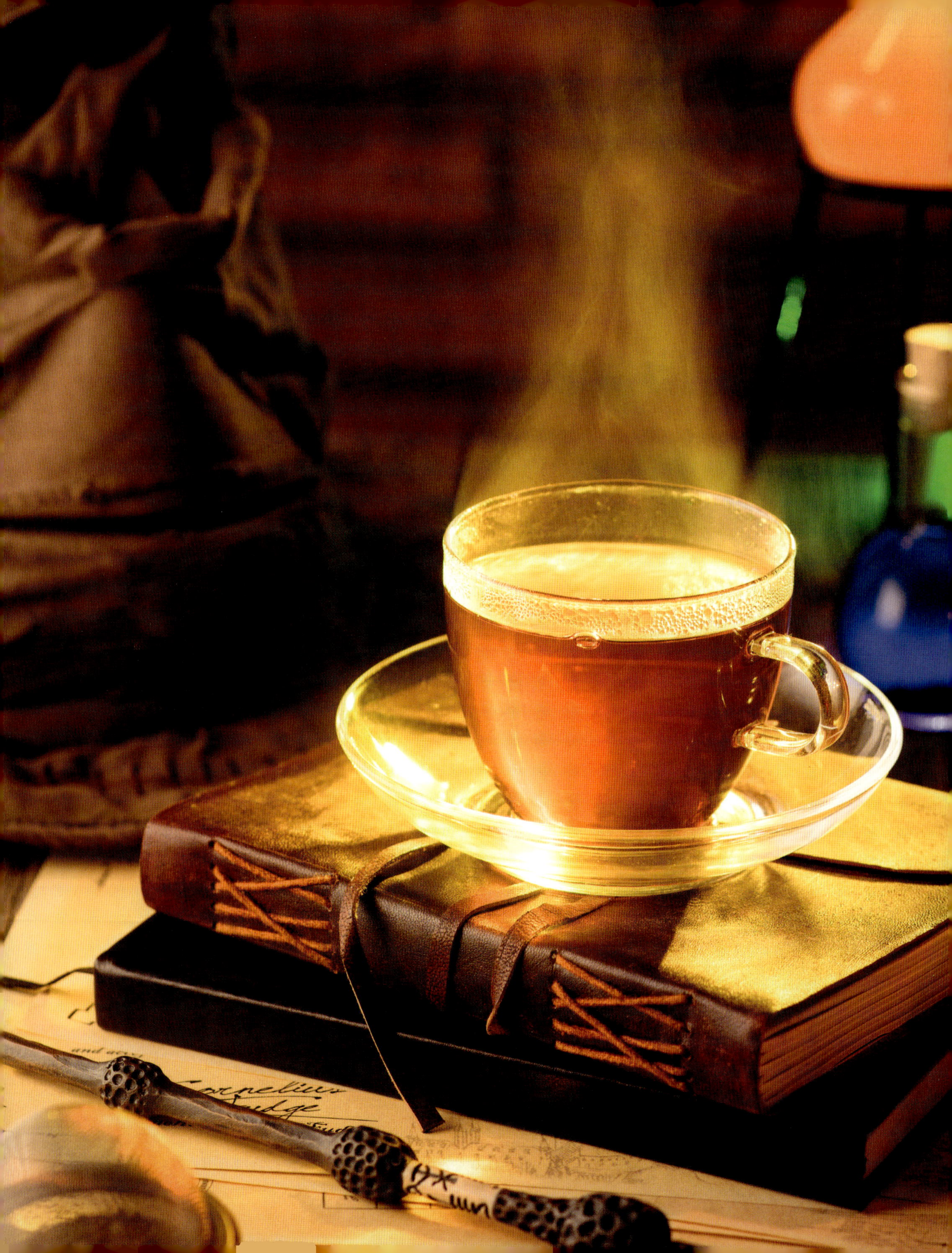

DUMBLEDORE'S FAVORITE TEA

**INGREDIENTS FOR
4-5 POTS OF TEA**
1 oz peppermint
0.5 oz lemon verbena
0.5 oz oregano (flowers and leaves)
0.5 oz mixed edible flowers
(e.g. elder, mallow, marigold)
1 tbsp grated licorice
1 vanilla pod, in small pieces
4 oz black tea honey (optional)

1. Line a baking tray with baking paper. Spread the mint, lemon verbena, oregano, and mixed flowers evenly over it. Either let dry for several days in a warm, dry place, or dry in the oven at 140 °F for about 3 hours. Then carefully pluck off the leaves and the flowers; discard the rest.

2. Coarsely grind the dried herbs with a mortar and pestle.

3. In a small bowl, mix the grated licorice and vanilla bean with the black tea. Add the ground herbs and mix everything together.

4. To prepare the tea, put 4-5 tsp in a tea infuser, hang it in the pot, pour boiling water, and let it brew for 5 minutes maximum. Then remove the tea infuser and serve immediately. It is best to pour the tea through a fine sieve into the cups to ensure that no residues get into it. Sweeten with a little honey if desired.

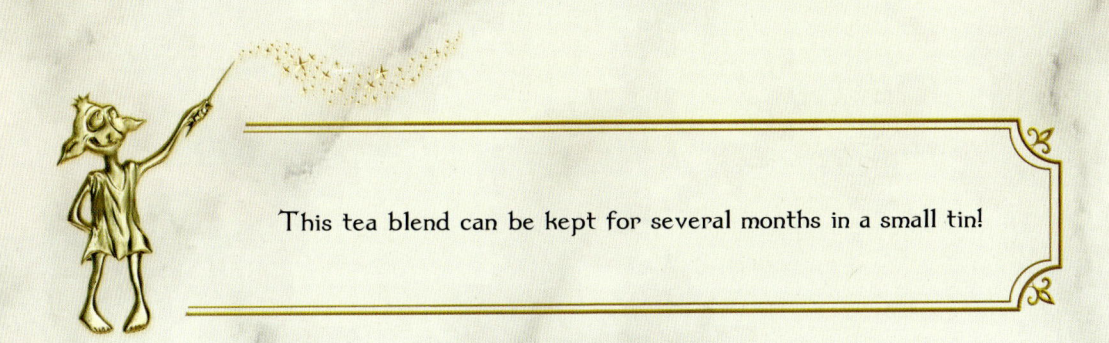

This tea blend can be kept for several months in a small tin!

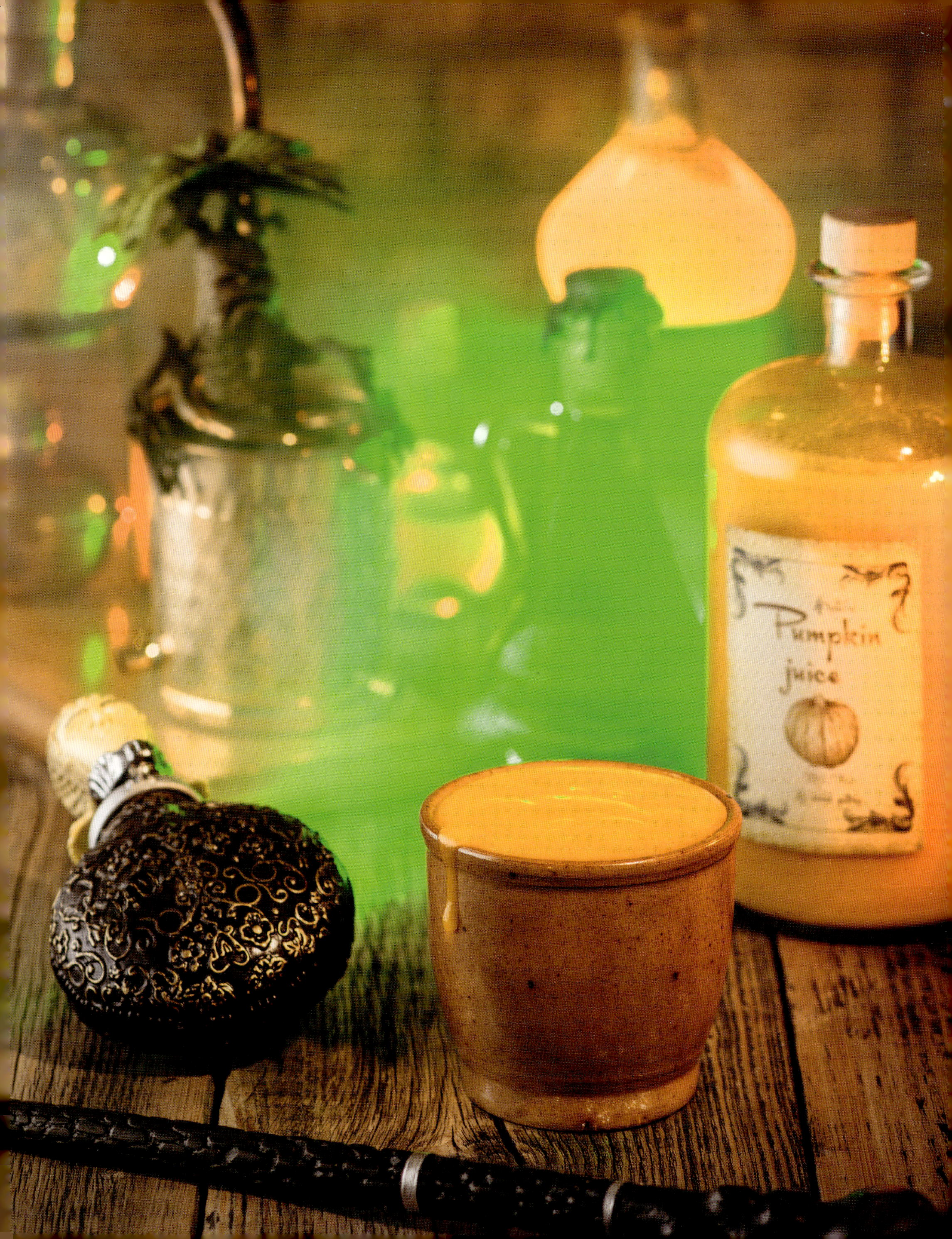
Pumpkin
juice

PUMPKIN JUICE

INGREDIENTS FOR APPROX. 8 ½ CUPS PUMPKIN JUICE

18 oz pumpkin, coarsely diced
7 oz cane sugar
6 cups water
1 packet citric acid
0.5 fl. oz apricot flavoring
1 tbsp vanilla extract
Sparkling mineral water (optional)
Also required: two empty bottles
(1 qt each)

1. Preheat the oven to 350 °F. Line a baking tray with baking paper.

2. Wrap the pumpkin cubes with aluminum foil, place them on the baking sheet and cook in the oven for about 20 minutes, until the pumpkin is soft and the skin can be easily removed from the flesh. Place the pumpkin flesh in a bowl and finely puree with a hand blender.

3. Put the pumpkin puree in a large saucepan with the sugar and water. Bring to a boil and simmer over low heat, stirring constantly, for about 20 minutes. Stir in the citric acid, apricot flavoring, and vanilla extract, mix well, and pour into two hot-rinsed 1 qt bottles. Close the bottles tightly and store in the refrigerator. When well-cooled, the pumpkin juice keeps for 3-4 days.

4. If the pumpkin juice is too thick for you, mix it with some mineral water immediately before use!

Unlike most other pumpkin juice recipes, this one is sweet instead of savory and tastes best chilled!

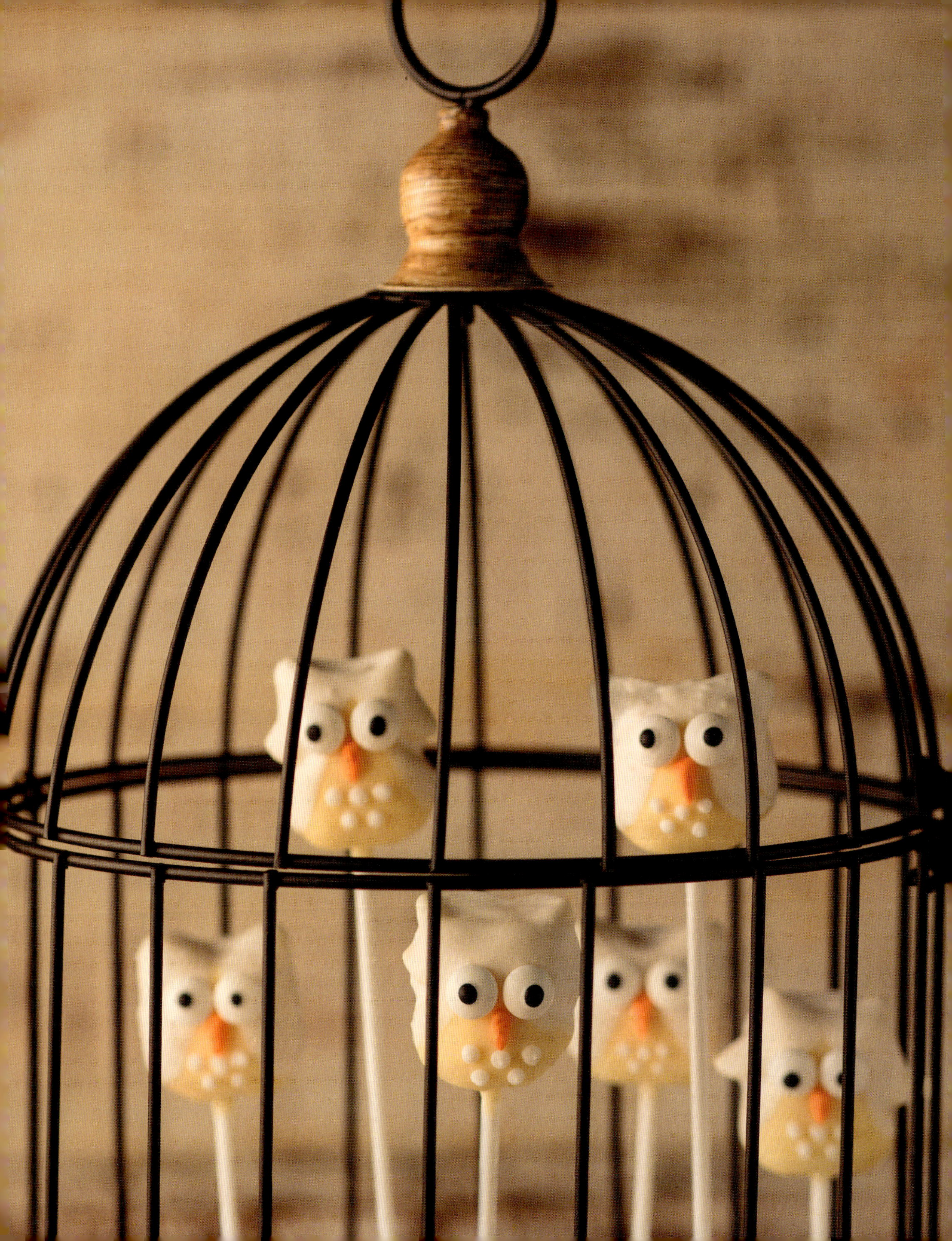

OWL POPS

INGREDIENTS FOR APPROX. 35 OWL POPS

9 oz soft butter plus a little more, for greasing the mold
5 oz sugar
1 packet vanilla sugar
1 pinch of salt
3 eggs
5 oz flour
2 tsp baking powder
2 tbsp milk
5 oz cream cheese
9 oz white chocolate, coarsely chopped
9 oz powdered sugar
4 tbsp water

Also required: approx. 35 cake pop stems, decorative sugar eyes, orange food pencil, white food pencil, cake pop stand, baking pan (any)

Prepare the cake:

1. Preheat the oven to 350 °F heat. Grease any baking pan with butter.
2. Put the softened butter, sugar, vanilla sugar, and salt in a mixing bowl and beat until creamy. One at a time, beat in the eggs.
3. In a small bowl, mix the flour with the baking powder and sift it into the batter. Add the milk and mix on low speed for one minute. Then pour the batter into the greased baking pan, smooth the top and bake for about 45 minutes. Remove and let cool completely in the pan.

Prepare the owl pops:

4. Trim the firm, dark edges of the cooled cake all around. Place the cake in a large bowl and crumble finely. Add the cream cheese and mix everything well with your hands.
5. Roll the sticky cake mixture into balls about 1" in size, carefully form two small, pointed ears each with your fingers, push a cake pop stem into the bottom of each one, and place them on a large, flat plate with a little distance between them. Place in the refrigerator for one hour.
6. In the meantime, melt the white chocolate over a water bath. Then dip each owl by the handle into the melted chocolate and coat all around. Gently drip off all excess chocolate. Place in a cake pop stand and return to the refrigerator until the chocolate has dried.
7. Meanwhile, place the powdered sugar in a small bowl, gradually add the water, and stir until smooth. Then dip each of the owl pops into the icing twice at an angle to create a white head and wings (see picture). Place in the cake pop stand and let dry for about 2-3 minutes.
8. Attach the decorative sugar eyes to the icing while it is still sticky. Allow to dry completely. Lastly, decorate with the food pencil as desired.

GRYFFINDOR

BUTTERBEER MACARONS

INGREDIENTS FOR APPROX. 35-40 MACARONS (BY SIZE)

For the macaron shells:
5 oz peeled, ground almonds
10 oz powdered sugar
1 oz cocoa powder
5 egg whites (from large eggs, at room temperature)
1 pinch of salt
1.5 oz sugar
Brown food coloring, to taste

For the butterbeer filling:
7 oz sugar
4 oz butter
4 oz whipped cream
3 fl. oz malt beer
½ tsp salt, to taste

Also needed: piping bag with wide-hole nozzle

Make the macaron shells:

1. Mix the ground almonds in a small bowl with the powdered sugar and cocoa powder and sift finely twice.

2. Beat the egg whites with the salt until stiff. Gradually sift in the sugar and continue to work through until you have a smooth, glossy cream. Add the brown food coloring and then fold the almond mixture into the colored egg whites in three batches until you have a homogeneous, viscous mixture that is not too runny, but not too firm either.

3. Pour the macaron mixture into a piping bag fitted with a wide hole nozzle and place small, coin-sized blobs of dough on a baking sheet lined with parchment paper.

4. Let rest for 30 minutes or until a fine "skin" forms on the macarons.

5. Meanwhile, preheat the oven to 300 °F heat.

6. Reduce the oven temperature to 290 °F and bake the macarons for about 14-16 minutes.

7. Remove the macaron shells from the oven, carefully pull them together with the baking paper from the baking tray onto a cold work surface and let them cool completely; this will make it easier to remove the macarons from the paper later. Meanwhile, prepare the filling.

Prepare the filling:

8. in a pan over low heat, melt the sugar to get light golden caramel. This can take up to 15 minutes. Attention: Do not stir during this time!

Continued on next page ...

9. Cut the butter into small pieces and stir one at a time into the sugar until you have a creamy caramel. Then add the salt and stir it in.

10. In a small saucepan, gently warm the cream with the malt beer. (Caution: Do not boil!) Then gently stir into the caramel mixture and simmer for 2-3 minutes, stirring occasionally. Pour into a jar, let cool slightly, and store in the refrigerator until ready to use.

11. Fill the butterbeer macarons:

12. Sort the finished macaron shells and make equal-sized pairs that fit well together. Place half of the macarons, "flat" side up, on a baking sheet lined with parchment paper.

13. Pour the caramel cream into a piping bag with a wide nozzle and pipe a blob on each of the "bottom" macaron shells. Place the matching "top" shell on top, press down lightly and refrigerate until ready to eat. Enjoy within 1-2 days!

AUNT PETUNIA'S WIND CAKE

INGREDIENTS FOR 1 WIND CAKE

For the meringue shells:
8 egg whites
2 tbsp lemon juice
1 pinch of salt
12 oz sugar

For the filling:
11 oz cold whipped cream
1 tbsp vanilla sugar
1 packet of cream stiffener
18 oz mixed fresh berries (e.g. blackberries, raspberries, currants)

For the cream:
14 oz cold whipped cream
4 tbsp sugar
2 packets of cream stiffener
A few drops of purple food coloring
A few drops of mint green food coloring
Candied cherries, as garnish

Also needed:
14 purple decorative flowers made of fondant or marzipan, piping bag with large hole nozzle and medium star nozzle

Prepare the meringue slices:

1. Preheat the oven to 210 °F.
2. Spread a piece of baking paper on the work surface and draw an 8" diameter circle and three 6" diameter circles on the paper with a pencil. Place them on two baking sheets with the marks facing up.
3. In an ungreased bowl, beat the egg whites at medium speed until foamy. Then add the lemon juice and salt, gradually adding the sugar. Continue beating until stiff peaks form. Put the meringue mixture into a piping bag with a large nozzle and pipe the meringue evenly into circles on the baking paper to make one large and three smaller meringue slices. Then bake for at least an hour, or until the meringue is set and can be easily removed from the baking paper. Meanwhile, prepare the filling and the cream.
4. Prepare the filling:
5. In a bowl, whip the cream. Once the cream becomes fluffy, sprinkle in the vanilla sugar and cream stiffener and continue beating until stiff peaks form. Then stir in the berries, cover with plastic wrap, and refrigerate until ready to use.
6. Prepare the cream:
7. In another bowl, beat the whipping cream at medium speed. Once the cream is fluffy, sprinkle in the sugar and cream stiffener and continue beating until stiff peaks form. Then remove ¾ of the whipped cream and place in a separate bowl with a few drops of food coloring to tint it purple. Color the rest of the whipped cream mint green. Place each of the colored whipped creams in separate piping bags fitted with medium star nozzles.

Continued on next page ...

8. Pipe everything together:
   Place the larger meringue slice on a serving plate or round pie plate. Spoon some of the fruit filling into the center and spread evenly, leaving about 2" to the edge. Place one of the smaller meringue slices on top, again spreading some of the filling on top and again leaving a 2" border. Repeat this procedure until you finish with the last meringue slice.

9. Using the piping bags, pipe large rosettes of green and purple cream alternately at regular intervals around the edge of the cake, starting with the bottom meringue slice. Decorate the edge of each cake layer in this manner. Add a continuous border of purple cream to the top edge. Place the candied cherries in the bottom and top tier and decorate the cake all around evenly with the purple decorative flowers (see picture). Serve promptly and earn lots of admiring glances!

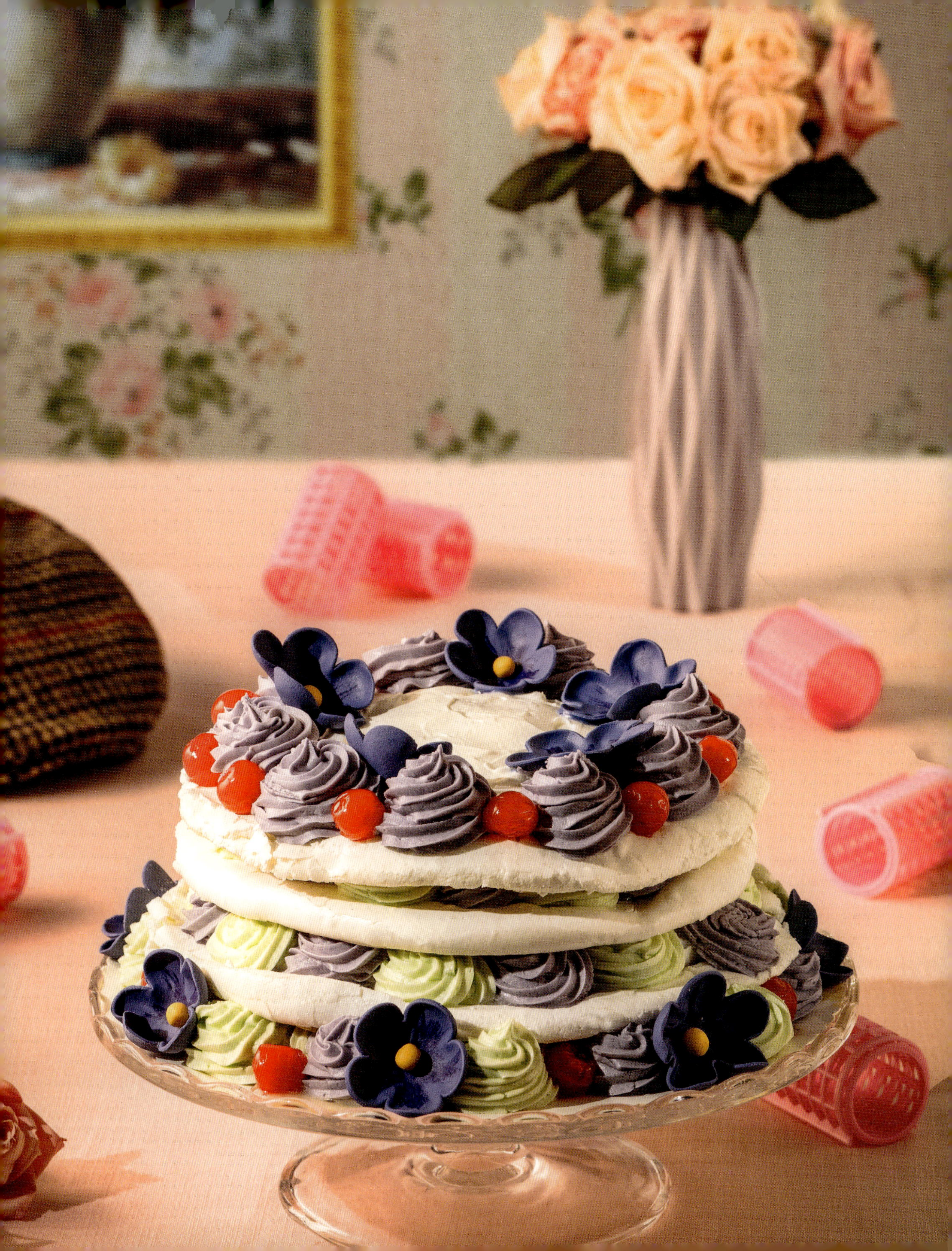

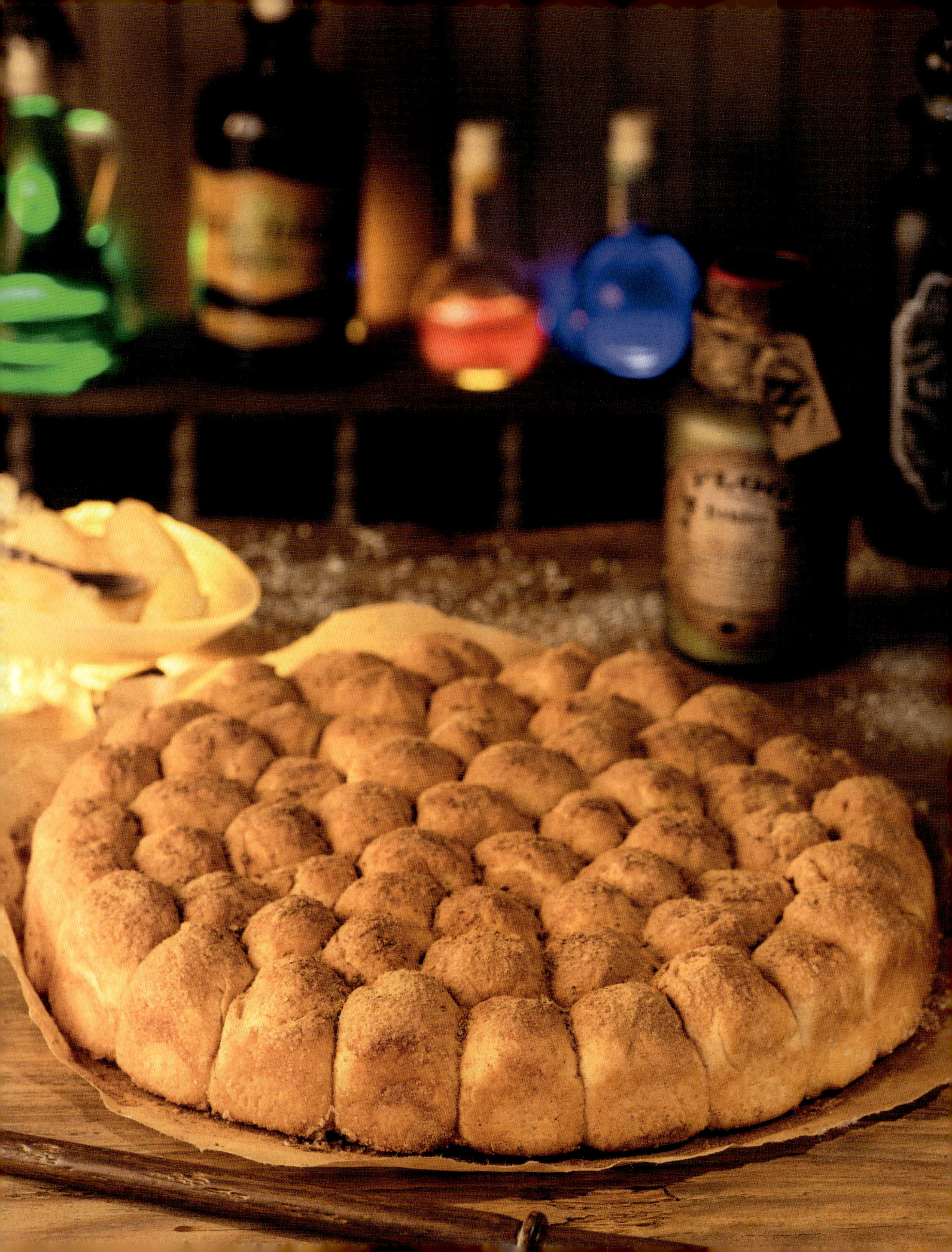

MAGIC BUBBLE BREAD

INGREDIENTS FOR 1 LOAF

For the dough:
18 oz flour
1 packet of dry yeast
1 tsp salt
3 oz sugar for the dough plus 2 tbsp for sprinkling
2 tbsp oil
10 fl. oz lukewarm water
1.5 oz melted butter plus a little more, for greasing the baking pan
1 packet vanilla sugar
1 tsp cinnamon

For the apple compote:
28 oz tart apples, peeled and cut into small pieces
1 tbsp lemon juice
7 fl. oz apple juice
2 tbsp sugar

Also required: round 11" baking tray or springform pan (approx. 11" diameter)

Prepare the dough:

1. In a bowl, combine the flour and dry yeast and place in a mixing bowl with the salt, 2.5 oz of sugar and the oil. Add the water and knead all the ingredients thoroughly for at least 10 minutes. Then let the dough rise for 50 minutes in a warm place, covered with a clean tea towel.

2. Grease a round baking sheet or springform pan generously with butter.

Prepare the apple compote:

3. Place the chopped apples in a large saucepan with the lemon juice, apple juice and sugar and bring to a boil over medium heat, stirring occasionally. Put the lid on and simmer for 15 minutes. Remove from heat and allow to cool. If the stewed apples are to be served chilled, refrigerate until ready to eat.

4. Preheat the oven to 350 °F.

5. Meanwhile, knead the risen dough thoroughly again and cut off 0.5 oz of dough at a time. Form golf ball-sized balls from the dough pieces with your hands and place them seamlessly together on the baking sheet or in the springform pan. Cover again and let rise for 15 minutes.

6. Mix the vanilla sugar, cinnamon, and the remaining 2 tbsp sugar in a small bowl.

7. Brush the bubble bread generously with the melted butter using a pastry brush and sprinkle with the sugar and cinnamon mixture. Bake in the preheated oven for about 20-25 minutes until golden brown. Remove and let cool for a few minutes. Then carefully remove from the pan.

8. Serve the bubble bread, preferably whole, with the apple compote.

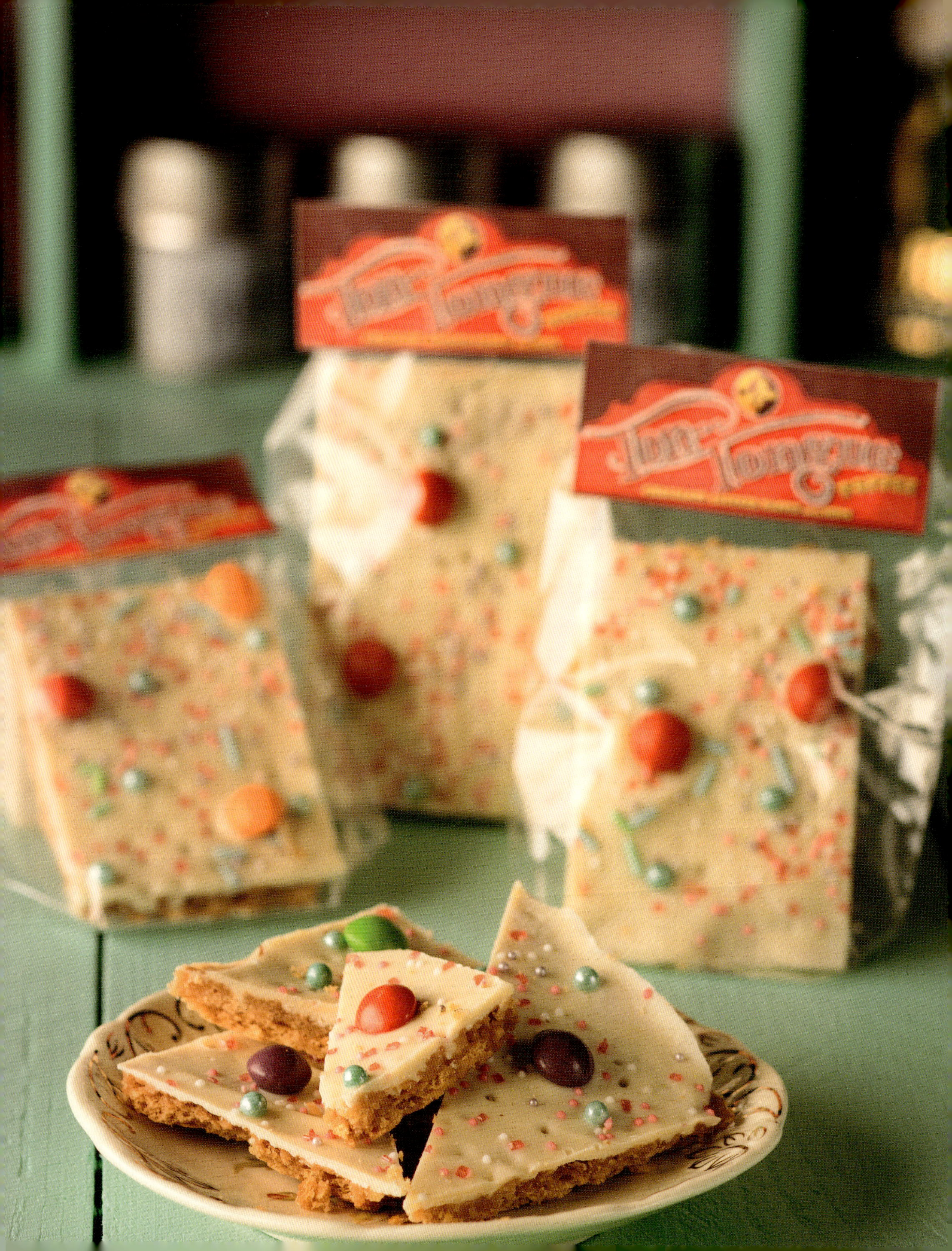

TON-TONGUE TOFFEES

INGREDIENTS FOR APPROX. 5-6 PORTIONS

Approx. 25 salted crackers
8 oz butter
7 oz sugar
12 oz white chocolate, coarsely chopped
Colorful chocolate candies
Colorful sprinkles

1. Line a small baking tray with baking paper and preheat the oven to 340 °F heat.

2. Spread the crackers in an even layer seamlessly over the entire tray. Break off pieces of the crackers from the edges of the pan, if necessary, so that they finish neatly.

3. Place the butter and sugar in a small saucepan and bring slowly to a boil over medium heat, stirring regularly. Simmer for two minutes.

4. Pour the butter-sugar mixture evenly over the crackers, smooth with a kitchen spatula, and place in the preheated oven for about 10 minutes. Then remove and let cool for a few minutes.

5. In the meantime, melt the white chocolate in a small bowl over a water bath. Make sure that the bottom of the bowl does not touch the water! Then pour the melted chocolate evenly over the cooled toffee crackers and gently smooth with a kitchen spatula. Decorate to your heart's content with the chocolate candies and colorful sprinkles, then let set.

6. Cut the ton-tongue toffees into pieces as desired on a cutting board with a large, sharp knife and store in an airtight container.

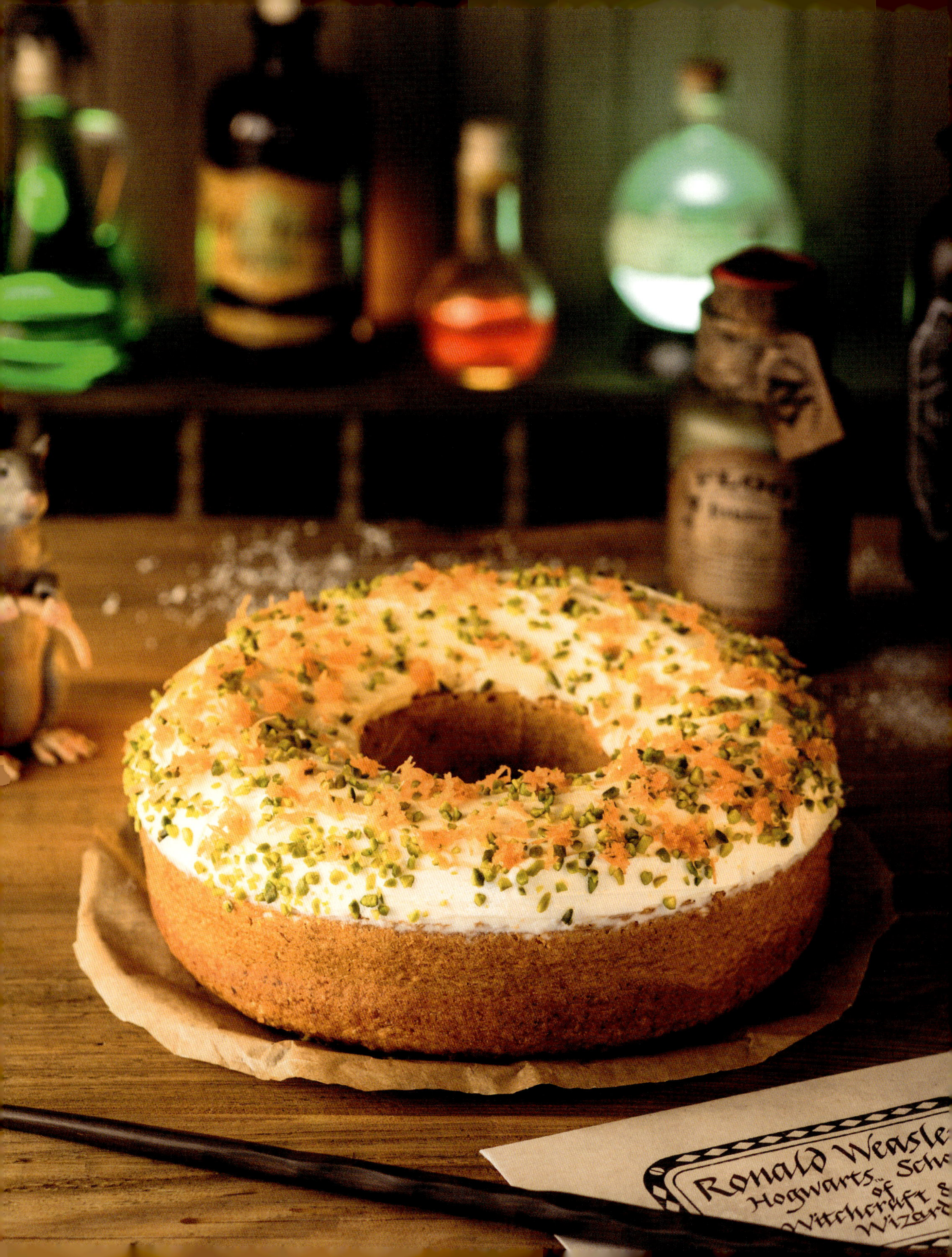
Ronald Weasle
Hogwarts Sch
of
Witchcraft &
Wizard

MRS. WEASLEY'S CARROT CAKE

INGREDIENTS FOR 1 CAKE

Butter for greasing the mold
9 oz flour plus a little more,
for sprinkling the mold
4 eggs
8 oz sugar
9 fl. oz neutral oil
1 tsp cinnamon
14 oz fresh carrots, grated
4 oz ground almonds
4 oz ground hazelnuts
2 tsp baking powder
11 oz cream cheese
1 squeeze of lemon juice
4 oz powdered sugar
Vanilla extract, to taste
Chopped pistachios, as garnish

Also required:
11" springform pan

1. Grease a 11" springform pan with a round bottom with butter and sprinkle with a little flour. Preheat the oven to 350 °F heat.

2. In a bowl, mix the eggs, sugar, oil, and cinnamon thoroughly with an electric mixer until smooth.

3. Set aside 2 tbsp of grated carrot as garnish. Add the remaining carrot, almonds, and hazelnuts to the bowl and beat until incorporated.

4. In a separate bowl, mix together the flour and baking powder and stir into the mixture as well.

5. Pour the batter into the prepared springform pan and bake in the preheated oven for 45-50 minutes, or until a toothpick inserted into the center comes out clean. Then remove the cake from the oven and let it cool in the pan.

6. In the meantime, put the cream cheese and lemon juice in a small bowl, mix until smooth, and gradually add the powdered sugar. Finally, add the vanilla extract to taste and incorporate thoroughly.

7. Remove the cake from the pan.

8. Place the frosting in a freezer bag, cut off one corner and spread evenly over the cake. Sprinkle with the remaining carrot shavings and the chopped pistachios. Serve promptly.

DROOBLE'S BEST

Blowing Gum

Guaranteed to never lose flavour!

DRUHBEL'S BEST BUBBLE GUM

INGREDIENTS FOR APPROX. 7 OZ OF GUM
4 oz chicle (natural chewing gum)
1 oz glucose syrup
1 tsp citric acid
8-10 drops of natural flavoring, to taste
1.5 oz glycerin (from the pharmacy)
A few drops of blue food coloring
5 oz sifted powdered sugar and some more, as a coating

1. Put the chewing gum raw mass together with the glucose syrup, the citric acid, and the natural flavoring of your choice in a plastic bowl and heat it at approx. 1,000 watts for 30 seconds in the microwave, or alternatively in a water bath. Stir the mixture thoroughly and heat again for 30 seconds until the natural gum is completely melted.

2. Now stir in the glycerin well and incorporate the food coloring until the mixture has taken on the desired blue color. Then add the sifted powdered sugar and knead with your hands until all the sugar is carefully incorporated. If possible, use disposable gloves, as the mixture is extremely sticky.

3. Roll out the mass on the work surface, remove small pieces at a time, form them into marble-sized balls, and turn them in powdered sugar so that the chewing gum pieces are coated with it all over. It is important to process the chewing gum as quickly as possible, as the more it cools down, the more difficult it becomes to shape the mass.

4. Keep for several months in an airtight container.

The easiest way to get chicle is over the Internet.

H. Potter
The Cupboard under the Stairs
4 Privet Drive
Little Whinging
SURREY

DUMBLEDORE'S FAVORITE LEMON DROPS

INGREDIENTS FOR APPROX. 14 OZ

11 oz sugar
5 oz dextrose
4 fl. oz water
2 tsp ascorbic acid
15 drops of natural lemon oil
3 drops of yellow food coloring
1 large pinch talcum powder

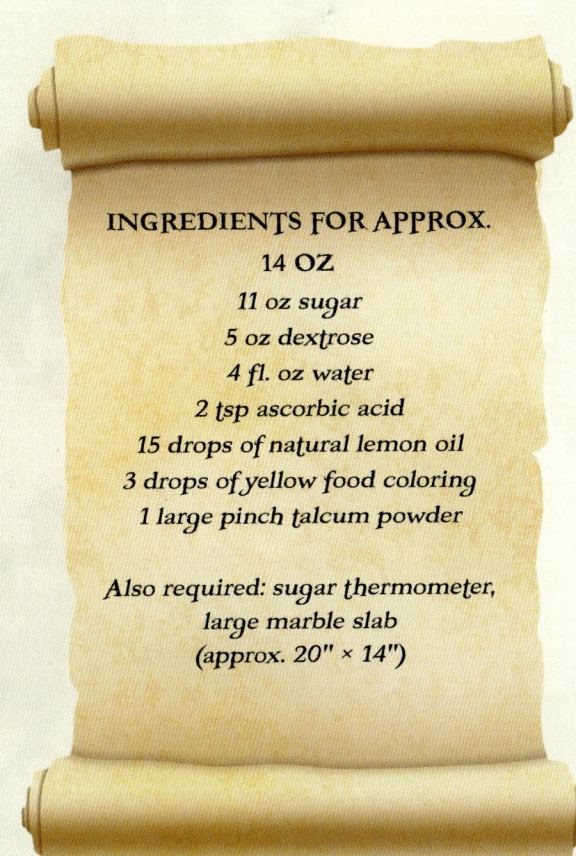

Also required: sugar thermometer, large marble slab (approx. 20" × 14")

1. Brush the marble plate thinly with oil.

2. Put the sugar, dextrose, and water in a small saucepan and bring to a boil gently over high heat. Be extremely careful here, as the sugar mixture is very hot and splashes on the skin can cause severe burns! Measure the temperature regularly with a sugar thermometer and heat the mixture until it reaches 310 °F (approx. 10 minutes).

3. Now pour the hot sugar mixture evenly onto the greased marble slab, taking care that nothing runs down the edge. At the same time, use a spatula to quickly loosen the mixture from the plate and knead it. While doing this, spread the ascorbic acid, lemon oil and food coloring evenly over the sugar mixture and quickly incorporate.

4. Once the candy mixture has cooled enough to handle safely, pull it into thin strands with your hands and cut off marble-sized pieces with household scissors. Place the drops in a freezer bag with the talcum powder, seal the bag, and shake well until the drops are coated all around with the powder; this will keep them from sticking together.

5. In an airtight container, Dumbledore's favorite lemon drops will keep for 1-2 months.

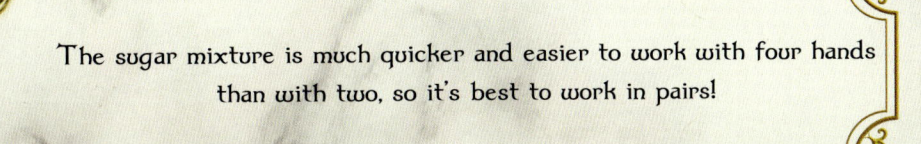

The sugar mixture is much quicker and easier to work with four hands than with two, so it's best to work in pairs!

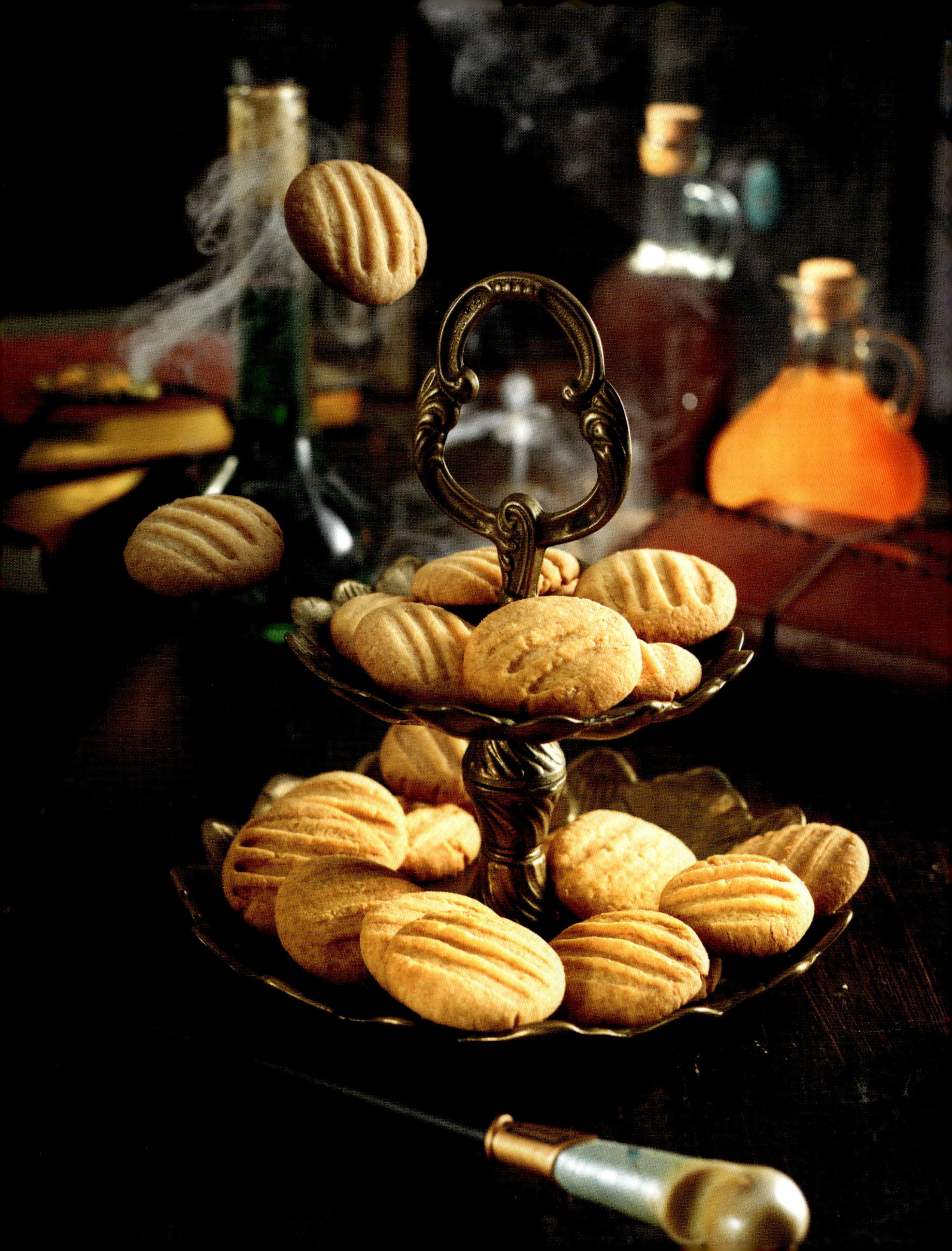

GINGER COOKIES

INGREDIENTS FOR APPROX. 25 COOKIES
8 oz soft butter
5 oz cane sugar
1 tsp ginger, freshly grated
12 oz flour
½ packet baking powder
2 oz candied ginger, finely chopped

1. Preheat the oven to 390 °F heat. Line a baking tray with baking paper.

2. Beat the soft butter with the cane sugar in a mixing bowl until creamy. Mix in the ginger. In a separate bowl, combine the flour and baking powder and sift into the butter and sugar mixture. Mix everything together thoroughly. Add the ginger and work with your hands until you have a smooth dough.

3. Form about 25 walnut-sized balls from the dough, place them on the prepared baking sheet and flatten them with a moistened fork or your hands to a thickness of about ½ inch. Then bake the ginger cookies approx.

4. Bake for 12-15 minutes until golden brown. Then remove from the oven and let cool completely on a cooling rack.

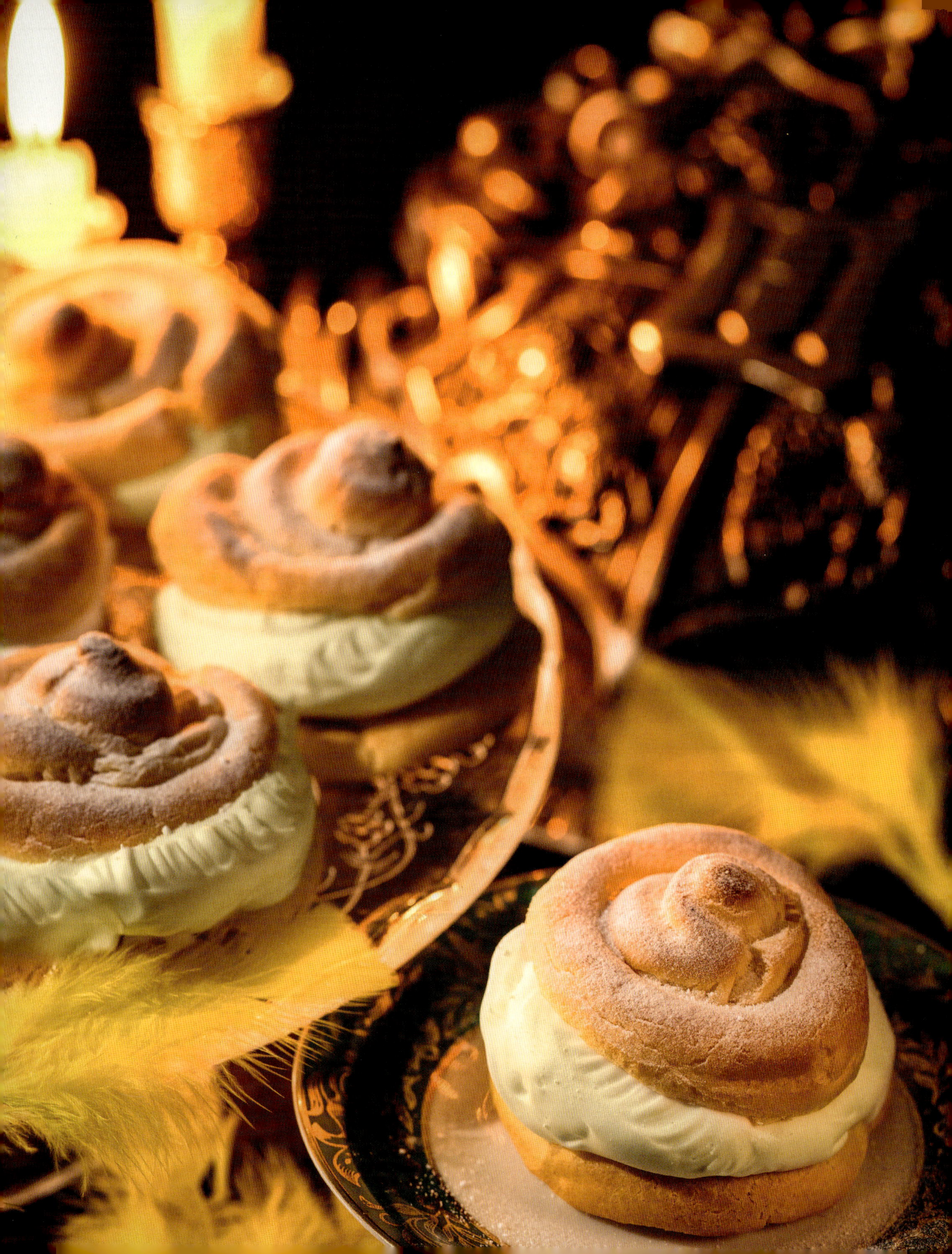

CANARY CREAM PUFFS

INGREDIENTS FOR APPROX. 10-12 CANARY CREAM PUFFS

For the dough:
4 fl. oz water
1 oz butter
0.5 oz flour
0.5 oz cornstarch
2 eggs
1 pinch baking powder

For the filling:
14 oz cream
2 packets of cream stiffener
1 oz powdered sugar
1 packet vanilla sugar
Juice of ½ lemon
5 drops of yellow food coloring

Also needed: piping bag with large star-shaped nozzle and filling nozzle

1. Preheat the oven to 390 °F heat. Line a baking tray with baking paper.

2. Bring the water and butter to the boil in a small saucepan. Remove from the heat.

3. Mix the flour with the cornstarch in a bowl and add to the pot with the melted butter. Stir until smooth, then heat for one minute, stirring constantly.

4. Pour the batter into a mixing bowl. One at a time, beat the eggs into the batter using a mixer with a dough hook attachment on high speed. Then mix in the baking powder.

5. Using a piping bag with a large star-shaped nozzle, pipe 10-12 heaps of dough onto the baking tray and bake in the preheated oven for approx. 20 minutes. Caution: Do not open the oven door during the baking time, otherwise the pastry will collapse!

6. After the baking time, remove the cream puffs immediately from the oven, cut off the "lids" with a sharp knife, and let everything cool completely on a cooling rack.

7. Meanwhile, prepare the filling. To do this, put the cream in a bowl, add the cream stiffener, powdered sugar, vanilla powder, lemon juice and food coloring and beat with a hand mixer until stiff. Once the cream puffs are finally cooled, pipe them into the pastry using a piping bag with a filling nozzle or a freezer bag with the corner cut off.

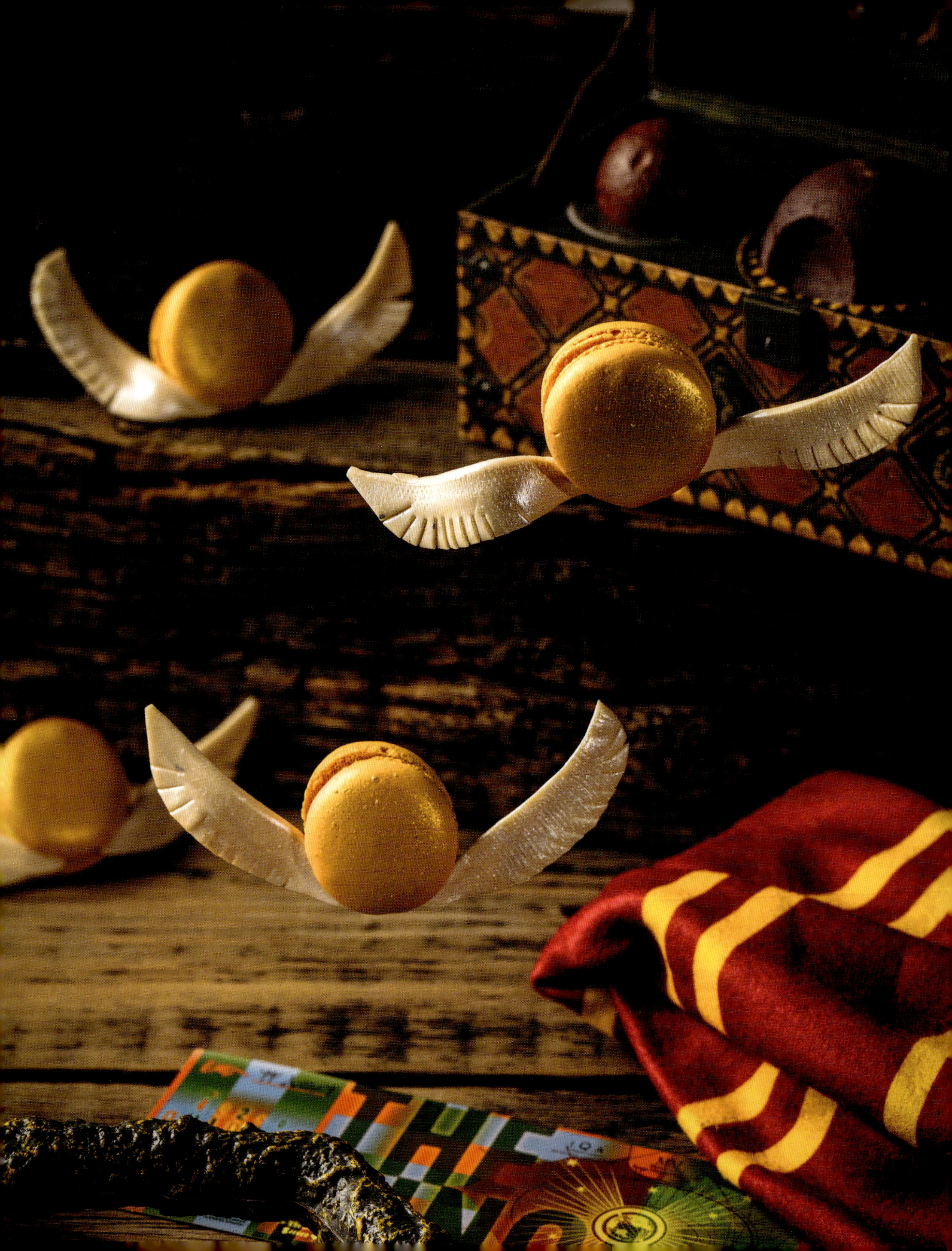

GOLDEN SNITCH

INGREDIENTS FOR APPROX. 12 SNITCHES

For the macarons:
1.5 oz ground almonds
3 oz powdered sugar
1.3 oz egg white (36g)
0.5 oz sugar
Yellow food coloring paste

For the ganache:
4 oz dark chocolate, finely chopped
1 tsp grated orange peel
4 fl. oz cream
24 narrow chewy candy strips, cut to size as wings

Also needed: edible gold powder, piping bag with hole nozzle

1. Put the almonds with the powdered sugar in a high cup, mix together and grind as finely as possible in a blender. Then sieve thoroughly twice.

2. Weigh the egg white exactly and beat with a mixer until stiff. Once the egg white becomes foamy, pour in the sugar, and continue beating until stiff peaks form.

3. Now add the yellow food coloring and continue beating for about 1 minute. Transfer all of this to a large bowl, gradually add the almond and powdered sugar mixture and gently fold in. Blend to a viscous, glossy mixture and pour into a piping bag fitted with a hole nozzle.

4. Line a baking tray with baking paper. Using the piping bag, pipe macaron blobs about 1" apart onto the sheet, spacing them slightly apart. Then gently tap the underside of the tray on the work surface to release any air bubbles.

5. Let rest for 30 minutes.

6. Meanwhile, preheat the oven to 300 °F heat. Put the tray in, reduce the heat to 290 °F and bake for about 12-14 minutes. Then remove and let the macarons cool on the tray.

7. Meanwhile, put the chocolate in a bowl. Bring the orange zest and cream to a boil once in a small saucepan over medium heat, stirring constantly, then pour over the chocolate. Let sit for two minutes. Then stir everything until no lumps are visible. Place in the refrigerator for at least one hour. Then mix well again and pour into a piping bag with any nozzle.

8. Remove the macarons from the baking paper and spread half of them out on the work surface, flat side up. Pipe a dollop of ganache on each, place two of the chewy candy strips on the left and right as wings so that they are held in place by the ganache, then (again, flat side up) place one macaron half on top of each and press down lightly. Refrigerate overnight and last but not least, brush all around with edible gold powder. Refrigerate and enjoy within 5-7 days.

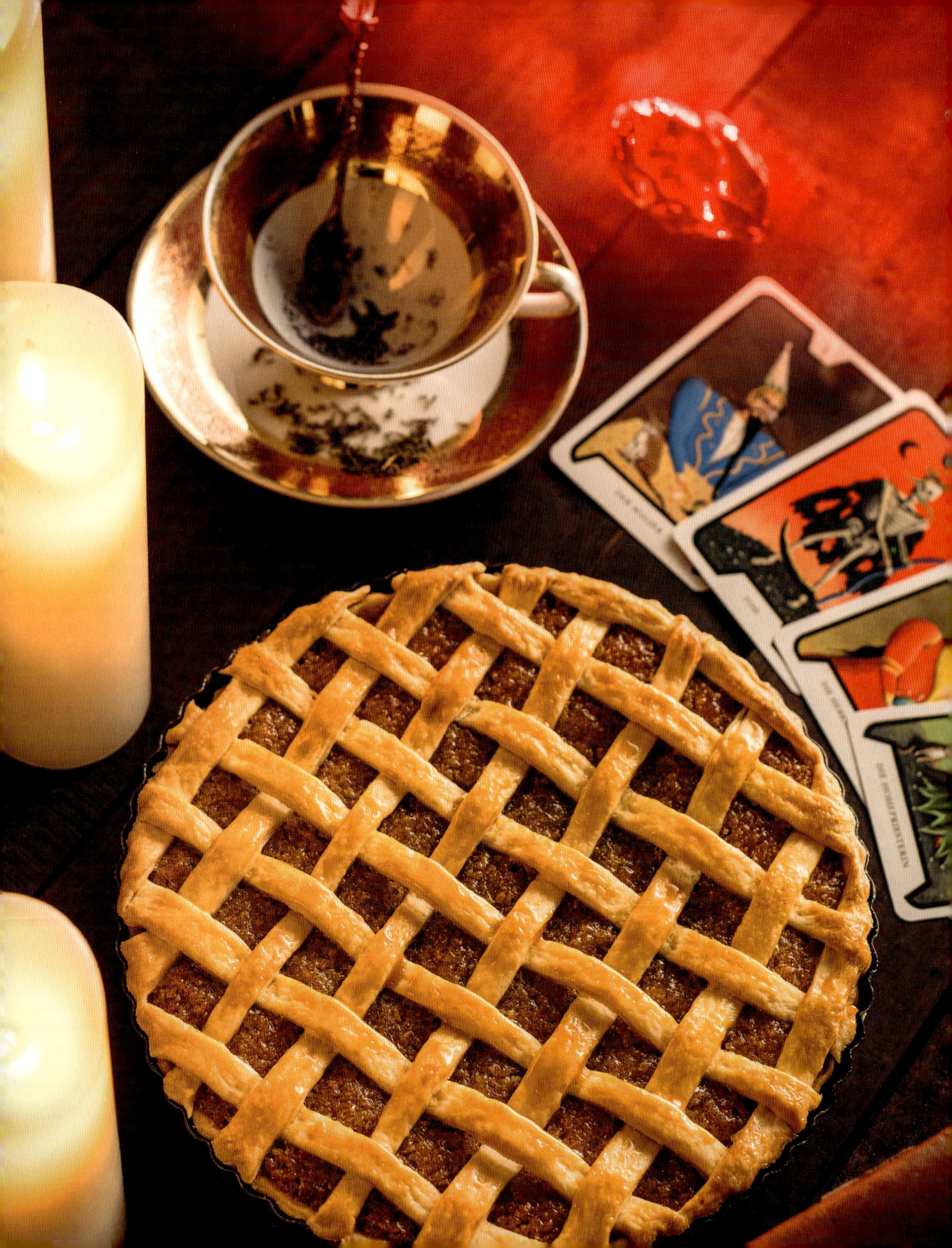

TREACLE TART

INGREDIENTS FOR 1 TART

For the cake base:
9 oz flour plus a little more, for dusting the work surface.
2 tbsp powdered sugar
Zest of 1 lemon
1 pinch of salt
6 oz cold butter, cubed
1 egg yolk
1-2 tbsp very cold water

For the filling:
20 fl. oz sugar syrup
1 pinch of ground ginger
5 oz fresh breadcrumbs
Zest and juice of 1 lemon
1 egg, beaten

Also required: cake pan (approx. 10" diameter), dried beans or other blind baking weights

Prepare the cake base:

1. Mix the flour, powdered sugar, lemon zest and salt in a bowl. Work in the cold butter cubes until the whole resembles breadcrumbs in consistency. Add the egg yolk and 1-2 tbsp of very cold water. Knead into a dough with your hands, turn out onto a lightly floured work surface, form into a ball, wrap tightly in plastic wrap and place for 30 minutes in the refrigerator.

2. Remove of the dough, wrap again with plastic wrap and return to refrigerator. Roll out the remaining dough on a lightly floured surface to a round of 12" diameter and a thickness of about ¼ inch. Then spread the dough across the baking pan and press it to the bottom and edges of the pan, making sure that the dough reaches all the corners. Seal any holes or gaps with a little extra dough. Finally, prick the bottom of the dough a few times with a fork and place it in the refrigerator for 30 minutes.

3. In the meantime, preheat the oven to 375 °F and preheat a baking tray in it.

4. Line the cooled cake base with baking paper and fill with baking beans or other blind baking weights. Place in the oven for 15 minutes, then remove the baking paper and weights and bake again for about 5 minutes or until the pie crust is golden brown.

5. Roll out the remaining dough as thinly as possible (approx. 1/8 inch) to a circle of approx. 10" in diameter. Cut into strips about ¼ inch thin.

Continued on the next page...

Prepare the filling:

6. Heat the sugar syrup and ground ginger in a saucepan over low heat until the mixture is hot but not boiling. Add the breadcrumbs, lemon zest, lemon juice,

7. stir in beaten egg, and mix everything well. Pour onto the cake base and spread evenly.

8. Use the pastry strips to create a lattice pattern on top of the cake. To do this, start on a piece of baking paper in one corner and then place the strips of dough over and under each other as if braiding. Then carefully lift the lattice onto the top of the cake and gently pull the paper away. This is easier than arranging the strips individually on top of the cake, as there is a risk of the dough falling into the filling.

9. Bake the tart for about 30-35 minutes, until the filling has set and the pastry is golden brown. Remove from oven and cool on a cooling rack for about 15 minutes. Gently remove from baking pan and serve warm.

10.
Heat the sugar syrup and ground ginger in a saucepan over low heat until the mixture is hot but not boiling. Add the breadcrumbs, lemon zest, lemon juice,

11. stir in beaten egg, and mix everything well. Pour onto the cake base and spread evenly.

12. Use the pastry strips to create a lattice pattern on top of the cake. To do this, start on a piece of baking paper in one corner and then place the strips of dough over and under each other as if braiding. Then carefully lift the lattice onto the top of the cake and gently pull the paper away. This is easier than arranging the strips individually on top of the cake, as there is a risk of the dough falling into the filling.

13. Bake the tart for about 30-35 minutes, until the filling has set and the pastry is golden brown. Remove from oven and cool on a cooling rack for about 15 minutes. Gently remove from baking pan and serve warm.

CANDIED PINEAPPLE

INGREDIENTS FOR ONE BATCH OF CANDIED PINEAPPLE
1 pineapple (approx. 2 lb)
1 qt water
2 lb sugar
Juice of 1 lemon
Some extra fine sugar

1. Remove peel and core from pineapple with a large, sharp knife or pineapple slicer. Cut into finger-thick slices and then into bite-sized pieces. Place in a saucepan with the water. Bring to a boil briefly over medium heat. Simmer for 18-20 minutes, stirring occasionally. Remove the pineapple chunks with a slotted spoon, drain thoroughly in a colander, and place in a large bowl.

2. Stir 9.5 oz sugar into the cooking liquid. Stir in the lemon juice and boil for about 3 minutes. Remove from the heat, let cool a bit, and pour over the pineapple chunks in the bowl. Place a plate, as heavy as possible, upside down on top so that all pieces are covered with liquid.

3. Let sit for 24 hours.

4. Remove the pineapple pieces from the bowl and drain thoroughly in a colander. Collect the juice, put it in a saucepan and add 4 oz of sugar. Bring to a boil, stirring constantly, and boil for about 2 minutes. Remove from heat and allow to cool slightly. Then return the drained pineapple to the bowl and pour the juice over it. As before, cover with a heavy plate and let sit for 24 hours.

5. Repeat step 3 the next day.

6. Repeat the same procedure (step 4) the next day and the day after that, but this time, add 5 oz of sugar.

7. Repeat again, this time adding 9.5 oz of sugar. Then let it rest for 48 hours. Put the pineapple chunks and the syrup into a saucepan.

Continued on the next page...

8. Bring to a boil over medium heat, stirring constantly, and simmer for about 5 minutes.

9. Meanwhile, line a baking tray with aluminum foil and place a baking rack on top. Preheat the oven to 210 °F.

10. Now carefully remove the pineapple pieces from the pot and place them on the baking rack to drain. Allow to dry in the oven for about 12-18 hours, holding the oven door open a crack with a wooden spoon to allow all moisture to escape. Then turn off the oven and let the pineapple cool in it for a bit.

11. Sprinkle the extra fine sugar in a large, deep plate. Roll the dry but still slightly sticky pineapple chunks all around in the sugar so they are completely covered by it. Store in an airtight container; place some wax paper between each pineapple layer to keep the pieces from sticking together. The candied pineapple will keep for up to 4 weeks.

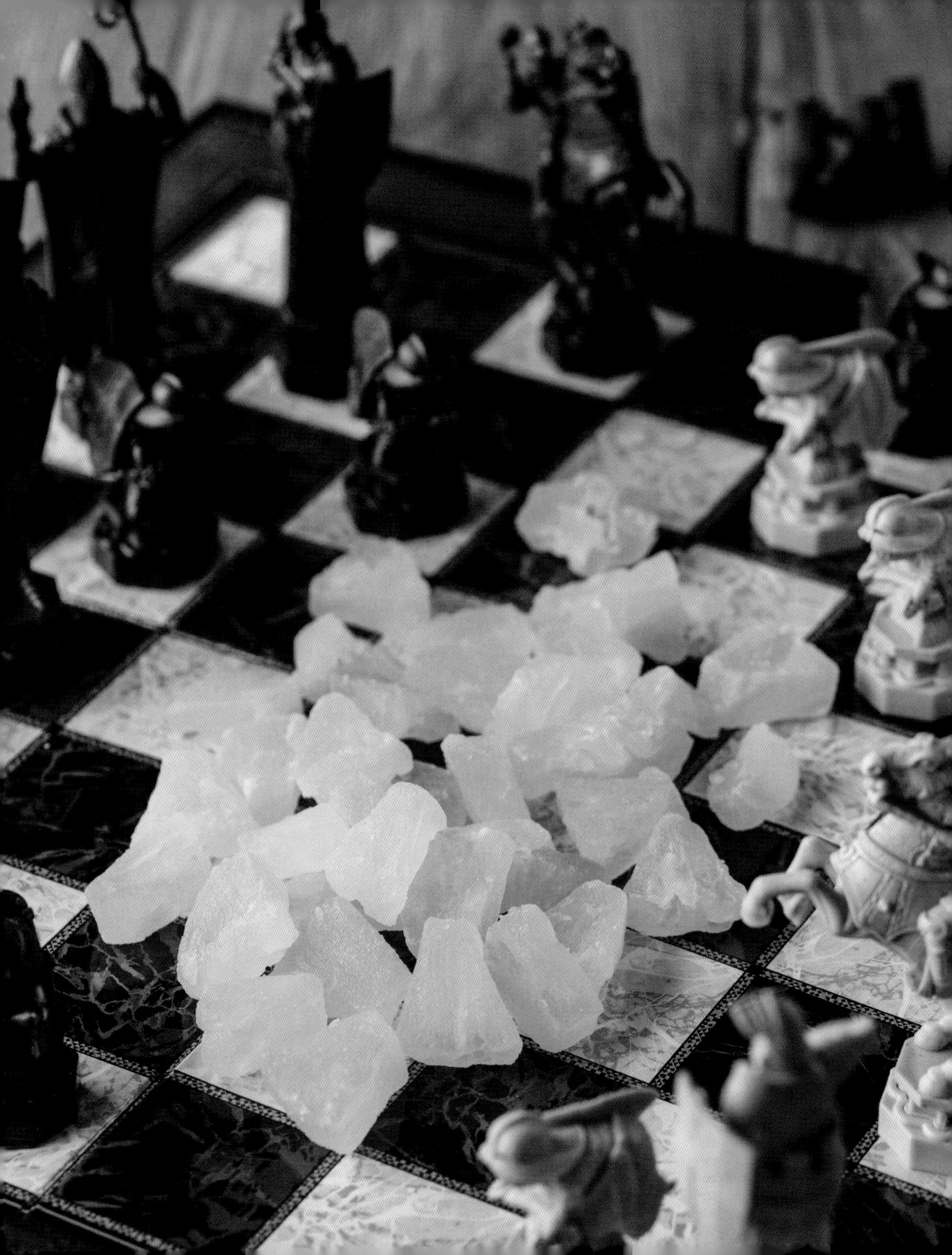

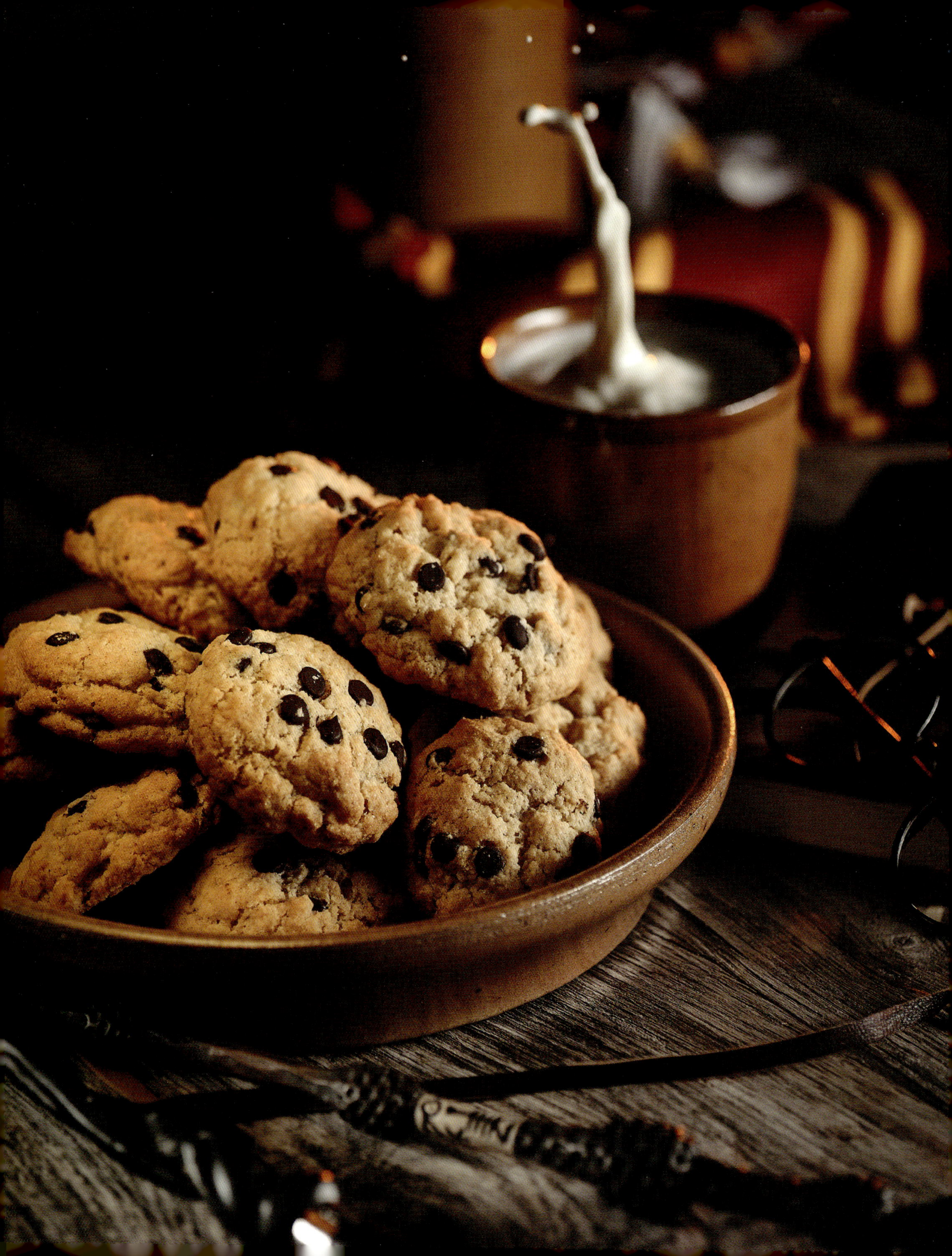

ROCK CAKES

INGREDIENTS FOR APPROX. 12 CAKES
8 oz flour
1 packet baking powder
4 oz very cold butter
4 oz sugar
1 level tsp cinnamon
1 pinch of nutmeg
1 pinch of salt
1 egg
1-2 tbsp milk
4 oz chocolate drops

1. Preheat the oven to 350 °F. Line a baking tray with baking paper.

2. Sift the flour finely and mix it with the baking powder in a bowl. Cut the butter into small pieces and knead into the flour until the mixture looks smooth. Add the sugar and spices and coarsely incorporate.

3. Beat the egg and, if necessary, add it to the dough mixture along with a little milk. Mix everything with a dough scraper until the dough resembles coarse breadcrumbs in consistency. Now gently incorporate the chocolate drops.

4. Using a tbsp, place ping-pong ball sized "blobs" of dough on the baking sheet, leaving about 2" between each cookie. Bake in preheated oven for about 17-20 minutes or until rock cookies are golden brown. Remove from oven and let cool on a cooling rack.

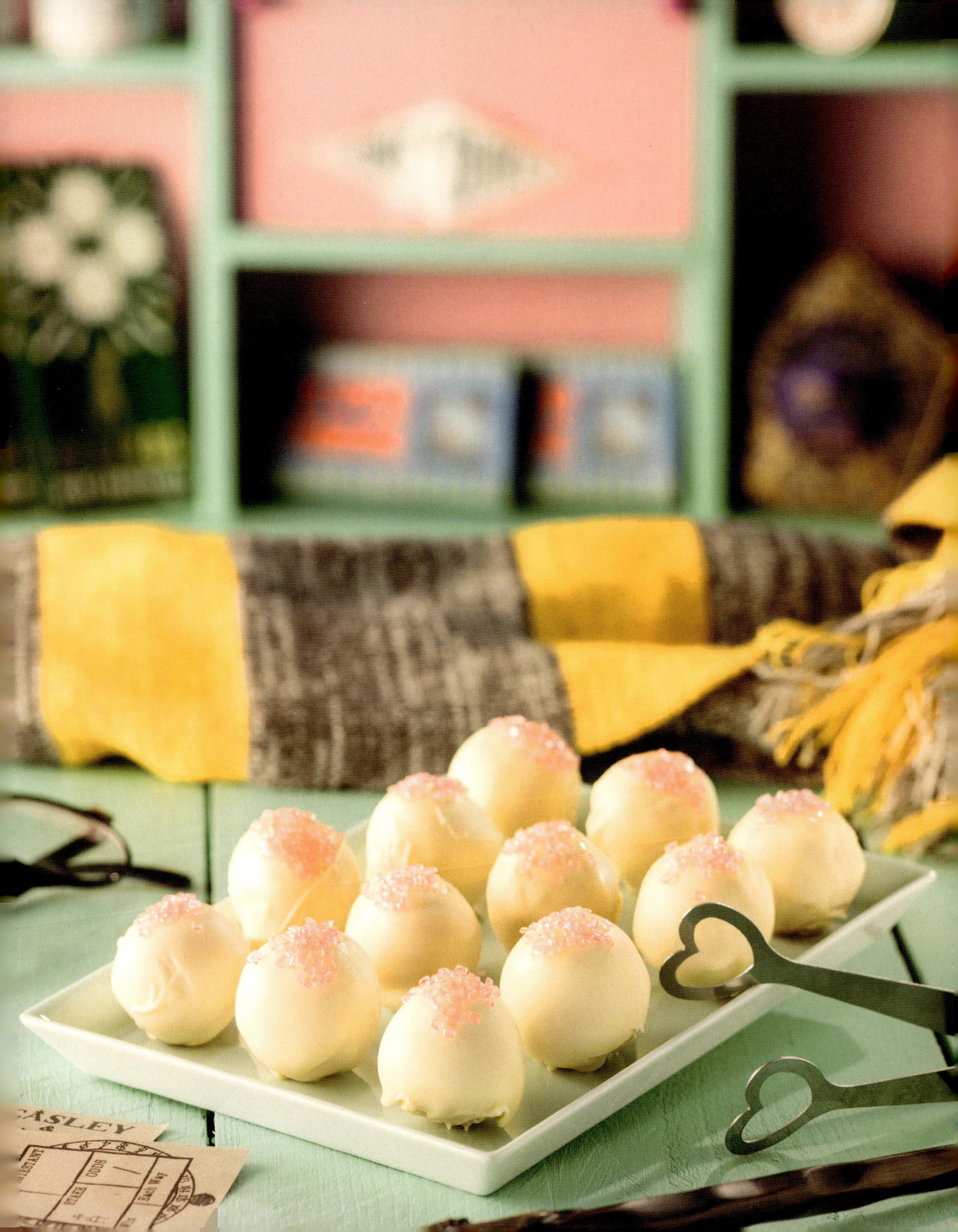

HICCUP DROPS

INGREDIENTS FOR APPROX. 25 DROPS
4 oz soft butter
6 oz sugar
2 eggs, Room Temperature
9 oz flour
1½ tsp baking powder
1 pinch salt
5 oz sour cream
Approx. 6 oz lemon curd
1 oz pop rocks
11 oz white chocolate, chopped
Glitter sugar, for decorating
Also required: Springform pan (approx. 8" diameter).

1. Preheat the oven to 350 °F heat. Line a springform pan with baking paper.

2. In a mixing bowl, beat the butter and sugar with an electric hand mixer until creamy white. Add the eggs one at a time, beating them in briefly at a time.

3. In a separate bowl, combine the flour, baking powder and salt, add to the mixing bowl and mix briefly. Stir in the sour cream. Pour the batter into the prepared springform pan and bake in the preheated oven for about 40 minutes, or until nothing sticks to a toothpick inserted in the center when you pull it out. Then remove from the oven and let cool completely in the pan.

4. Remove the cake from the pan, crumble it into a large bowl, and knead it with enough lemon curd to form golf ball-sized balls with your hands. To do this, make sure the cake mix is not too moist! Press some pop into each of the balls and smooth the opening. Place on a large flat plate and place in the freezer for 20 minutes.

5. During this time, melt the white chocolate coating over a hot water bath and remove from heat. Then, using two forks, dip each cooled cake ball into the liquid chocolate, let it drip off a bit, and place it on a small rack or baking sheet lined with parchment paper to dry. As long as the chocolate coating is not completely set, decorate with the glitter sugar. Place in the refrigerator to set.

6. Store in an airtight container.

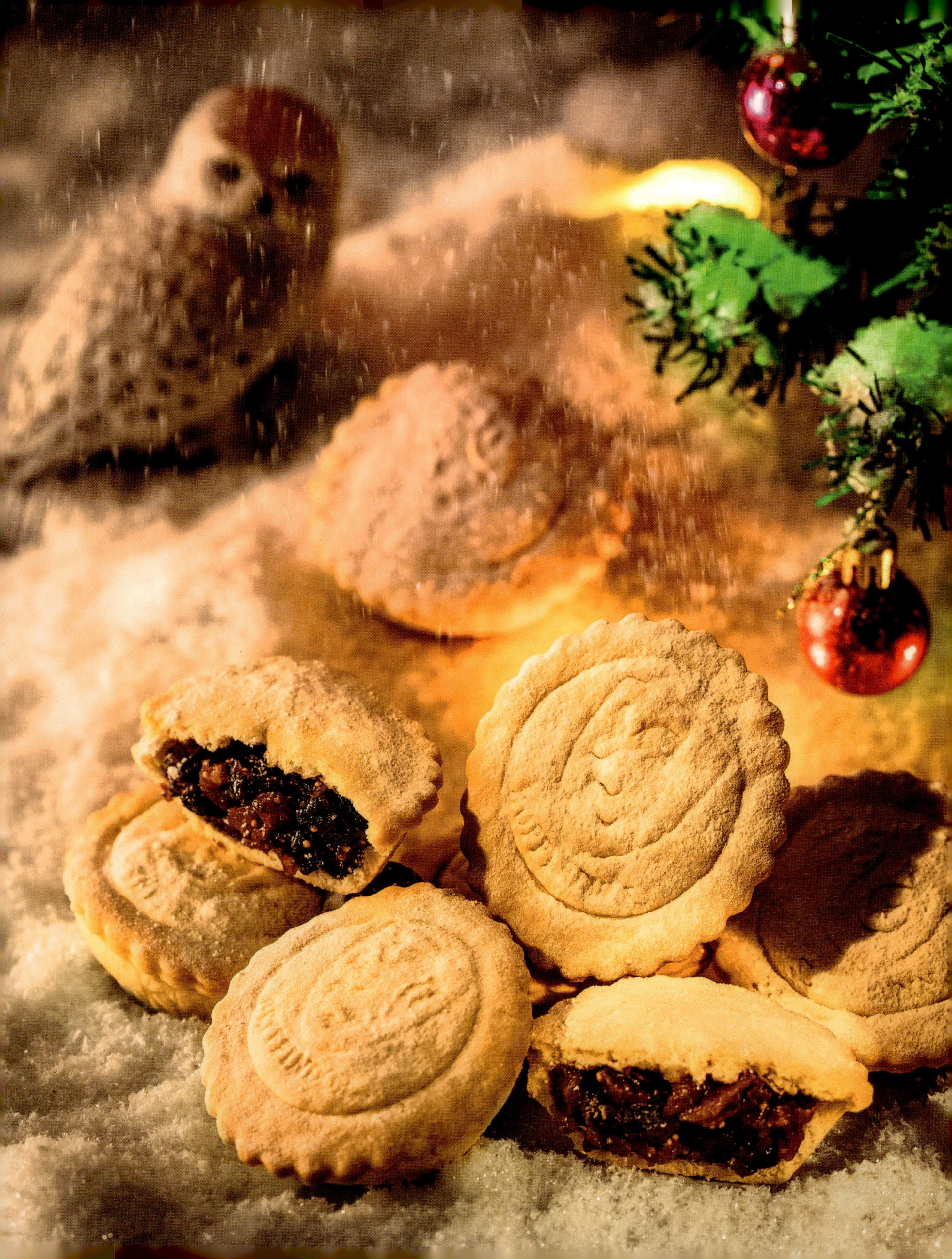

MINCE PIES

WITH ALCOHOL

INGREDIENTS FOR 8 MINCE PIES

For the filling:
11 oz mixed dried fruit, finely diced.
5 oz raisins
Zest of 1 orange
3 oz cane sugar
1 tsp cinnamon
1 tsp ginger
½ tsp ground cloves
4 fl. oz rum
A few drops of almond extract
½ tsp vanilla extract
2 tbsp honey

For the short crust pastry:
9 oz soft butter plus a little more, to grease the mold.
13 oz flour plus a little more, for sprinkling the mold
5 oz sugar
1 pinch of salt
2 eggs powdered sugar

Also needed: round cookie cutter (approx. 4" diameter), round cookie cutter (approx. 3" diameter), Hogwarts silicone cookie stamp, 8-cavity muffin tin

1. Mix the finely diced dried fruit, raisins, orange zest, sugar, cinnamon, ginger, and ground cloves in a bowl and mix well with the rum, almond extract, vanilla extract and honey. Cover with plastic wrap and let sit in the refrigerator for at least 12 hours.

2. Put the butter and the flour in a bowl, add the sugar, the salt and one egg and mix everything with a hand mixer with dough hook until you have a smooth dough. Cover with a clean kitchen towel and chill in the refrigerator for 10 minutes.

3. Grease the muffin tin with a little butter and sprinkle with flour. Preheat the oven to 430 °F.

4. Roll out the dough as thinly as possible (about 3 mm) on a well-floured surface and, using a round cookie cutter, cut out eight circles large enough to cover the bottom and sides of the wells of the muffin tin. Then carefully place the dough circles in the troughs and press down lightly. Re-knead the leftover dough, roll it out again, and cut out the same number of smaller circles. Carefully emboss these with the Hogwarts silicone stamps.

5. Pour the dried fruit filling into the muffins, seal each with an embossed dough round and press the edge down a bit all around. In a small bowl, whisk the second egg and brush it on the top of the mince pies. Bake in the preheated oven for 20 minutes. Let cool slightly and sprinkle with powdered sugar. Enjoy warm or cold.

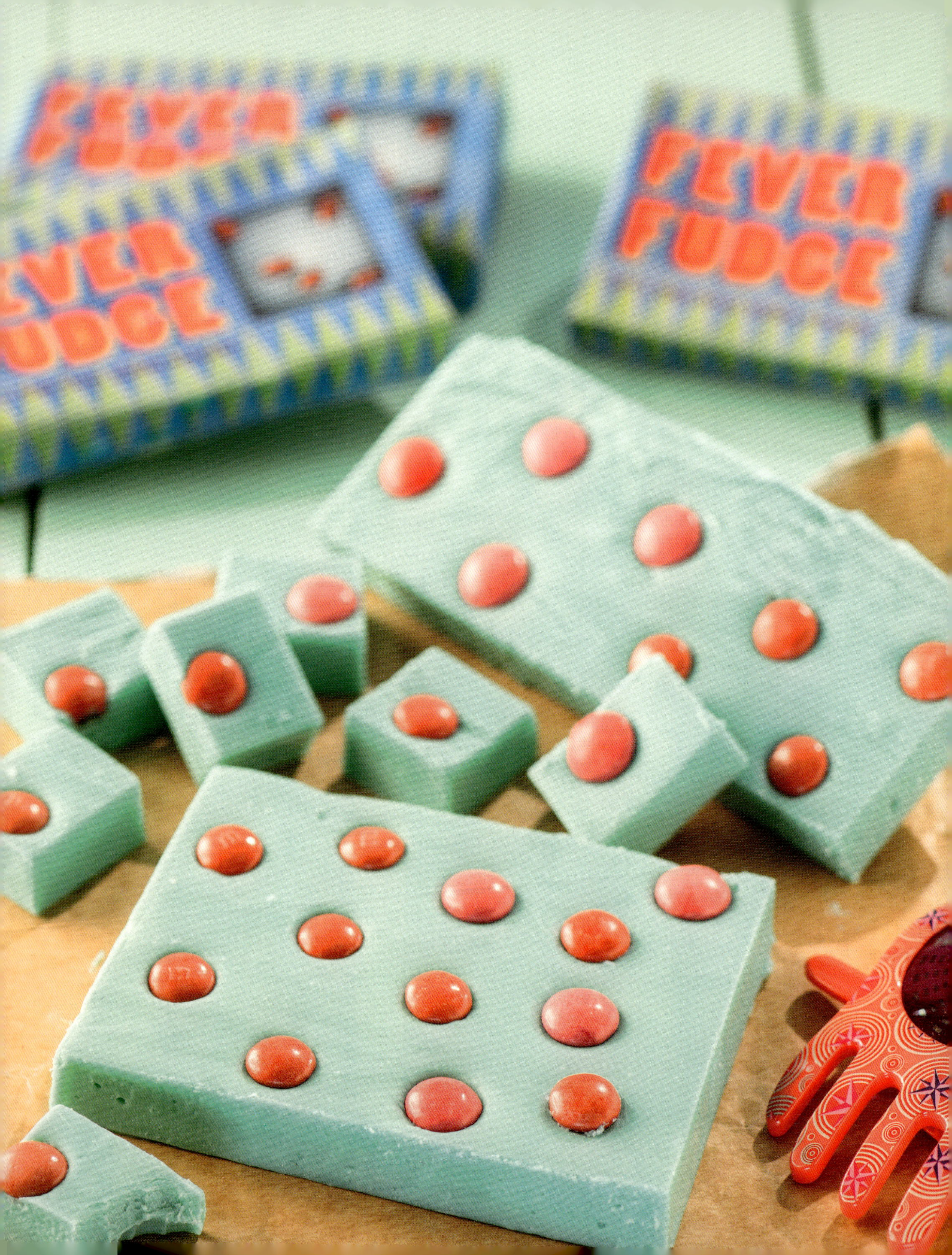
FEVER
FUDGE

FEVER FUDGE

INGREDIENTS FOR 5-6 PORTIONS
Vegetable oil
14 oz sweetened condensed milk
14 oz white chocolate, finely chopped
1 tsp vanilla extract
Blue food coloring, to taste
Red candy-coated chocolates
Also required: Baking or casserole dish (approx. 7" x 7").

1. Line a baking or casserole dish with baking paper and brush with a little oil.

2. Heat the sweetened condensed milk in a saucepan over medium heat, stirring constantly. Add the chopped chocolate and melt, stirring regularly. Blend until smooth and homogeneous. Stir in the vanilla extract and (depending on the desired color intensity) the blue food coloring.

3. Pour the fudge mixture into the prepared mold and smooth it out with a kitchen spatula. Spread the red chocolate candies on top at irregular intervals and place in the refrigerator to set for about 2 hours.

4. Remove the fever fudge from the refrigerator, transfer to a cutting board, and cut into the desired shape with a large, sharp knife. Store in an airtight container.

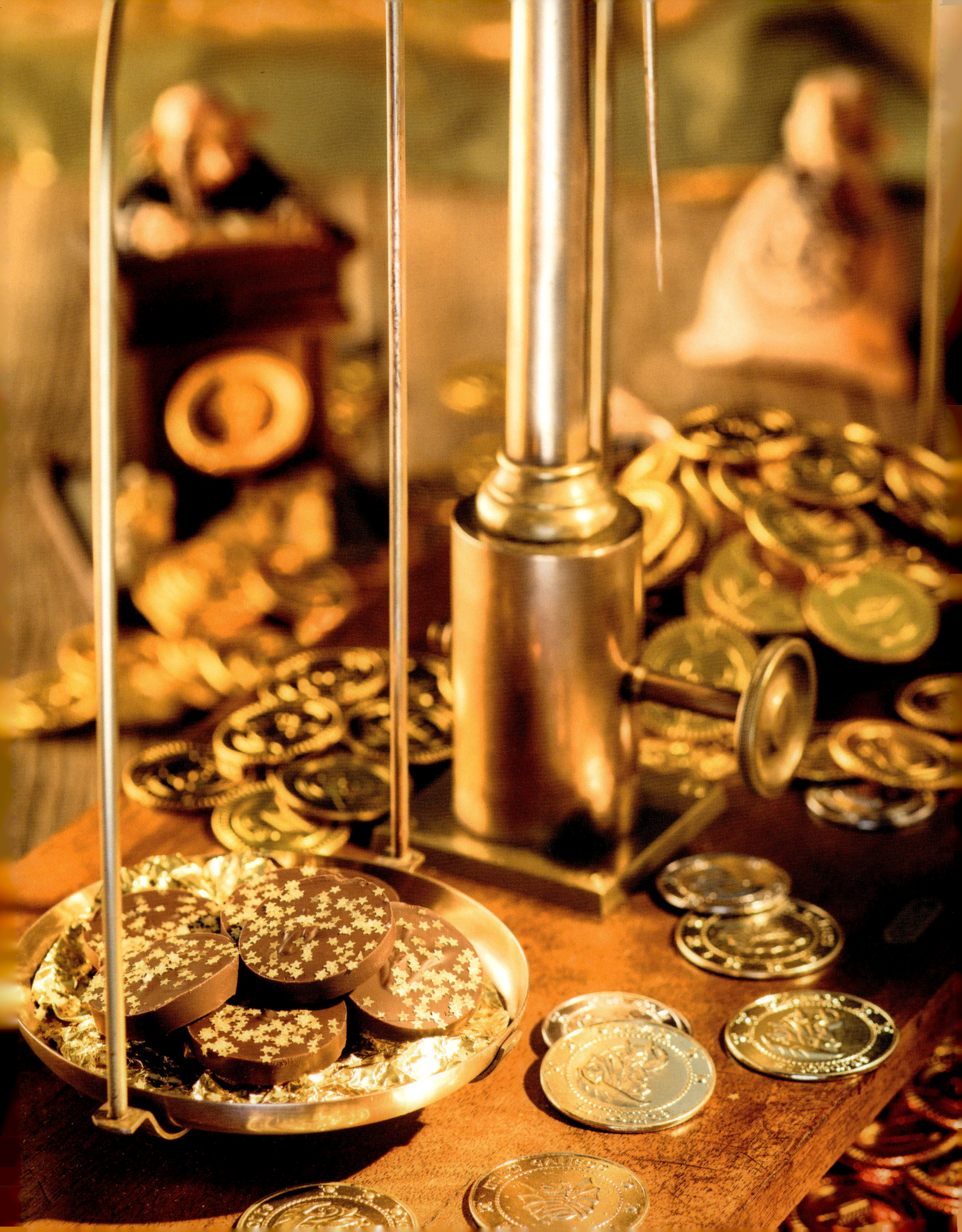

GRINGOTTS GOLD COINS

INGREDIENTS FOR APPROX. 20 GOLD COINS
7 oz plain chocolate coating
2-3 drops of orange extract
Edible golden glitter
Also needed: sugar thermometer, coin silicone mold (if available), gold foil (optional)

1. Roughly chop the chocolate and melt in a bowl over a water bath on medium heat, stirring constantly. Use a candy thermometer to check the temperature. Heat the liquid chocolate once to about 115 °F, then remove from the heat and cool to about 80 °F while stirring evenly. Finally, place over the water bath once more and heat again to a temperature of approx. 90 °F. This repeated tempering gives the chocolate a nice shine and a crunchy break.

2. Stir a few drops of orange extract into the chocolate.

3. Line a tray or baking sheet with baking paper. Spoon the melted chocolate onto the baking paper with a small spoon, spread into even coins, and let dry. Or, if available, pour them into an appropriate silicone mold and let them cool in it. Decorate with edible gold glitter while the chocolate is still setting.

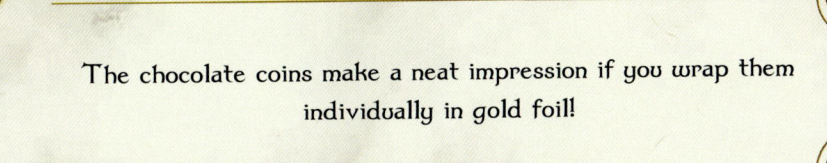

The chocolate coins make a neat impression if you wrap them individually in gold foil!

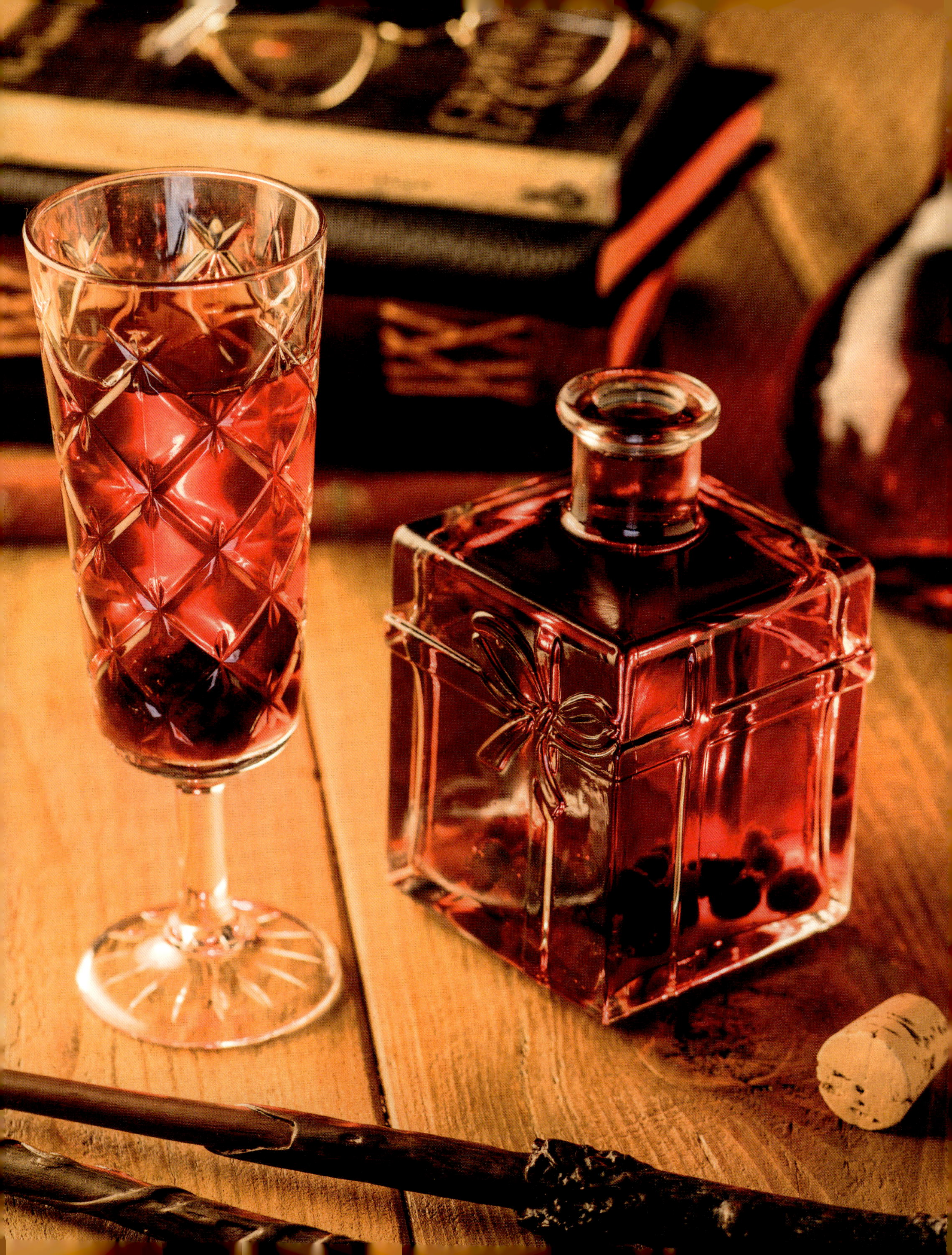

RED CURRANT RUM

INGREDIENTS FOR APPROX. 3 CUPS RUM

18 oz fresh red currants
18 oz rock candy
1 mace
1 star anise
½ vanilla pod, scraped out
3 cups white rum

Also required: sealable container with at least 1 qt capacity.

1. Wash the currants and remove the stalks. Put them together with the rock candy in an appropriately sized container thoroughly rinsed with hot water.

2. Add the mace, star anise and half a vanilla pod scraped out. Pour in the white rum and stir carefully to mix everything together well.

3. Close the jar airtight and leave to infuse in a cool, dark place for four weeks. Shake vigorously every 3-4 days so that the rock candy dissolves completely.

4. After four weeks, taste the currant rum. If you want the taste to be even more intense, let it infuse for a few days longer.

5. Finally, strain through a kitchen sieve into a clean, sealable container, discard the mace, star anise and vanilla bean, and add what's left of the currants back into the rum. Enjoy in moderation.

6. If you want to speed up the procedure or make it a little less work for yourself, you can also simply replace the currants and rock candy with 9 fl. oz of currant syrup (see p. 166). This reduces the infusion time by half.

If you want to speed up the process and make yourself a little less work, you can remove the currants and rock candy simply replace it with 250 ml currant syrup (see p. 166). This reduces the brewing time by half.

Florean Fortesque's **ICE CREAM**

FLOREAN FORTESCUE'S CHILI ICE CREAM

INGREDIENTS FOR APPROX. 8 PORTIONS OF ICE CREAM

6 oz coffee cream
1.5 oz milk
1 vanilla pod, scraped out
7 oz sweet cream
2 oz fine crystal sugar
1 oz powdered sugar
1 packet vanilla sugar
2-3 drops of pink food coloring
Some chili powder
(or red decorating sugar)

1. Put the coffee cream, milk and vanilla pulp in a small saucepan and gently bring to a boil over medium heat, stirring constantly. Then remove from the heat and allow to cool.

2. Meanwhile, place the sweet cream, granulated sugar, powdered sugar, and vanilla sugar in a small bowl and beat with a hand mixer until stiff. Gradually increase the speed, i.e. start slowly and increase the speed by one every 30 seconds, until the cream becomes more compact and stiff peaks gradually form.

3. Once the vanilla milk has cooled a bit, add the cream-sugar mixture and the food coloring and mix well. Pour into a container and place in the freezer for a few hours, but preferably overnight. During this time, stir regularly so that the ice cream remains as creamy as possible.

4. Just before serving, remove from freezer, place in small cups or bowls and serve sprinkled with a little chili powder.

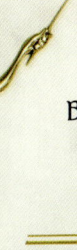

Brave muggles take chili powder as a garnish. Everyone else – and Ron, who we all know doesn't like it spicy – can easily use red decorating sugar as an alternative.

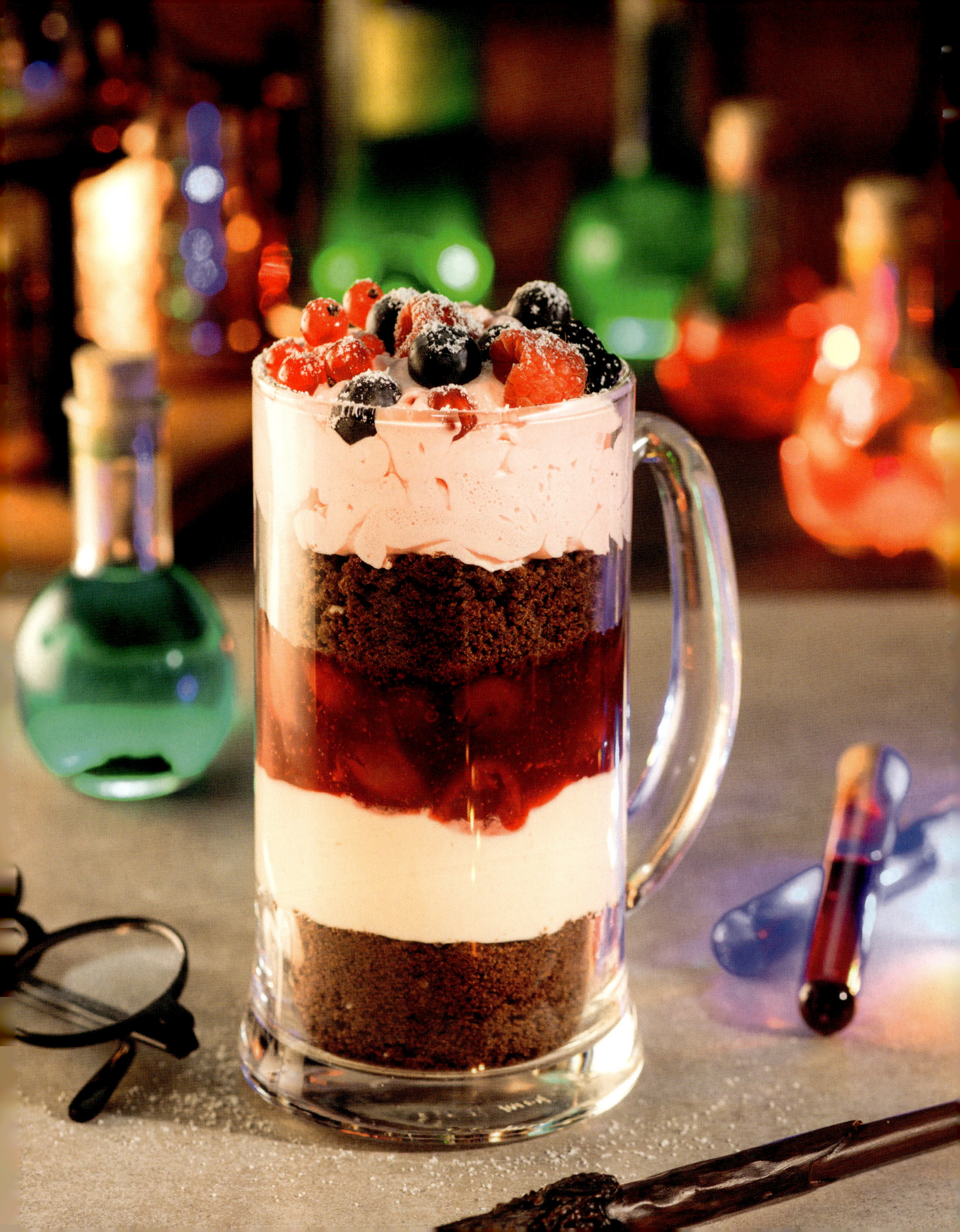

FIVE-LAYER TRIFLE

INGREDIENTS FOR 4 PORTIONS

For the chocolate cake:
5 oz wheat flour
5 oz ground hazelnuts
2 tsp baking powder
1 pinch of salt
2 oz baking cocoa
3 oz chocolate shavings
11 oz soft butter
6.3 oz sugar
5 eggs

For the cherry jam:
1 jar of cherry compote (24 oz drained)
14 fl. oz cherry juice
1 packet of vanilla pudding powder
1 tbsp cane sugar
1 tbsp cherry brandy

For the mascarpone yogurt cream:
7 oz mascarpone
5 oz yogurt
2 oz powdered sugar, sifted
5 fl. oz cream, whipped

For the whipped cream:
2 fl. oz sweet cream, chilled
1 oz powdered sugar
1 tbsp vanilla sugar
2-3 drops of pink food coloring

For the garnish:
7 oz fresh mixed berries (e.g. raspberries, blueberries, blackberries)
4 oz powdered sugar, sifted
Also needed: four beer mugs, two piping bags with a ½ inch diameter nozzle, loaf pan (approx. 11")

Prepare the chocolate cake:

1. Preheat the oven to 350 °F heat. Grease a large loaf pan with a little butter and dust with flour. Mix the hazelnuts, flour, baking powder, salt, and baking cocoa. Beat the butter with the sugar with a hand mixer until fluffy, then one by one add the eggs. Then gradually add the flour-cocoa mixture and beat in well. Finally, fold in the chocolate shavings, pour the batter into the pan and smooth the top. Bake for about 50 to 60 minutes. Remove, let cool in the pan, then turn out and crumble coarsely.

Prepare the cherry jam:

2. Drain the cherries through a sieve, reserving the juice. Pour into a measuring cup and add enough "prepared" cherry juice to reach 2 cups. Mix well, reserving 3 tbsp, and heat the rest in a saucepan over medium heat. Add the sugar and the cherry brandy and stir until smooth. Once boiling, remove from heat and whisk in the custard powder. Bring to a boil briefly, remove from the heat again and stir in the cherries. Allow to cool slightly and place in the refrigerator to cool completely.

Prepare the mascarpone yogurt cream:

3. Mix the mascarpone and yogurt with the powdered sugar until smooth and fold in the cream. Pour into a piping bag.

Prepare the whipped cream:

4. Place the cream in a bowl. Add the powdered sugar, vanilla sugar and food coloring and beat with a hand mixer until stiff. Pour into a piping bag.

5. When all the elements are ready, layer the trifle. To do this, pour the crumbled chocolate cake into the mug at the bottom. On top, using the piping bag, add a layer of the mascarpone yogurt cream, followed by the cherry jam. Layer a layer of chocolate cake on top of this and top with spray cream. Garnish with fresh berries, sprinkle with powdered sugar and enjoy!

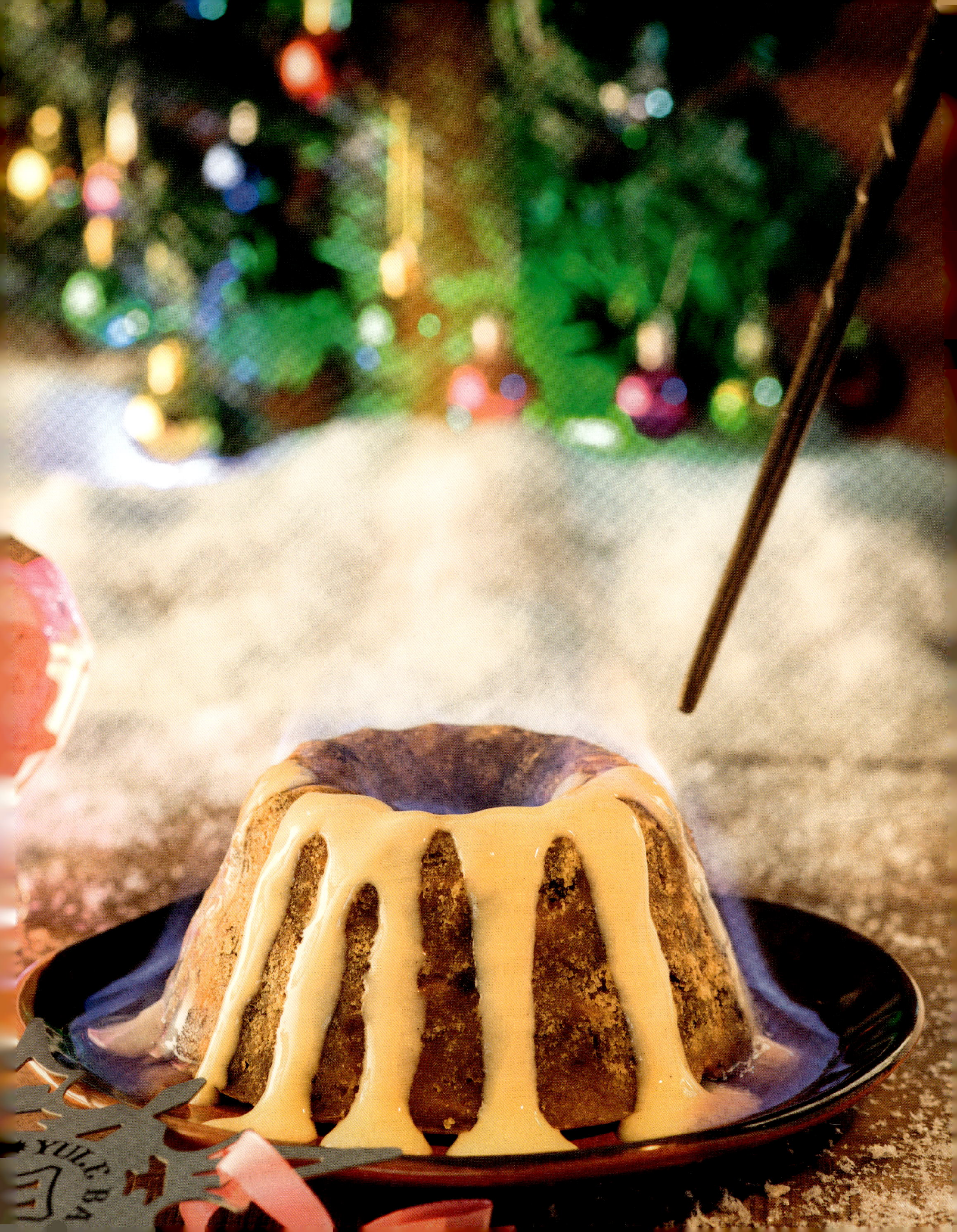
YULE

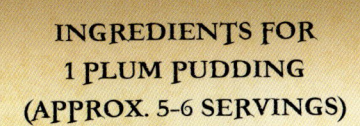

PLUM PUDDING

WITH ALCOHOL

**INGREDIENTS FOR
1 PLUM PUDDING
(APPROX. 5-6 SERVINGS)**

3 oz prunes
6 oz raisins
2 tbsp rum
1 apple
2 oz candied lemon peel
2 oz candied orange peel
2 oz breadcrumbs plus a little more, for sprinkling the pudding mold
2 oz flour
2 oz butter or margarine plus a little more, for greasing the pudding mold
1.5 oz brown sugar Juice and zest of one untreated lemon
2 eggs
A pinch each of ground pepper, nutmeg, cloves, cinnamon and ginger
2 oz ground hazelnuts
Vanilla sauce, for serving

Also required: sealable pudding mold (capacity 27 fl. oz)

1. Cut the prunes into small cubes, put them in a bowl together with the raisins, sprinkle with the rum, and leave to infuse for about 30 minutes.

2. In the meantime, peel the apple, remove the core, and cut the apple into small cubes.

3. In a large bowl, knead the candied lemon peel, candied orange peel, breadcrumbs, flour, butter, brown sugar, lemon zest, lemon juice, eggs, spices, and ground hazelnuts with the dough hook of a hand mixer. Then add the diced apples, prunes and raisins and incorporate.

4. Bring a large saucepan of water to a boil. Reduce the heat so that the water is only gently boiling.

5. Pour the pudding mixture into a greased pudding mold sprinkled with breadcrumbs and press down lightly. Close the mold tightly and place in a hot water bath for 2½ hours. If necessary, add a little hot water every now and then.

6. Remove the pudding mold from the water and let it rest for ten minutes. Finally, gently turn the plum pudding out of the mold onto a serving plate and let it cool completely.

7. Serve garnished with vanilla sauce.

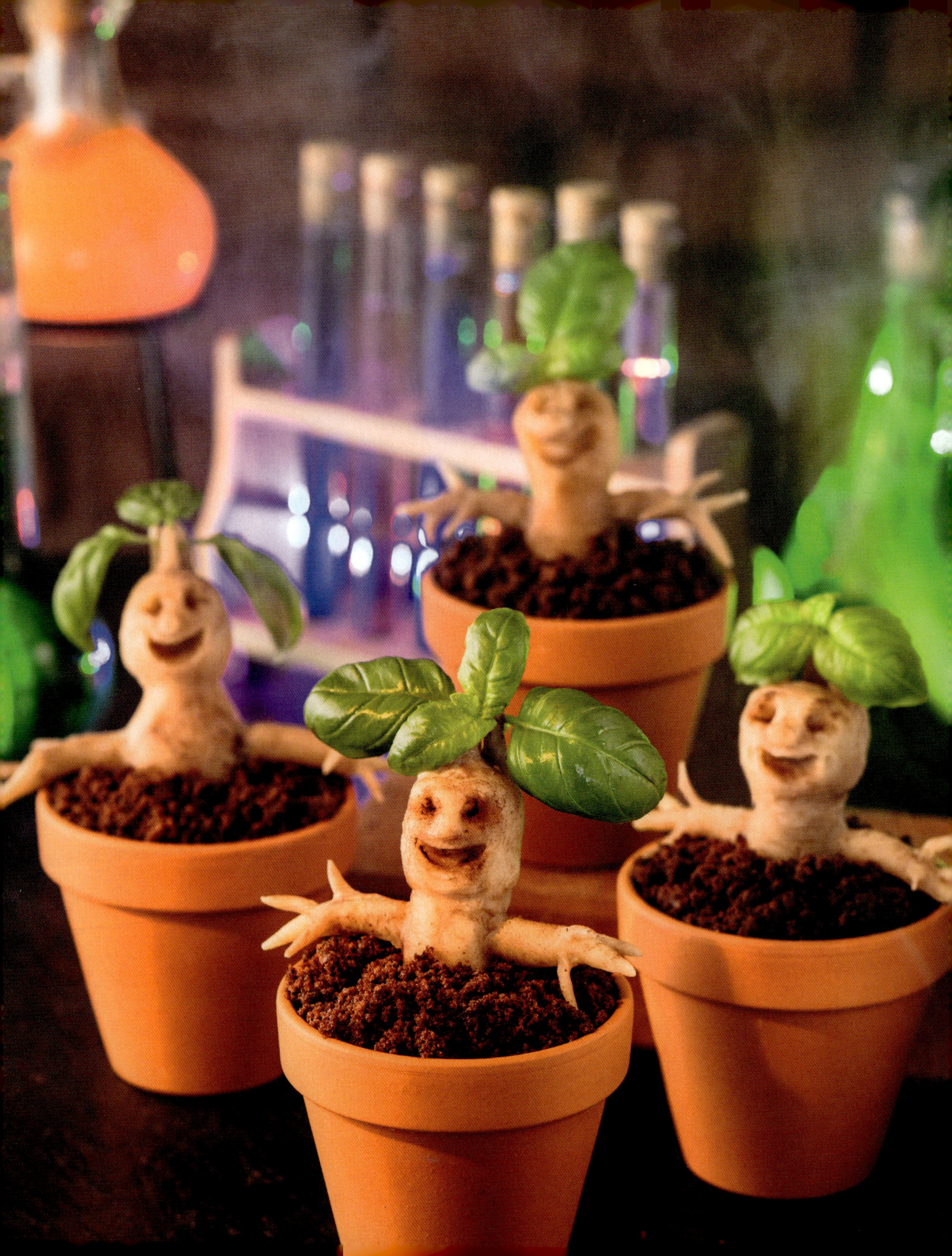

MANDRAKE

INGREDIENTS FOR 10 MANDRAKES

For the muffins:
11 oz flour
3 oz baking cocoa
1 tsp baking powder
1 tsp baking soda
1 pinch of salt
4 oz soft butter
8 oz sugar
1 tsp vanilla extract
2 eggs
9 fl. oz buttermilk
5 oz dark chocolate, coarsely chopped

For the mandrakes:
14 oz marzipan paste
Some baking cocoa, for dusting
20 herb leaves (e.g. basil, mint)

For the chocolate frosting:
5 oz cream cheese
0.5 oz powdered sugar
1 heaped tbsp baking cocoa

Also needed: three paper muffin tins, ten small clay pots.

1. Soak the clay pots in water for about an hour. Cut out suitably sized circles from baking paper and place in the bottom of the pots. Preheat the oven to 390 °F degrees.

2. Mix the flour, cocoa, baking powder, baking soda and salt in a small bowl. In a separate, larger bowl, beat the butter, sugar, and vanilla extract with a hand mixer. Add the eggs one at a time and continue beating until fluffy. Stir in the buttermilk thoroughly.

3. Mix the dry ingredients from the smaller bowl into the butter mixture. Remove enough batter for three muffins and pour into plain muffin tins. Fold the chopped chocolate into the remaining batter and pour into the prepared clay pots. Place the pots and muffin tins in the oven for about 25 minutes. Then remove from the oven and let cool completely. Then remove the muffins from the pans and crumble them coarsely in a bowl.

4. Divide the marzipan into ten equal pieces and shape each into a rough mandragora. Flatten the underside a little. Give the mandragora "character;" To do this, score small grooves crosswise with a knife, press in the eyes with a toothpick, work out the mouth with a spoon and, if necessary, form more or less pronounced little arms. To make the whole thing look as "alive" as possible, powder it with cocoa using a brush. Finally, poke a hole in each "head" with a toothpick, into which you can later insert the edible leaves. Place in the refrigerator.

5. Combine the cream cheese, powdered sugar and baking cocoa in a small bowl and beat until smooth. Generously spread the frosting on the top of the muffins in the clay pots, stick the mandrakes on top, and decorate all around with crumbled "cake soil". Tuck the herb leaves into the previously pricked ones. Perfect!

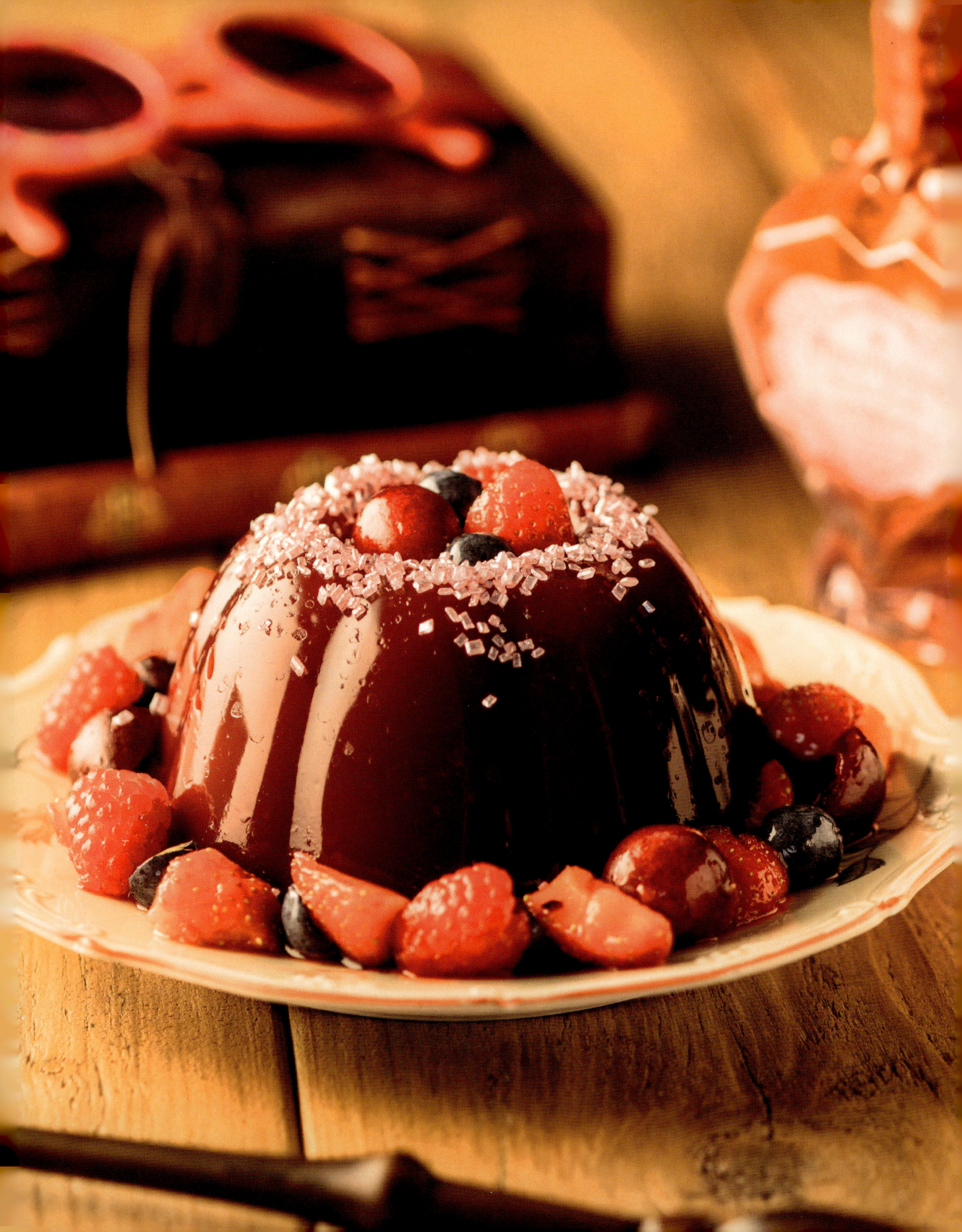

LUNA'S LOVELY FRUIT PUDDING

INGREDIENTS FOR 4 SERVINGS
9 oz fresh blueberries
2 tbsp lemon juice
Approx. 10 fl. oz water
3 oz sugar
1 packet vanilla pudding powder
Fresh berries, as garnish

Also required: glass bowl or pudding mold

1. Put the blueberries and lemon juice in a pot with 4 fl. oz of water and bring to a boil over low heat. Simmer for one minute.

2. Strain the contents of the pot through a kitchen sieve, pour the collected juice into a measuring cup and add cold water up to the 14 fl. oz mark. Return the whole to the pot, add the sugar, and take a little of the fruit liquid to mix with the custard powder. Bring the rest to a boil over low heat, stirring regularly.

3. Mix the pudding powder with the removed fruit liquid, add it to the simmering juice, and boil for one minute, stirring constantly.

4. Pour the pudding into a cold-rinsed, heat-resistant glass bowl or a special pudding mold and let cool for a few minutes. Then chill in the refrigerator for about 4-5 hours.

5. To serve, gently turn out onto a large, flat plate and garnish with fresh berries.

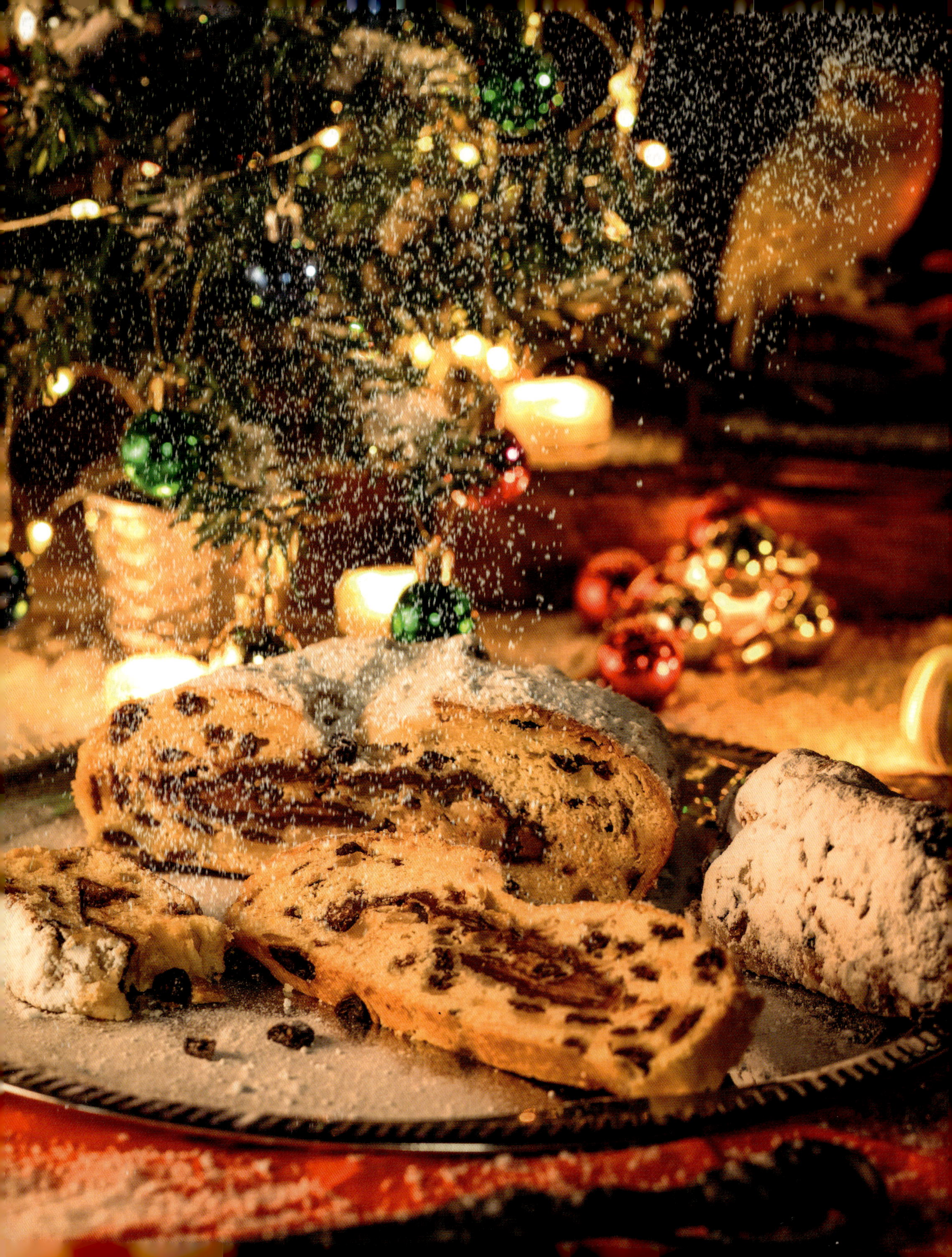

CHRISTMAS CAKE

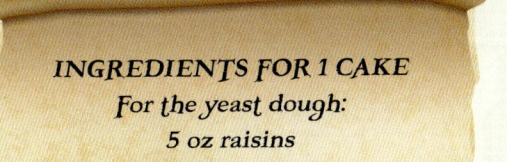

WITH ALCOHOL

INGREDIENTS FOR 1 CAKE

For the yeast dough:
5 oz raisins
½ tsp lemon zest
2 oz candied orange peel
2 oz candied lemon peel
2 fl. oz rum
2 oz ground almonds
15 oz flour
½ cube fresh yeast
5 tbsp lukewarm milk
2 oz sugar
4 oz butter
1 egg
1 packet vanilla sugar
½ pinch salt
½ tsp cinnamon
¼ tsp cardamom
¼ tsp nutmeg

To coat:
1.5 oz butter
3 oz powdered sugar

1. In a large bowl, mix the raisins, lemon zest, candied orange peel and candied lemon peel with the rum and ground almonds. Leave to infuse for at least an hour, better overnight.

2. Put the flour in a large bowl and crumble in the yeast. Add 2 tbsp of the lukewarm milk and a pinch of sugar and mix in briefly. Cover and let rise in a warm place for about 30 minutes.

3. Add the butter in small pieces to the flour. Gradually add the egg, remaining sugar, vanilla sugar, salt, cinnamon, cardamom, and nutmeg, mixing each in briefly, then knead well with a hand mixer with dough hook on highest speed for at least 10 minutes. Meanwhile, gradually knead in the remaining milk. Finally, incorporate the fruit-rum-nut mixture and let rise, covered with a clean tea towel, for another 30 minutes.

4. Line a baking tray with aluminum foil, then with baking paper.

5. Knead the dough briefly and shape into an oblong loaf. Using a rolling pin, flatten the stollen slightly halfway over the long side. Fold the thicker side over and shape the loaf into the desired shape with your hands. Place on the prepared baking sheet and let rise, covered, for another 30 minutes. Meanwhile, preheat the oven to 390 °F.

6. Bake the cake for about 40-45 minutes. After 30 minutes, reduce the temperature to 350 °F. If the cake gets too dark, cover it with aluminum foil until it is done baking.

7. In the meantime, melt the 1.5 oz butter in a saucepan over low heat. Remove the cake from the oven and immediately brush with the butter. Let cool slightly, then brush again with melted butter and sprinkle generously with powdered sugar. Allow to set for 24 hours before eating.

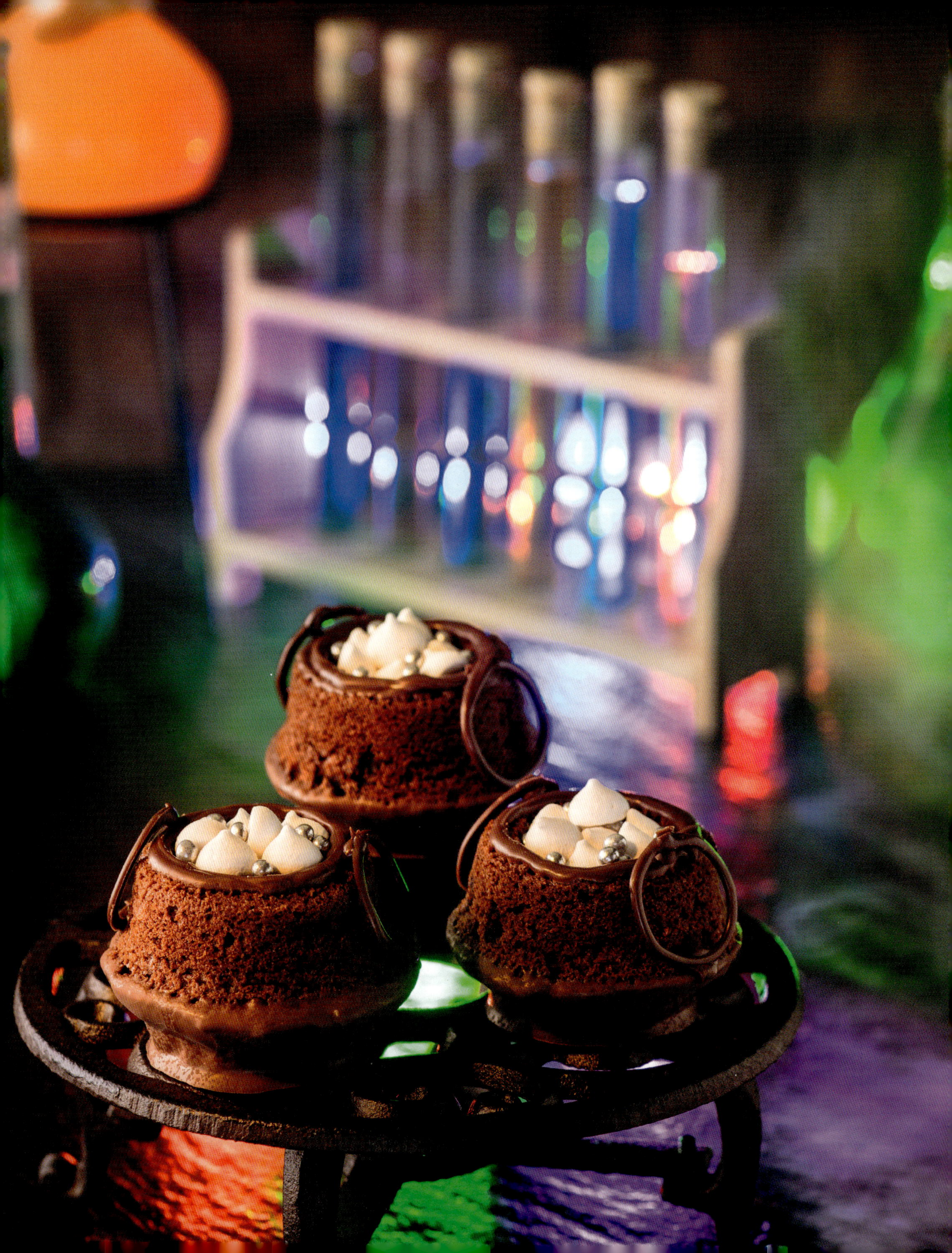

MAGIC CAULDRON

INGREDIENTS FOR APPROX. 10-12 CAULDRONS

5 oz soft butter plus a little more, to grease the muffin tin
5 oz sugar
1 packet vanilla sugar
1 pinch of salt
3 eggs
9 oz flour
½ packet baking powder
5 fl. oz milk
2 tsp baking cocoa
14 oz milk chocolate, coarsely chopped

For decorating:
White chocolate drops Sugar pearls

Also needed:
12-cavity muffin tin, piping bag with very fine nozzle

1. Preheat the oven to 350 °F heat. Grease the cups of the muffin tin with butter.

2. In a bowl, beat the butter with the sugar, vanilla sugar and salt using an electric hand mixer. Then, one at a time, beat in the eggs.

3. In a separate bowl, mix together the flour and baking powder and add a little at a time, adding a little milk at a time (4 fl. oz in total). Work everything thoroughly. Then pour ¾ of the batter into the prepared muffin tin.

4. Mix the rest of the batter with the remaining milk and the baking cocoa. Spread the chocolate batter evenly over the light batter in the muffin tins. Gently mix the batter in the baking cups with a small cake fork. Then bake in the preheated oven for about 25-30 minutes. Remove as soon as nothing sticks to a toothpick poked into the center when pulled out. Let cool completely in the pan.

5. When the muffins have cooled, carefully remove them from the pan and turn them upside down on the work surface. (Straighten the "bottom" a bit with a sharp knife if necessary to help the "cauldron" stand up). Then, using a small, sharp knife and a small spoon, carefully cut out the cauldron opening and hollow out the muffin to a depth of about 1-2 inches. Be careful to leave the "cauldron walls" intact.

6. In a bowl over a water bath, melt the chocolate. Place some of the chocolate coating in a piping bag fitted with a very fine nozzle. Line a baking tray with baking paper and pipe the kettle handles onto it using the piping bag. To do this, it is best to draw two circles per muffin on the baking paper with a pencil. Allow the chocolate coating to set.

7. Meanwhile, dip the bottom third of the cauldron into the melted chocolate, let it drip off a bit, and place it on the baking tray lined with baking paper to dry. Then use the piping bag to pipe the rim of the cauldron and use the chocolate coating to attach the handles (see picture). Finally, decorate with sugar pearls and chocolate drops.

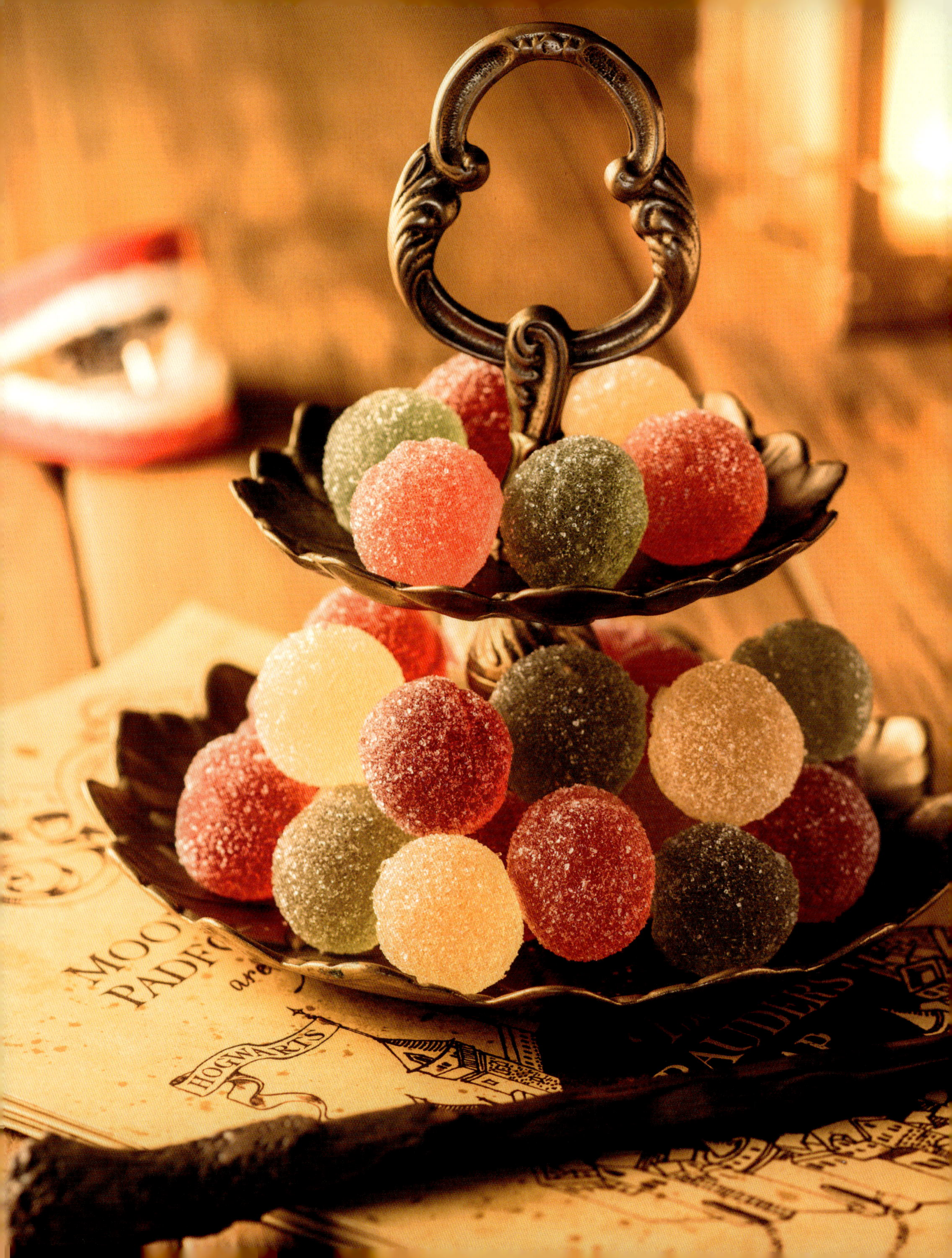
HOGWARTS

SOUR DROPS

**INGREDIENTS FOR APPROX.
2¼ LB SOUR DROPS**

1¾ lb fruit of your choice
(e.g. raspberries, strawberries, oranges)
4 fl. oz water
1½ lb sugar
5-6 drops of food coloring (optional)
2 tbsp cornstarch
2 tbsp powdered sugar
Some butter, to grease the mold
Juice of 1 lemon

Also needed:
2-3 candy silicone molds

1. Thoroughly wash the desired fruits and remove any stems. Place in a large pot, add the water and bring to a boil over medium heat. Then reduce the heat to low and simmer until the fruit is soft, about 10 minutes. Pour into a kitchen strainer, drain off any excess liquid, and return the fruit to the pot.

2. Increase the heat again and add 18 oz of sugar. Allow the fruit puree to reduce for about 30 minutes; stir constantly with a whisk. This is now the time to add, if desired,

3. Stir in 1-2 drops of food coloring of your choice. Once you have a viscous paste that separates itself from the bottom of the pot, remove from heat and set aside briefly.

4. In a small bowl, mix together the cornstarch and powdered sugar.

5. Butter the candy silicone molds thinly and dust with the starch mixture. (If you only have one mold on hand, repeat the following an appropriate number of times). Pour the fruit mixture evenly into the silicone mold, smooth it out and let it cool completely in the refrigerator for about 2-3 hours.

6. Remove the cooled fruit jelly halves from the mold, moisten the flat side with a little water, "glue" two halves together at a time and let them dry for a few minutes.

7. In the meantime, prepare the lemon sugar. To do this, mix the remaining sugar with the lemon juice in a small bowl. Roll the fruit jellies all around in the lemon sugar.

8. The sour drops will keep for several weeks in an airtight container.

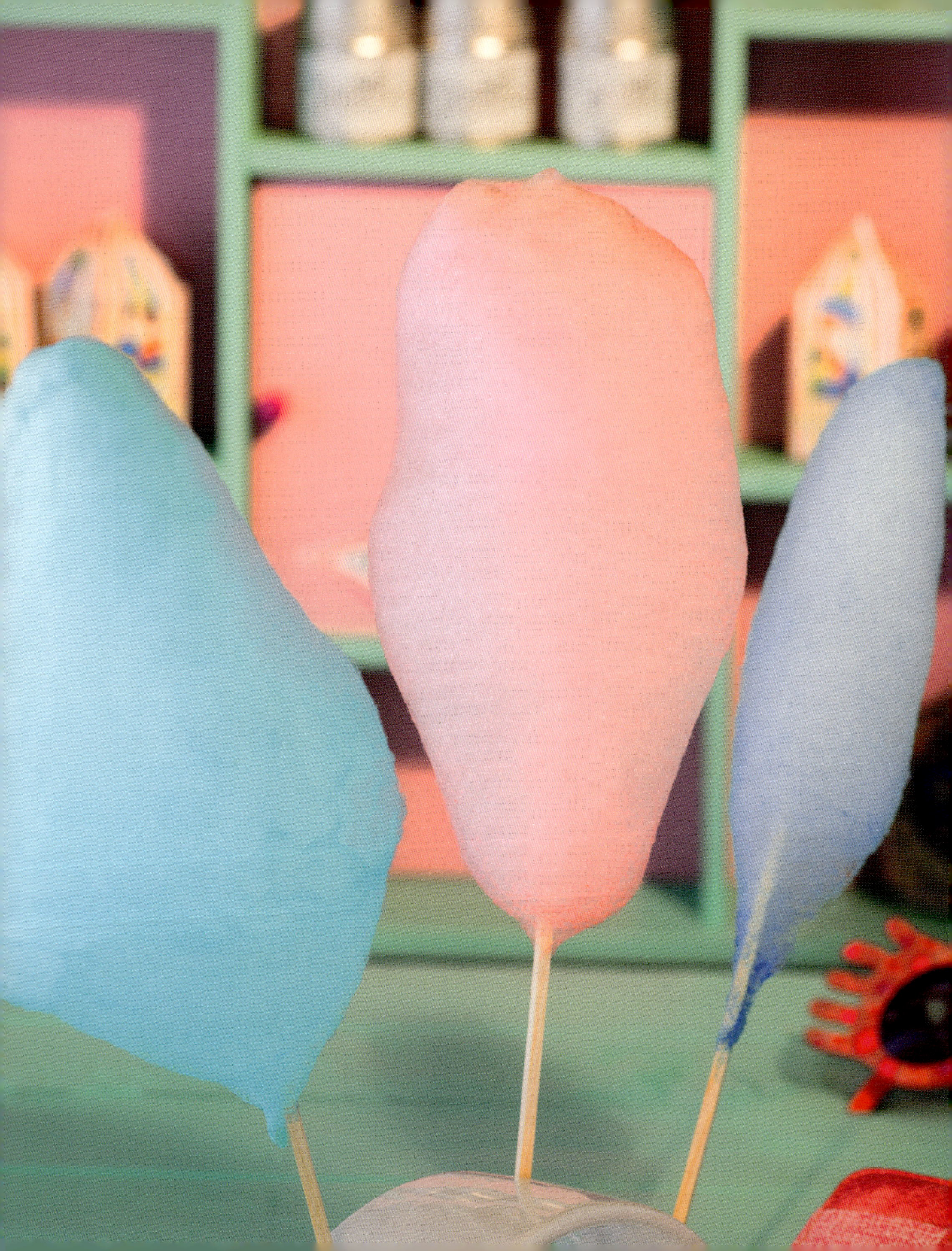

COTTON CANDY

INGREDIENTS FOR 1 PORTION
2 tbsp sugar
2 drops of food coloring, to taste
2 drops of flavoring, to taste
(e.g., butter vanilla, raspberry, woodruff, cherry, etc.)

Also needed:
cotton candy machine,
cotton candy sticks.

1. Preheat the cotton candy machine according to the manufacturer's instructions.

2. Meanwhile, in a bowl, mix the sugar with the food coloring and flavoring as desired. There are no limits to your imagination here: You can combine all the colors and flavors that come to mind. The only important thing is that you follow the quantity guidelines.

3. Once the machine is ready, add the sugar and prepare the cotton candy according to the manufacturer's instructions. After about 1 minute, when the first strands of sugar start to form, insert a cotton candy stick and run it around the outside of the bowl to get the most uniform oval cotton candy possible. Continue this until no more threads form (about 2-3 minutes). Enjoy as soon as possible.

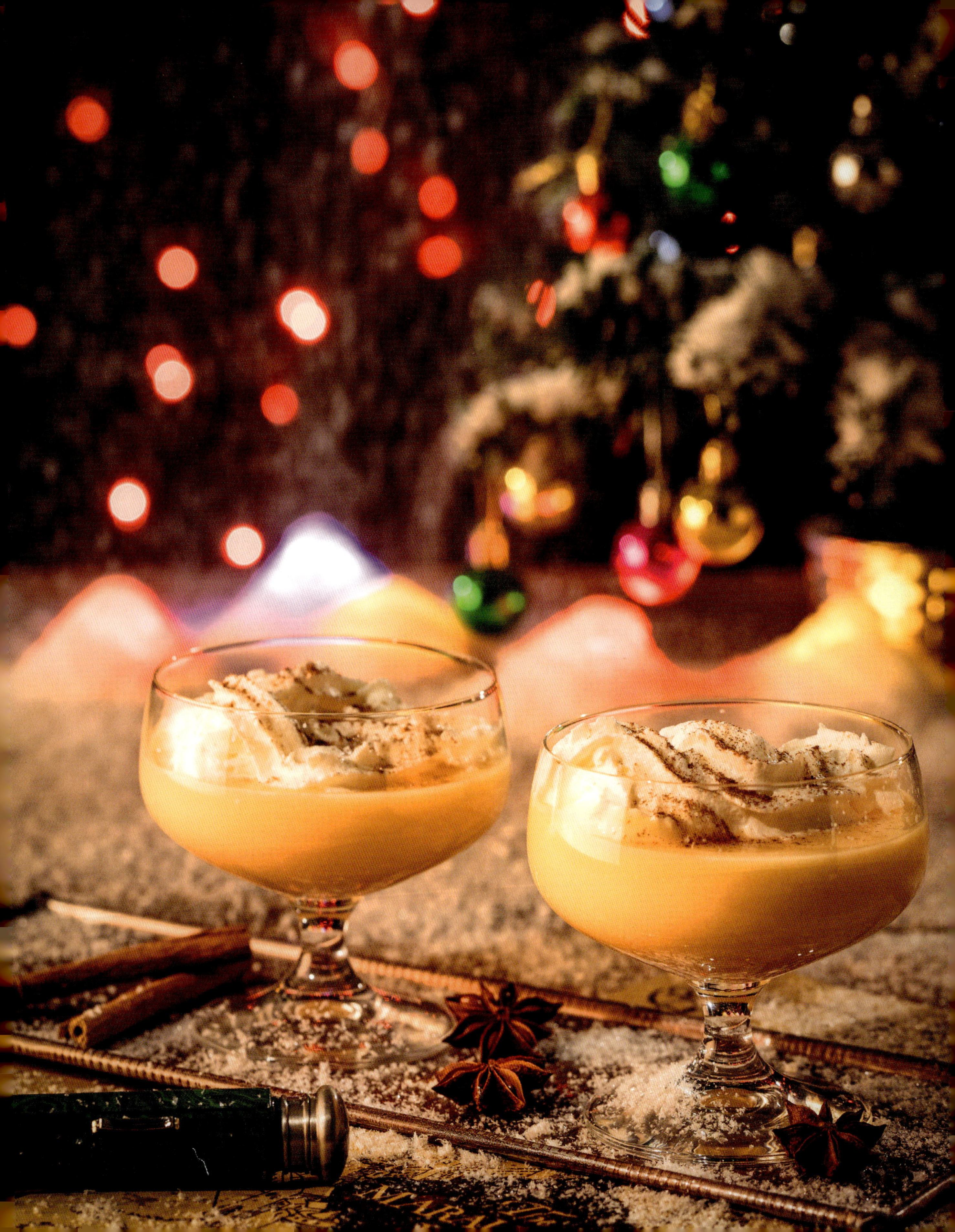

EGGNOG

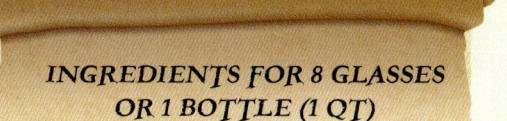

WITH ALCOHOL

INGREDIENTS FOR 8 GLASSES OR 1 BOTTLE (1 QT)

8 egg yolks
5 oz sugar
½ tbsp cinnamon plus a little more, for garnish
2-3 tbsp lemon juice
4 oz cream
27 fl. oz dry white wine
2 fl. oz rum

Also needed: sealable bottle with 1 qt capacity (optional).

1. Place the egg yolks in a mixing bowl and whisk together with the sugar, cinnamon and lemon juice for approx.

2. Beat for about 10 minutes until fluffy.

3. In a separate bowl, whip the cream.

4. Pour the egg cream into a high saucepan. Stir in the white wine and rum. Heat over low heat, stirring constantly so that nothing burns or sets. Finally, whisk again briefly and pour into the glasses or into a hot-rinsed, sufficiently large bottle, if the eggnog is to be enjoyed later; in this case, be sure to store in the refrigerator!

5. Top the eggnog (whether hot or cold) with a dollop of whipped cream, sprinkle with a little cinnamon and serve immediately!

This recipe can also easily be made without alcohol. Instead of white wine, just use the same amount of whole milk and replace the rum with some black tea!

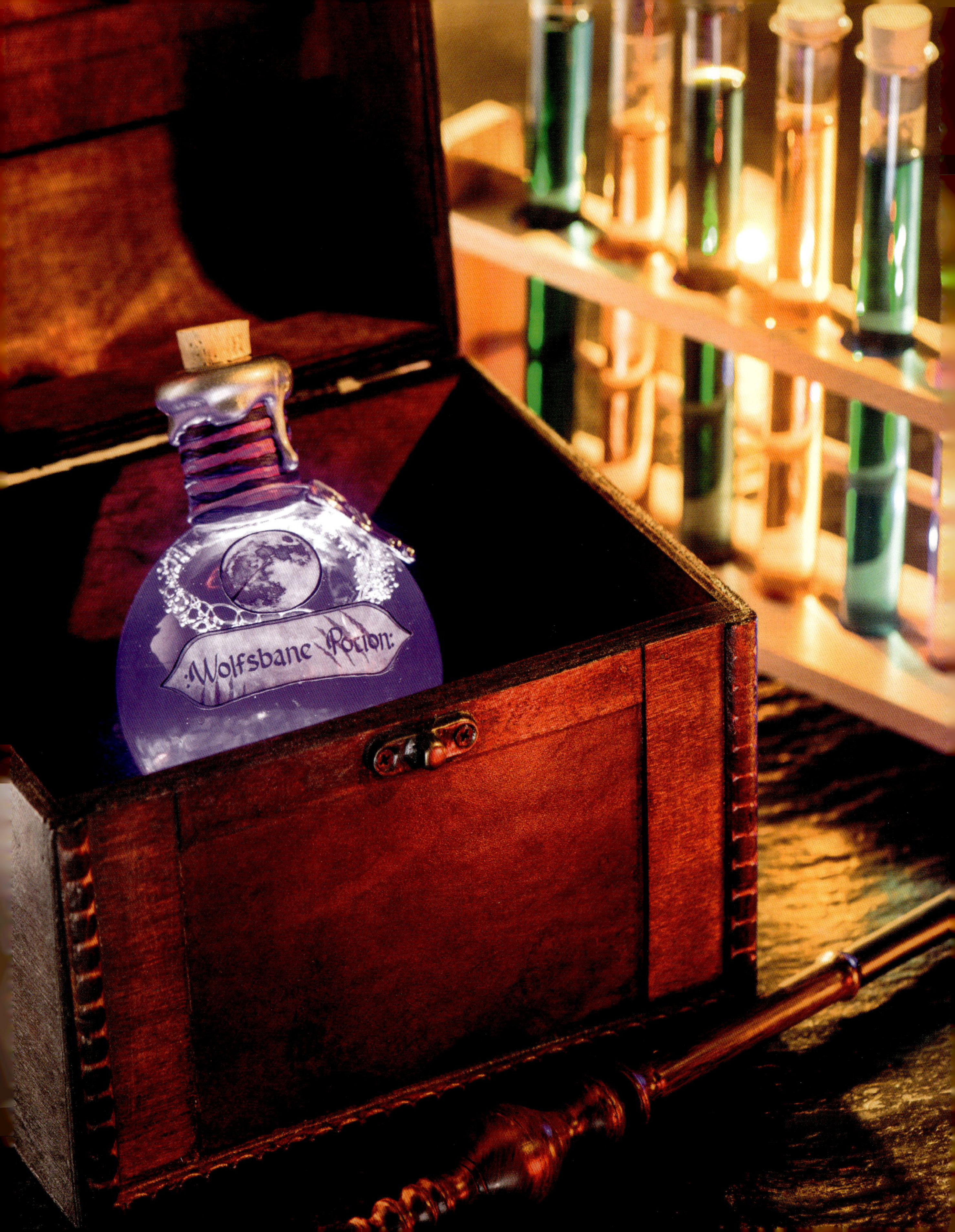
Wolfsbane Potion

WOLFSBANE POTION

WITH ALCOHOL

INGREDIENTS FOR 3-4 DRINKS
2 fl. oz vodka
4 fl. oz Blue Curaçao
5 fl. oz cranberry juice
2 fl. oz Grenadine syrup
3 fl. oz sweet & sour syrup
Black food coloring (optional)
Ice cubes

1. In a small pitcher, combine the vodka, Blue Curaçao, cranberry juice, grenadine, and sweet & sour syrup. If the coloring is not purple enough, add 1-2 drops of black food coloring.

2. Pour a few ice cubes into rocks glasses, top with wolfsbane potion, and serve immediately.

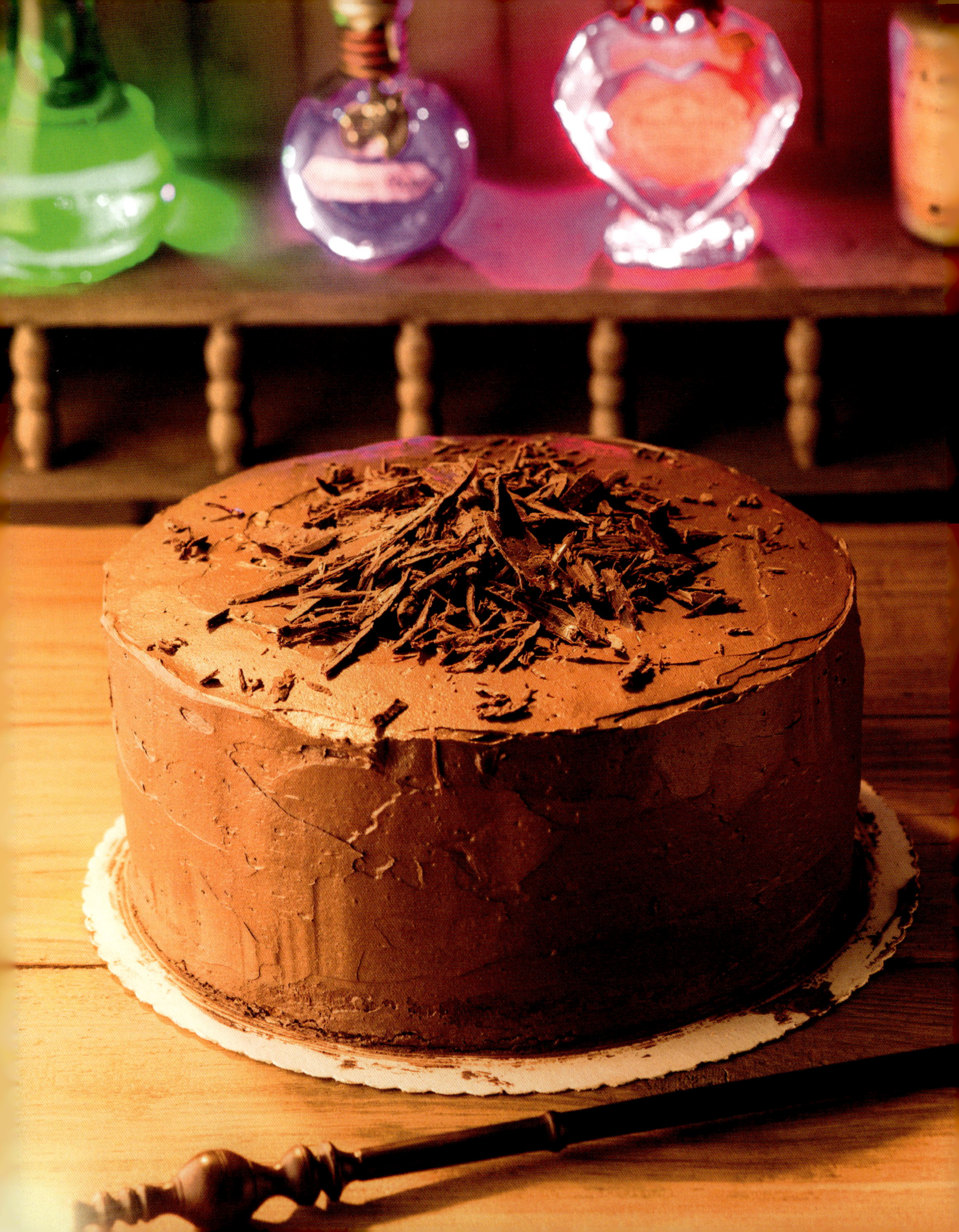

CHOCOLATE GATEAU

INGREDIENTS FOR 1 CAKE

For the pastry:
9 oz softened butter plus a little more, to grease the mold.
7 oz sugar
1 pinch of salt
1 packet vanilla sugar
3 eggs
7 oz sour cream
7 oz cake flour
6 tbsp cocoa powder
3 tsp baking powder
4 tbsp milk
4 oz dark chocolate chips

For the butter cream:
5 fl. oz cream
7 oz dark chocolate, coarsely chopped
4 oz soft butter
3 oz powdered sugar, sifted
3 tbsp cocoa powder, sifted
1 tsp vanilla extract
If necessary, a little room-temperature milk

For decorating:
3 tbsp chocolate shavings

Also needed:
8" springform pan

1. Preheat the oven to 350 °F heat and grease the 8" springform pan with butter.

2. In a mixing bowl, cream the butter with the sugar, salt and vanilla sugar. Then, one at a time, add the eggs and mix them in. Add the sour cream and beat until thoroughly incorporated.

3. In a separate bowl, mix the flour with the cocoa powder and baking powder. Add the flour-cocoa mixture and the milk to the butter-vanilla-sugar mixture and mix thoroughly. Fold in the chocolate chips, pour everything into the prepared springform pan, smooth the top and bake the cake in the preheated oven for about 45 minutes. Then remove from the oven and let cool.

4. Meanwhile, prepare the buttercream. To do this, bring the cream to a boil in a small saucepan over medium heat, stirring constantly.

5. Put the chopped chocolate in a bowl and pour the warm cream over it. Let stand for a few minutes, then whisk to make a creamy ganache. Set aside and let cool at room temperature.

6. Meanwhile, in a separate bowl, beat the softened butter together with the powdered sugar, cocoa powder, and vanilla extract with a handheld electric mixer on low speed until creamy. Add the cooled ganache, beating constantly, and beat for a few minutes until noticeably lighter and fluffier. Then beat on high speed for five minutes. If the buttercream is too firm, add a little milk.

7. Spread the buttercream evenly all over the cooled chocolate cake and decorate with chocolate shavings as desired.

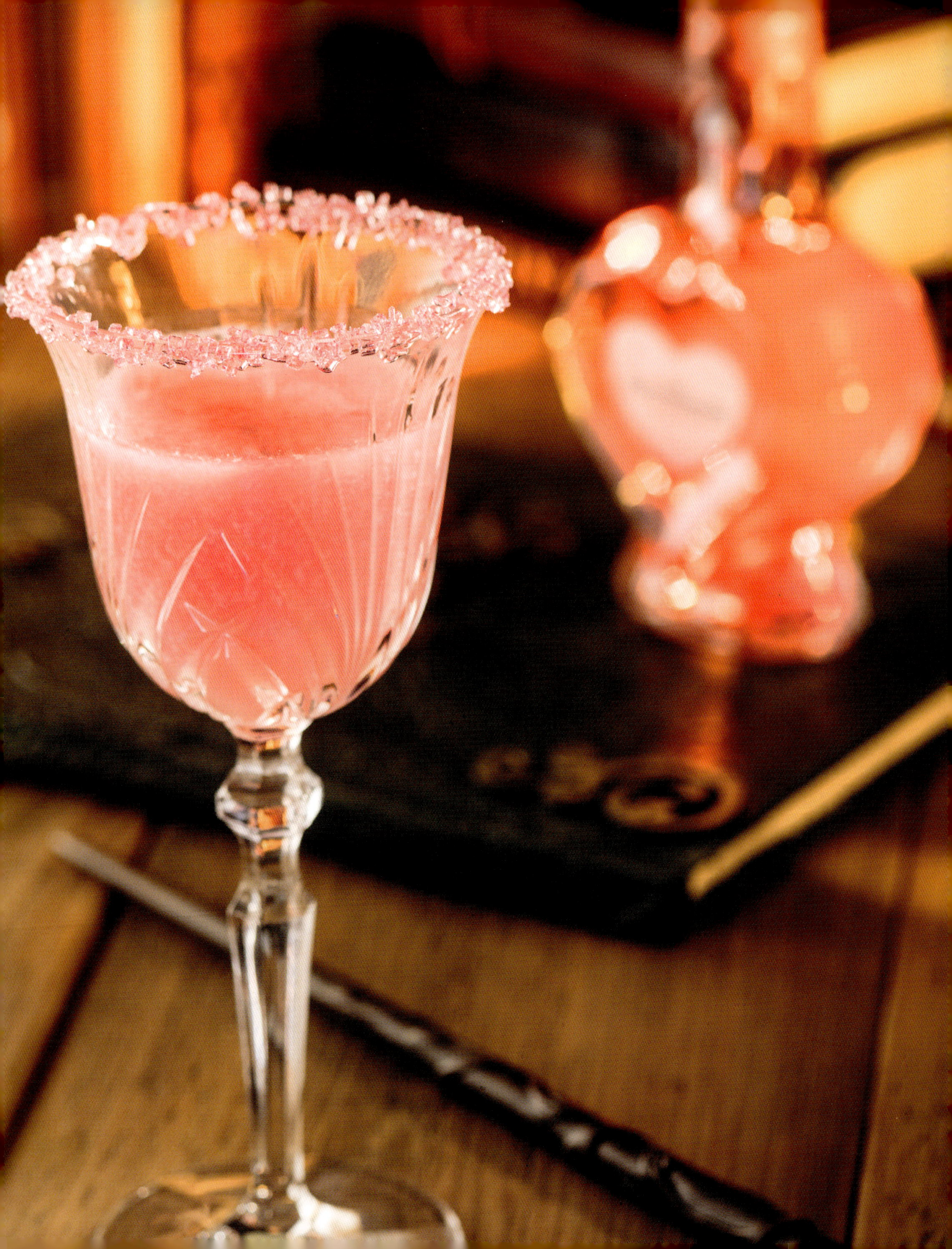

AMORTENTIA

WITH ALCOHOL

**INGREDIENTS FOR
1 LOVE POTION**

Pink decorating sugar
2 oz lemon juice, freshly squeezed, plus a little more, for the garnish
2 oz gin
1 tsp grenadine
1 egg white
1 tsp whipped cream
Ice cubes

1. Sprinkle the pink decorating sugar on a saucer. Pour some of the lemon juice into another saucer. Dip the rim of your glass upside down into the lemon juice, then into the decorating sugar. Let it dry a bit.

2. Add the lemon juice, gin, grenadine, egg whites and cream to a shaker with ice cubes. Shake vigorously for 30 seconds, then strain into the glass. It is best to use a small funnel for this so as not to ruin the sugar garnish. Serve immediately.

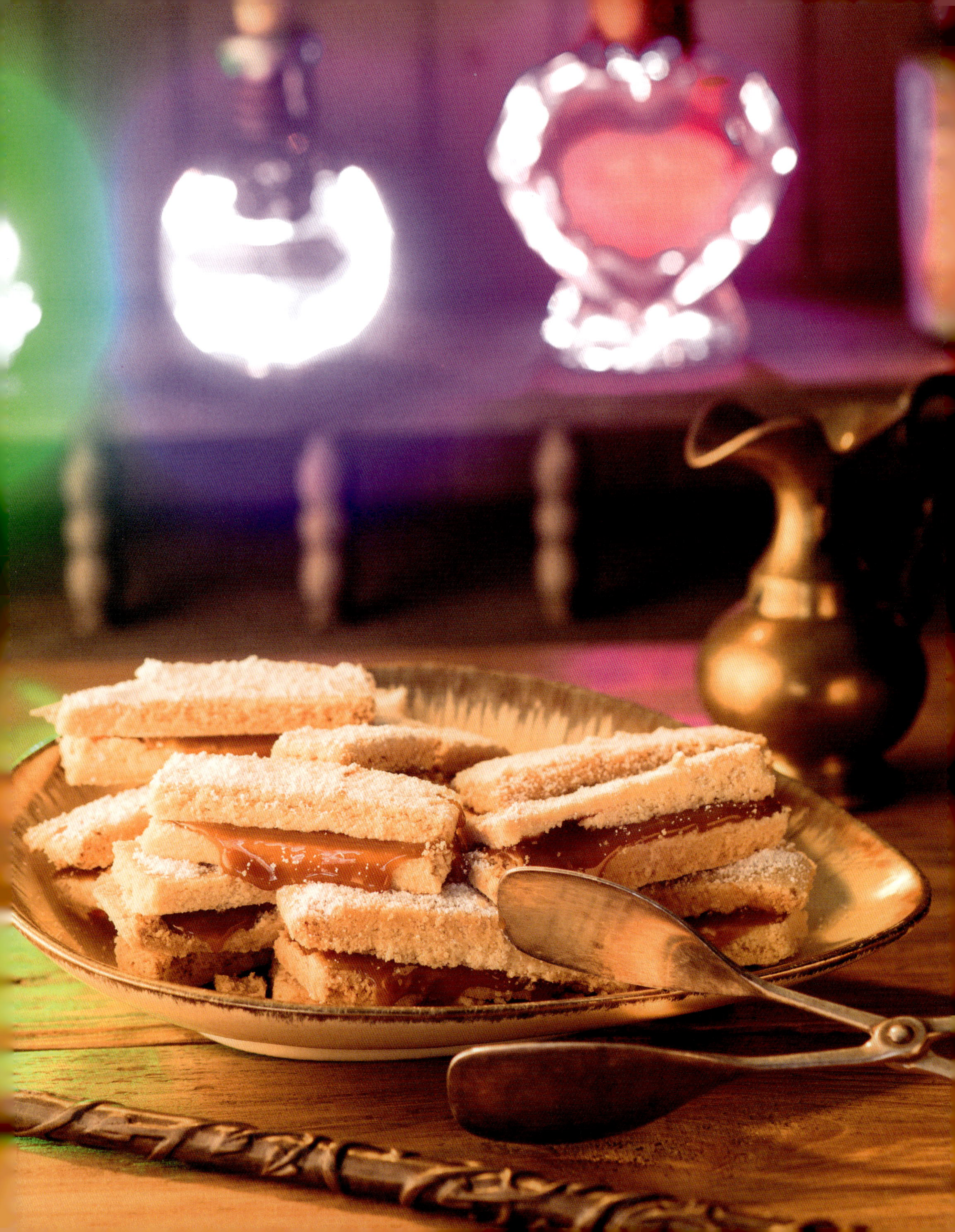

BUTTERBEER SHORTBREAD

INGREDIENTS FOR APPROX. 20 PIECES

5 oz soft butter plus a little more, to grease the baking frame
1.5 oz sugar
1 oz powdered sugar plus a little more, for sprinkling
8 oz flour
1 pinch of salt
1 tbsp rose water
Butter beer sauce (see p. 34)

Also required: baking frame (approx. 10" x 10")

1. In a bowl, beat the butter with the sugar using an electric hand mixer until creamy.
2. Add the powdered sugar, flour, salt, and rose water and mix with the dough hook of the mixer until a smooth dough is formed. Form the dough into a ball with your hands, wrap it in cling film and put it in the fridge for 30 minutes.
3. Preheat the oven to 320 °F heat. Line a baking tray with baking paper.
4. Remove the dough from the refrigerator, unwrap it from the cling film and place it a finger's width high in a baking frame greased with a little butter. Smooth the top, prick all over with the tines of a fork and bake for approx.
5. 30 minutes in the preheated oven.
6. Remove from the oven, let cool in the baking frame, and only then remove from the frame. Transfer to a cutting board and cut into finger-length, oblong pieces with a large, sharp knife.
7. Spread half of the shortbreads evenly on one side with a little butterbeer sauce, place the remaining shortbread on top and sprinkle generously with powdered sugar.
8. If stored in a tin, this shortbread will keep for a few days.

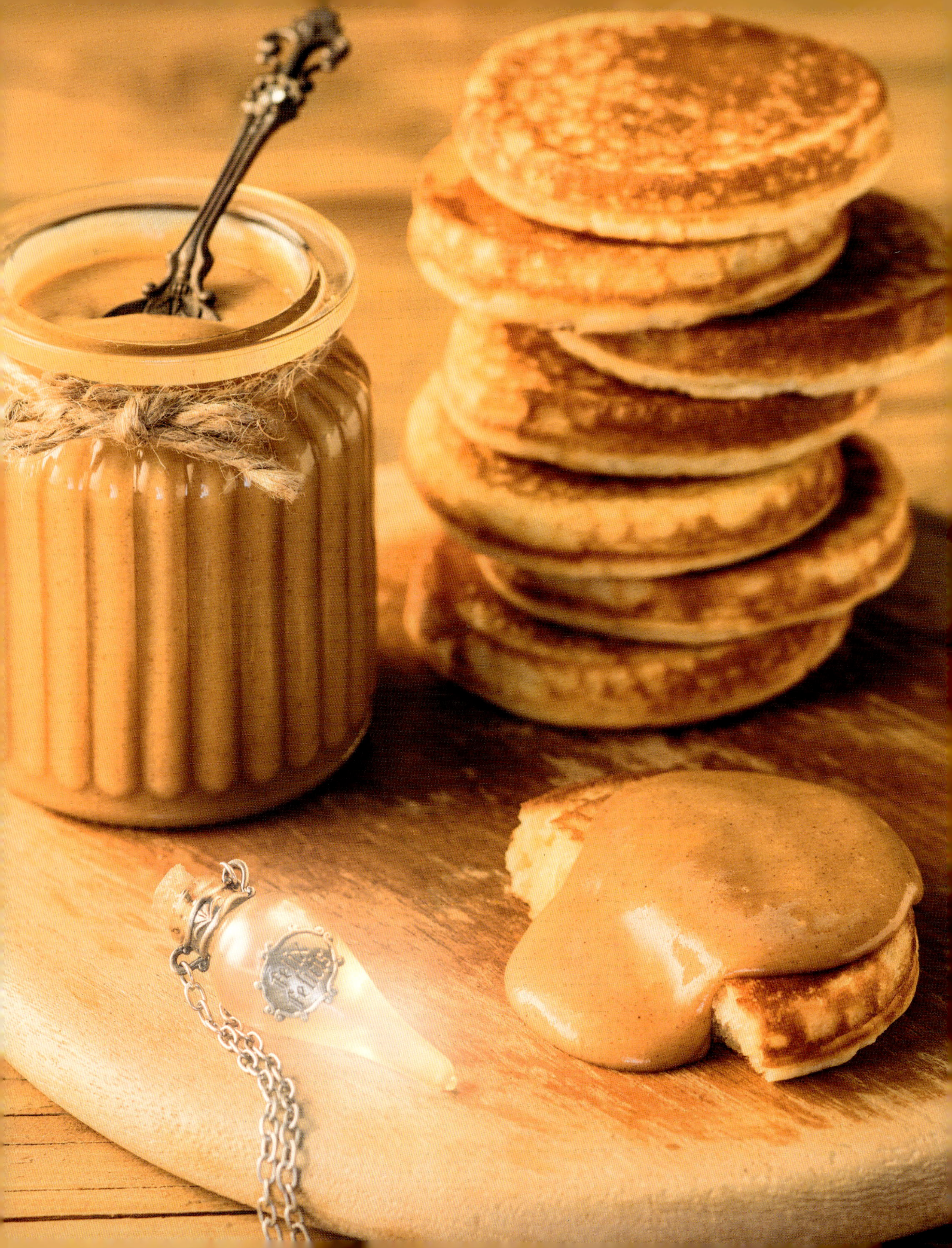

CINNAMON-CARAMEL MAGIC

INGREDIENTS FOR APPROX. 1 LB
14 oz sweetened condensed milk, canned
9 oz room-warm butter
1 tbsp coconut blossom sugar
2 tsp cinnamon

Also required: canning jar or screw-top jar with 17 fl. oz capacity

1. Place the can of sweetened condensed milk in a covered saucepan with enough water to fully cover the can. Bring to a boil over medium heat, then reduce the heat to low and simmer gently for about 3½ hours. Carefully remove the can from the pot with tongs and allow to cool completely before opening. Caution: Very hot!

2. Meanwhile, in a bowl, using an electric hand mixer, lightly beat the butter. Then add the coconut blossom sugar, the cinnamon, and the cooled condensed milk and work everything thoroughly until you have a smooth, homogeneous cream. Pour into a hot-rinsed canning jar or screw top jar.

3. Keeps in the refrigerator for about 2-3 weeks.

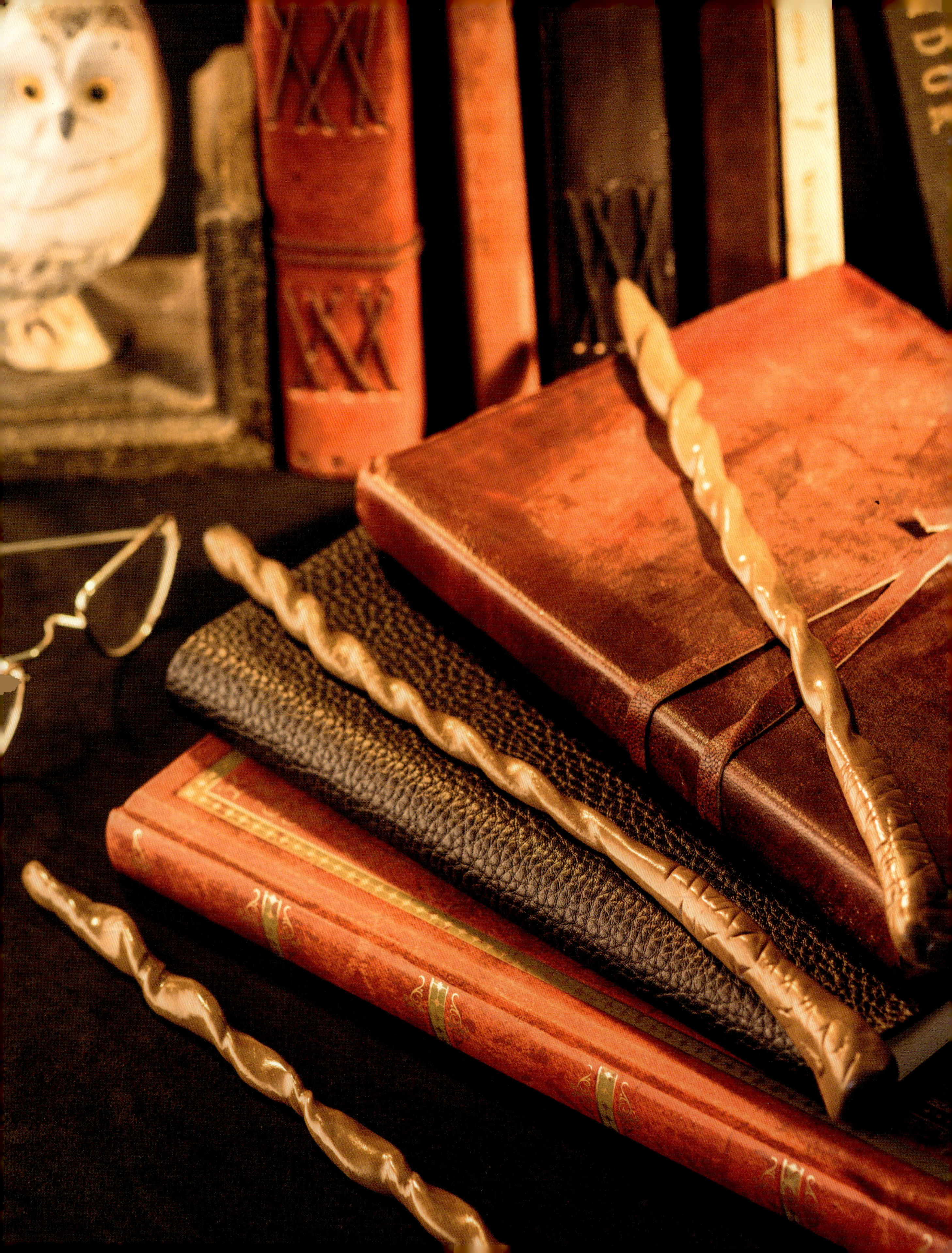

LICORICE WANDS

INGREDIENTS FOR 10 WANDS
50 licorice candies

1. Let the licorice candies soften in a warm place for about 1-2 hours before processing, so that they are easier to knead. If that is not enough, soften them individually with your hands using your own body heat if needed. And if that is still not enough, put them in the oven for a few minutes at the lowest heat setting.

2. When the candies are soft and malleable, shape them into a ball, five at a time. Then roll them with the flat of your hand into a "snake" about 5-10" long. Use your fingers to form a "handle" at the bottom and gently twist the mass to form the wand into the desired shape.

3. Allow the wands to set in a cool place (but not in the refrigerator!).

4. Then store in a cool place in an airtight container.

For those of you who don't like licorice, you can easily make these wands from pure soft caramel candies. The method of preparation is exactly the same.

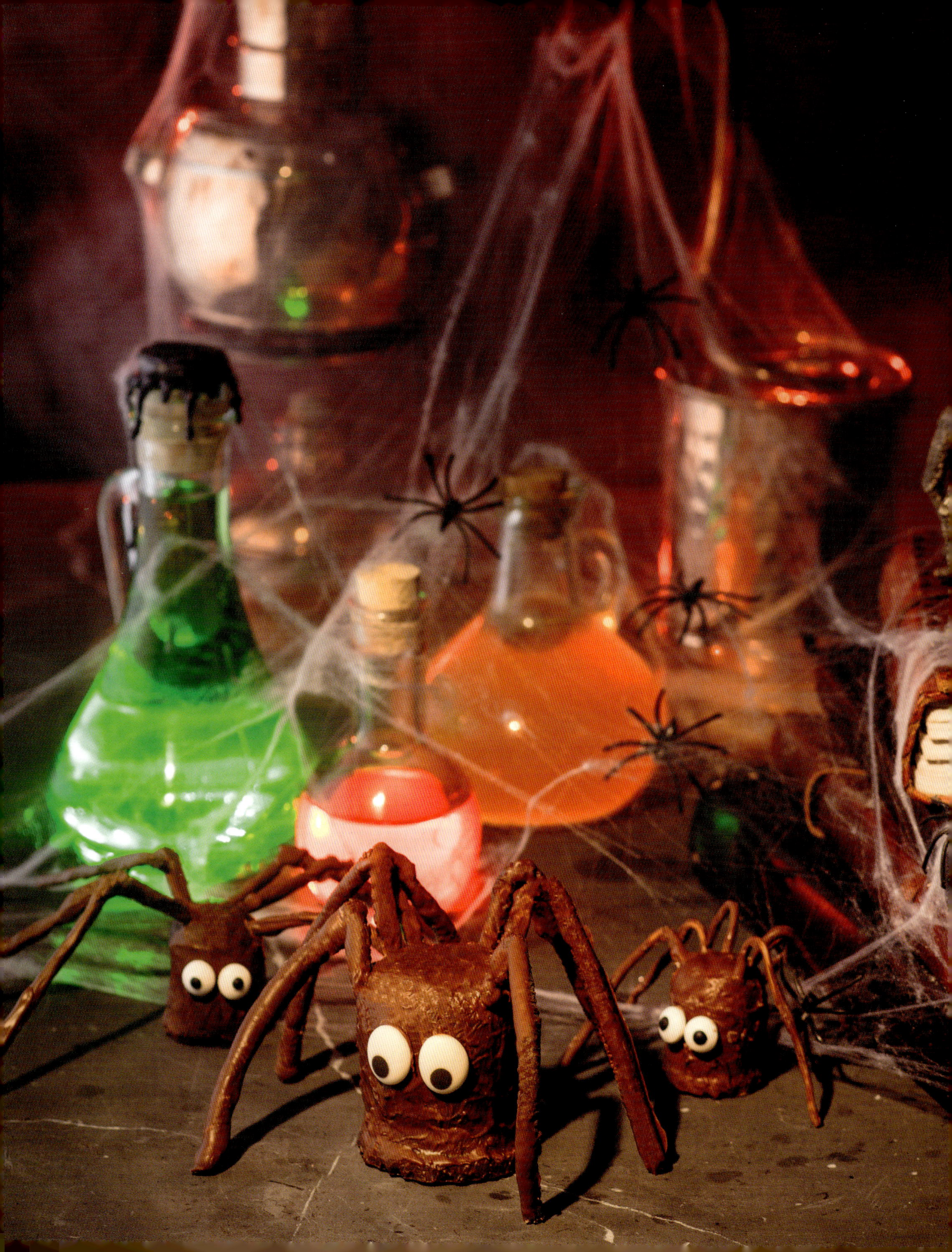

CHOCOLATE ACROMANTULAS

**INGREDIENTS FOR
5 ACROMANTULAS**
7 oz dark chocolate coating,
coarsely chopped
30-40 pretzel sticks
5 large and/or small chocolate kisses
10 sugar eyes, to taste

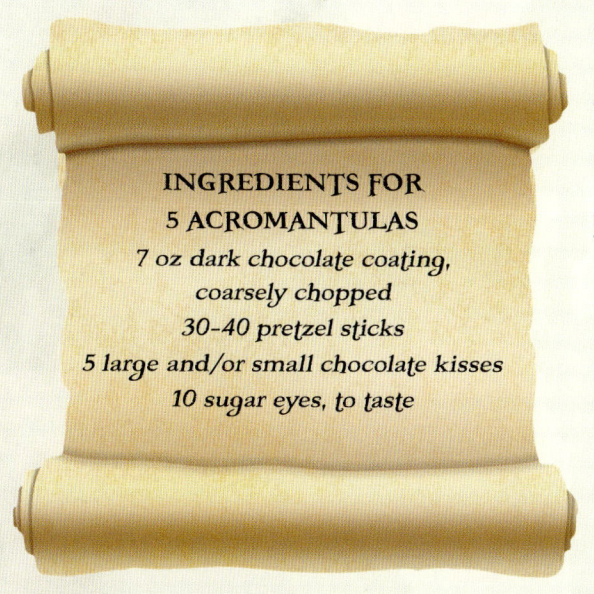

1. Line a baking tray or board with baking paper.
2. Place the coarsely-chopped chocolate coating in a bowl and melt over a water bath. Make sure the bottom of the bowl does not touch the boiling water.
3. Carefully break the pretzel sticks so that you get a short piece and a much longer piece. Using the melted chocolate coating, "glue" these two pieces back together so that you have a bent spider leg. To do this, place the pretzel sticks on the baking tray, cover them completely with the chocolate on the top side and carefully press on the "joint" at the desired angle until the glue has dried. Then gently turn the "spider leg" and coat the other side with the chocolate. Allow to dry completely.
4. Now prepare the chocolate kisses. To do this, very carefully melt holes in the chocolate shell (three on each side) with a slightly warmed pointed knife or a warmed tin pricker in the places where the spider legs are to be placed. Then insert the dried spider legs into the holes with the short "joint" side and gently seal with melted chocolate coating. Allow to harden on the baking sheet in the refrigerator.
5. Melt the remaining couverture again and brush the acromantulas all over with a small pastry brush to give them a bit more texture. Lastly, carefully place two sugar eyes on each of the still sticky chocolate and allow to dry. Store in the refrigerator until ready to eat.

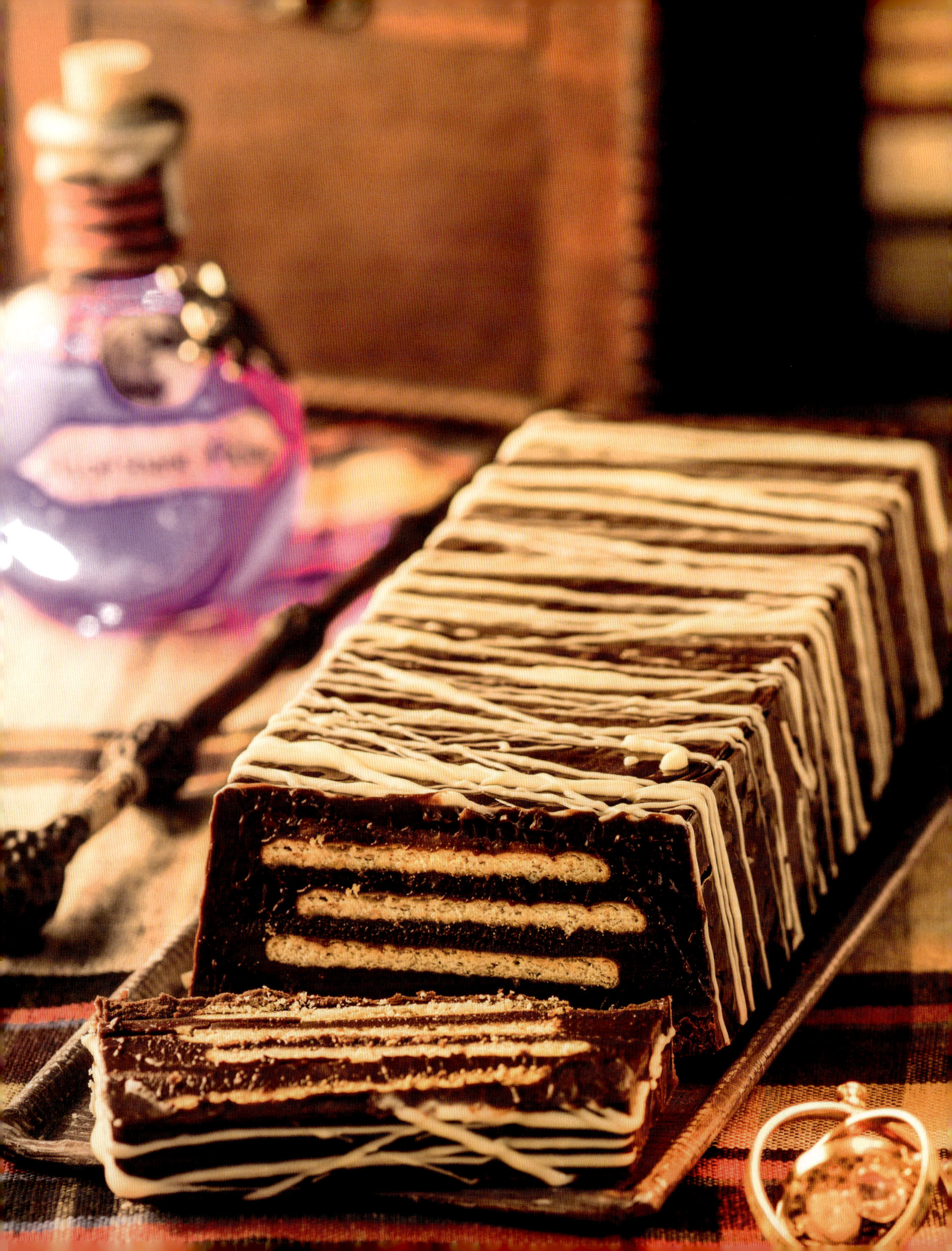

ANIMAGUS CAKE

INGREDIENTS FOR 1 CAKE

9 oz dark couverture chocolate, coarsely chopped

7 oz milk couverture chocolate, coarsely chopped

9.5 oz coconut oil

2 eggs

2 oz powdered sugar

2 tbsp baking cocoa

5 oz butter cookies

1 oz white couverture, for decorating

Also required: loaf pan (approx. 12" x 4")

1. Line the loaf pan with plastic wrap.
2. Melt the coarsely chopped chocolate (plain and milk) and the coconut oil over a water bath on low heat, stirring constantly. Make sure that the bottom of your bowl does not touch the boiling water! Mix everything thoroughly and let cool slightly.
3. In a separate bowl, beat the eggs, powdered sugar, and baking cocoa with an electric hand mixer until fluffy. Stir in the liquid chocolate-coconut oil mixture.
4. Pour a thin, even layer of the lukewarm chocolate mixture into the loaf pan and smooth it out. Place a layer of butter cookies on top and spread enough chocolate cream to completely cover the cookies with it. Continue in the same way, alternating layers of cookies and chocolate cream in the loaf pan. Finally, place the filled mold in the refrigerator for at least 3-4 hours, but preferably overnight.
5. Gently turn out the set cake onto a serving plate, carefully remove from the mold and peel off the cling film.
6. Melt the white chocolate coating over a water bath and place in a small freezer bag. Cut off one corner of the bag and decorate the top and sides of the cake with it as desired. Let the chocolate dry for a few minutes. Finally, cut into not-too-thick slices with a large, sharp knife on a cutting board. Best enjoyed slightly chilled.

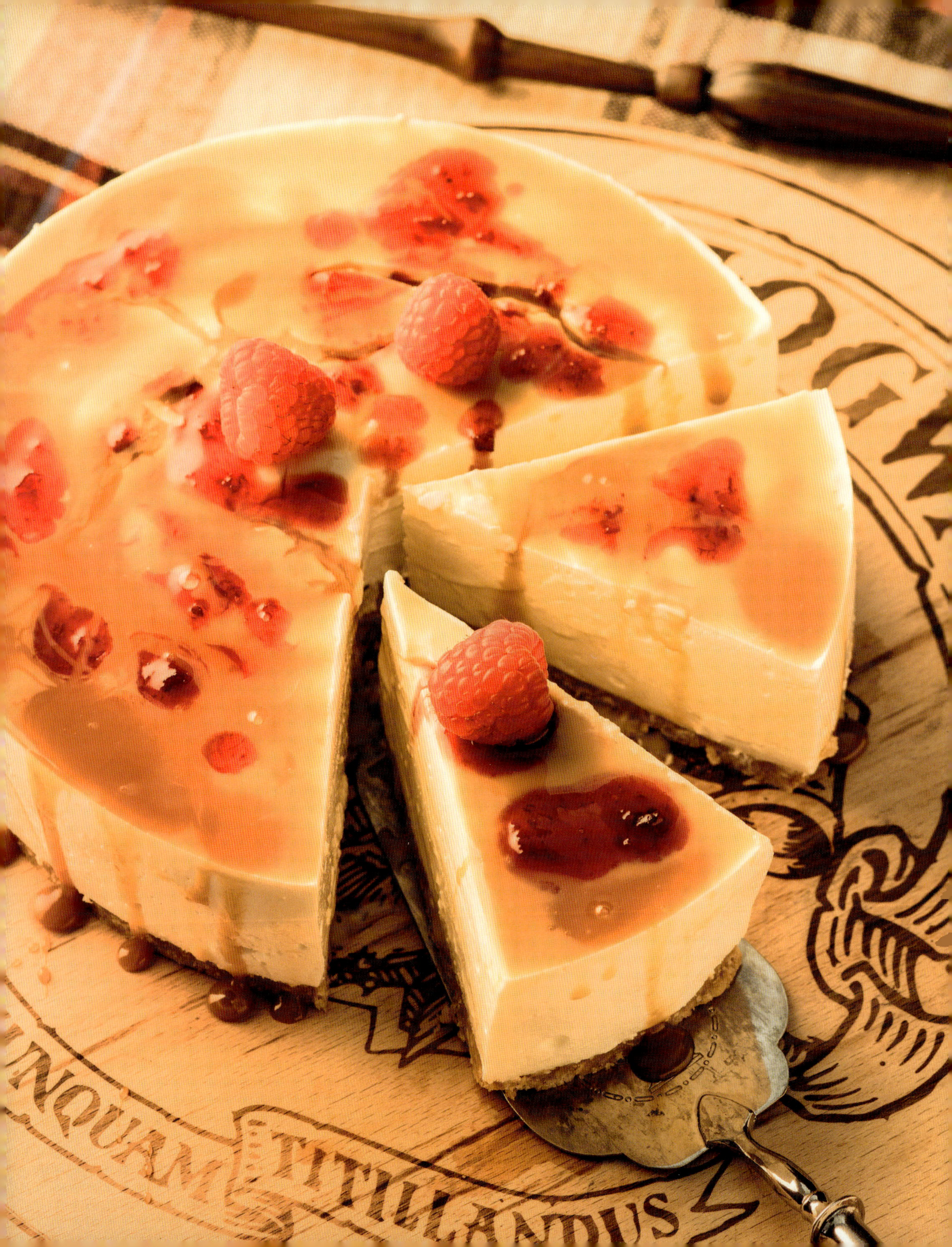
NQUAM
TITILLANDUS

BUTTERBEER CHEESECAKE

**INGREDIENTS FOR
1 CHEESECAKE**

For the cheesecake:
4 oz butter plus a little more,
to grease the baking dish.
7 oz butter cookies
7 oz cream
21 oz cream cheese
5 oz sour cream
5 oz sugar
1 packet vanilla sugar
4 fl. oz malt beer
4 leaves gelatin Juice of ½ lemon

For the fruit sauce:
7 oz raspberries, finely chopped, plus a
few whole raspberries, as garnish
1 oz sugar
1 squeeze of lemon juice

Also needed:
10" springform pan

1. Line a 10" springform pan with baking parchment and grease the sides with butter.

2. Finely grind the butter cookies in a food processor and transfer to a bowl.

3. In a small saucepan over low heat, melt the butter and add to the cookie crumbs. Work everything together well and mix thoroughly. Then press the mixture evenly as a base into the prepared springform pan and smooth all around.

4. In a bowl, whip the cream with an electric hand mixer until stiff and chill in the refrigerator.

5. In a separate bowl, mix the cream cheese, sour cream, sugar, vanilla sugar, and malt beer.

6. Soak the gelatin leaves in a small bowl of cold water for five minutes. Then take out the gelatin and gently squeeze it.

7. Heat the lemon juice in a small saucepan, but do not boil it! Add the squeezed gelatin and dissolve completely. Add 1-2 tbsp of the cream cheese mixture to the gelatin and incorporate thoroughly. Then add it all to the cream cheese mixture and stir everything well. Fold in the whipped cream. Finally, spread the mixture evenly over the cookie base in the springform pan and place in the refrigerator for at least six hours.

8. During this time, prepare the fruit sauce. To do this, place the raspberries in a tall container with the sugar and lemon juice and puree very finely with a hand blender. Refrigerate until ready to use.

9. Pour the fruit sauce generously over the butterbeer cheesecake and serve garnished with fresh raspberries.

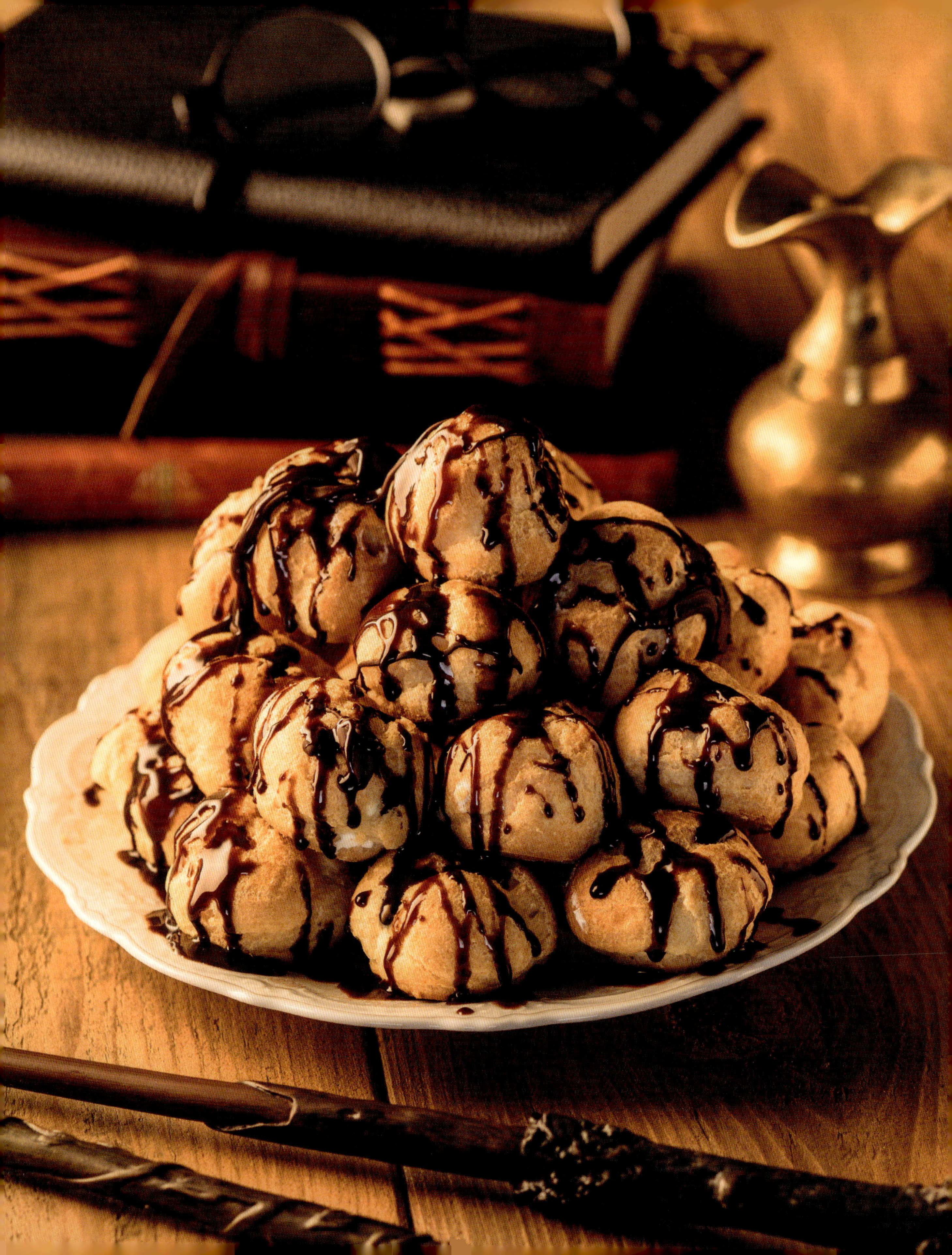

SLUG CLUB PROFITEROLES

INGREDIENTS FOR 5-6 PORTIONS

For the batter:
4 fl. oz milk
4 fl. oz water plus a little more, to coat the dough
1 oz sugar
1 packet vanilla sugar
1 pinch of salt
3 oz butter
5 oz flour
3-4 eggs, room temperature, plus 1 more egg, to coat the dough
Chocolate sauce

For the filling:
7 fl. oz cold whipped cream
1.5 oz powdered sugar
1 packet vanilla sugar

Also needed: piping bag with round nozzle and filling nozzle

1. Put the milk, water, sugar, vanilla sugar, salt, and butter in a saucepan and bring to a boil over medium heat. Remove from the heat, add all the flour in one sweep and stir through until you have a thick paste with no lumps. Return to the heat and stir until a firm lump of dough forms and a white layer has formed on the bottom of the pot. Then transfer the dough to a mixing bowl and let cool slightly.

2. In the meantime, preheat the oven to 350 °F and line a baking tray with baking paper.

3. Whisk in the eggs one at a time until the mixture resembles mashed potatoes. Pour into a piping bag fitted with a round nozzle and pipe walnut-sized dots onto the prepared baking sheet, spacing them slightly apart (as the batter is still rising).

4. In a small bowl, whisk the remaining egg with a little water and brush the dots with it. Bake for about 15-20 minutes until golden. Note: Do not open the oven door!

5. Meanwhile, prepare the filling. To do this, place the cold whipped cream in a chilled mixing bowl and whip with an electric hand mixer, first on low speed, then on high speed. Once the cream is creamy, add in the powdered sugar and vanilla sugar and continue beating just until the cream is stiff. Place in the refrigerator until ready to use.

6. Once the mini cream puffs are baked, remove them from the oven and let them cool completely on the baking sheet.

7. Place the filling in a piping bag with a long nozzle and fill the cream puffs. Pile into a pyramid on a flat plate and serve topped with chocolate sauce.

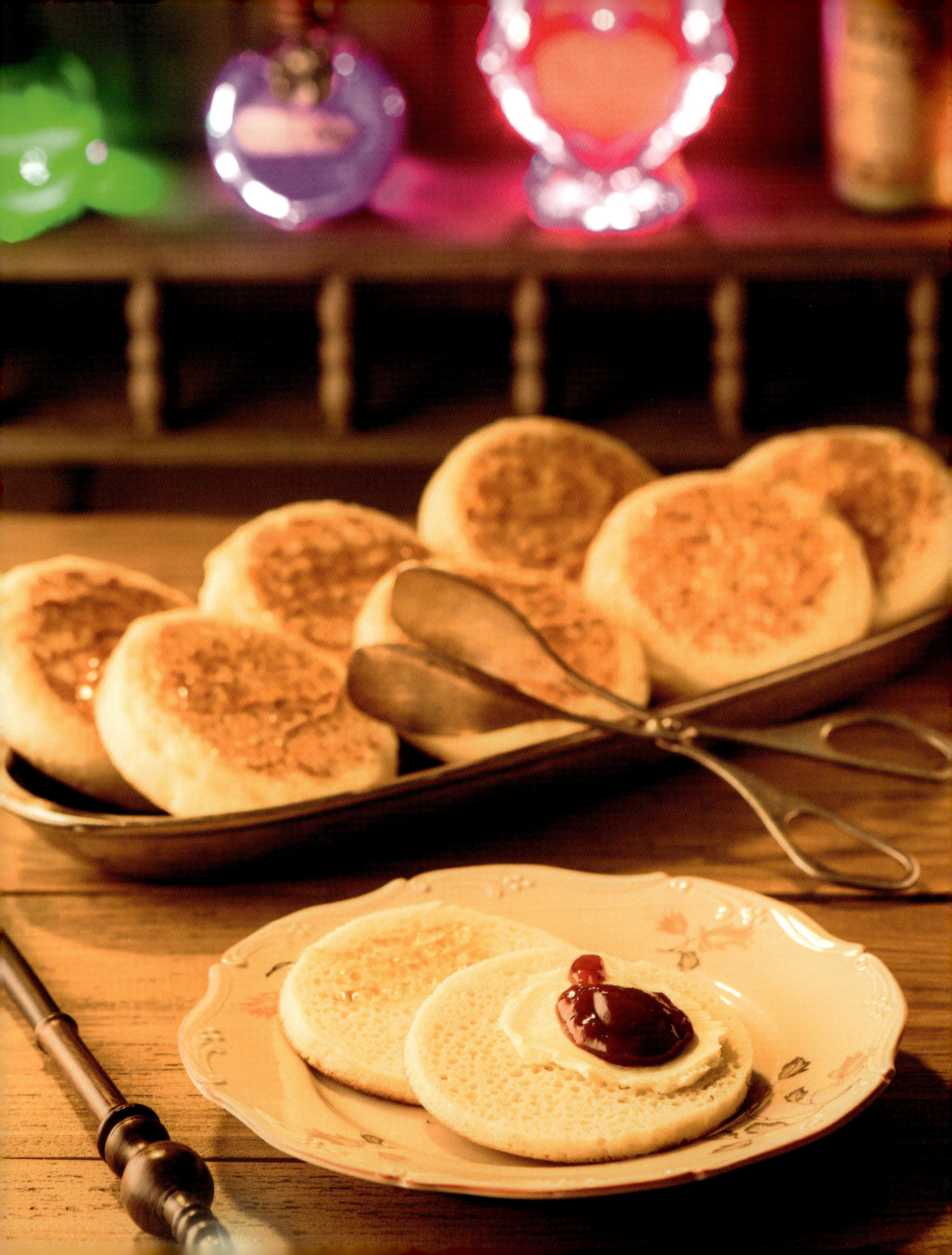

CRUMPETS

INGREDIENTS FOR APPROX. 10-12 CRUMPETS
5 oz flour
½ tsp salt
1 oz yeast
15 fl. oz milk
5 oz whole wheat flour
Some butter

Also needed:
crumpet rings
(alternatively pancake
or fried egg molds).

1. Mix the flour and salt together well in a large bowl. Form a well in the center, crumble in the yeast, and add a dash of milk. Let rest for ten minutes.

2. Heat the remaining milk in a small saucepan over low heat and add to the bowl. Mix everything until a homogeneous dough is formed. Let rest in a warm place for about 35-40 minutes.

3. Meanwhile, grease the crumpet rings generously with butter.

4. Once the dough has rested sufficiently, heat some butter in a large frying pan over medium heat, place the crumpet rings inside and ladle enough batter into each one so that it stands about ½ inch high in the ring. Now bake until small bubbles form on the surface of the crumpets and burst open. Then remove from the pan, flip and bake again for two minutes from the other side. Finally, transfer to a plate lined with paper towels to drain.

5. Serve with raspberry jam (see p. 180) or cinnamon-caramel magic (see p. 128).

You can either enjoy the crumpets fresh from the pan or eat them later. In this case, store them in an airtight container and toast them briefly before serving.

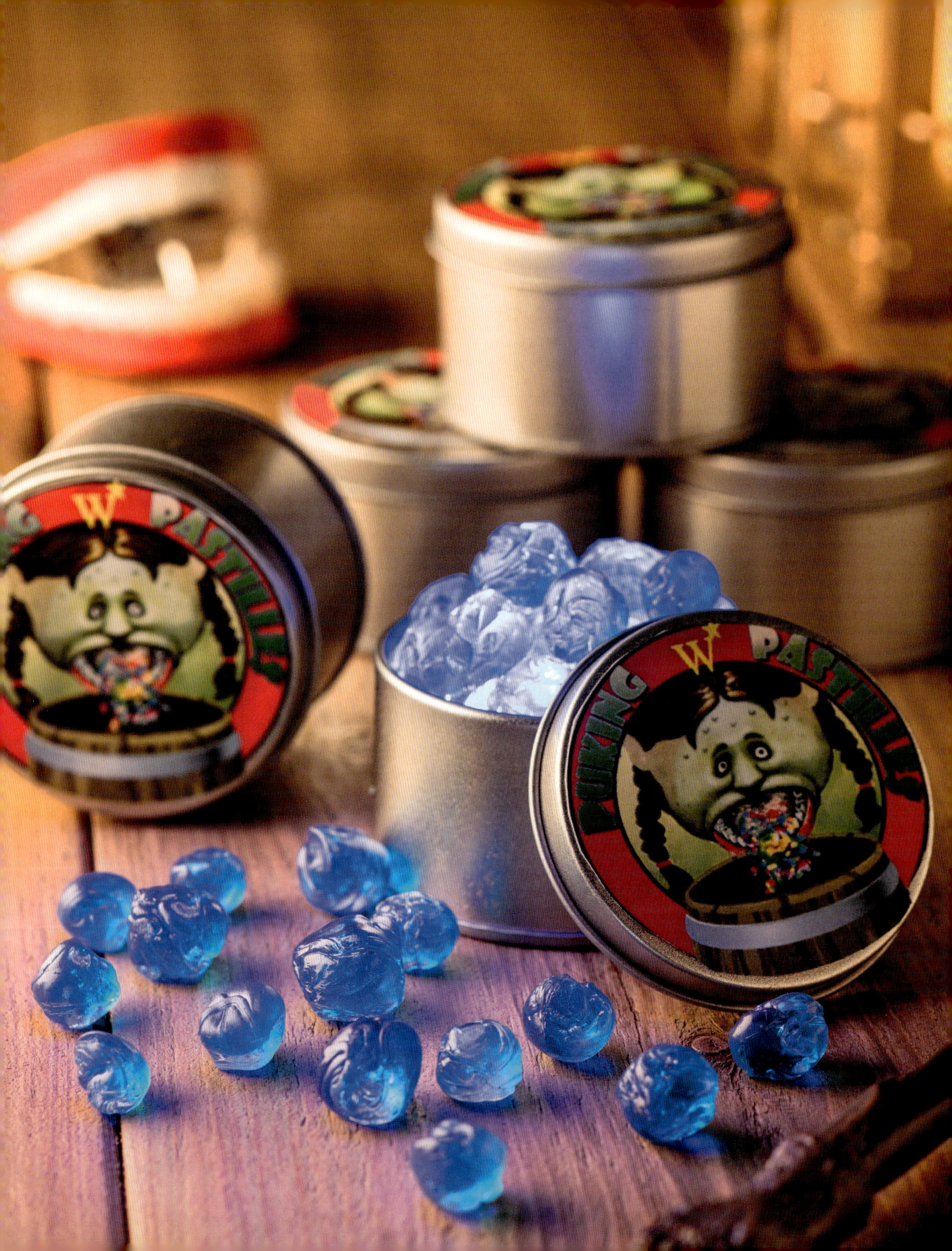
PUKING W PASTILLES

PUKING PASTILLES

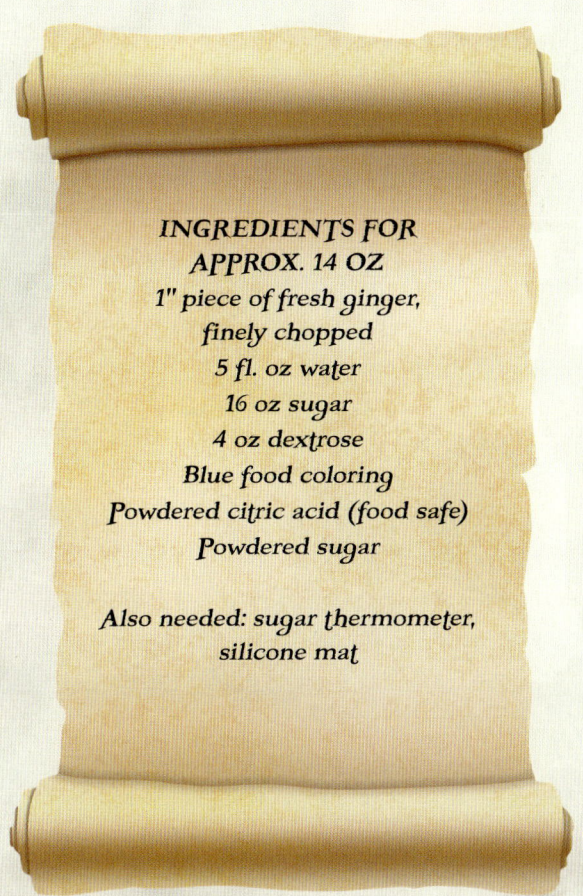

INGREDIENTS FOR APPROX. 14 OZ
1" piece of fresh ginger, finely chopped
5 fl. oz water
16 oz sugar
4 oz dextrose
Blue food coloring
Powdered citric acid (food safe)
Powdered sugar

Also needed: sugar thermometer, silicone mat

1. Put the ginger and water in a small pot, bring to a boil over medium heat and simmer for 15 minutes.

2. Drain the ginger water through a kitchen strainer preferably into a saucepan. Discard the ginger.

3. Add the sugar and dextrose to the ginger water, heat over medium heat and simmer gently, stirring constantly, until the sugar is completely dissolved.

4. Once the syrup begins to boil, stop stirring and place a sugar thermometer in the pot. When the temperature reaches 300 °F, immediately remove from heat, place on a heat-resistant surface and quickly stir in the blue food coloring and citric acid. Caution: Very hot!

5. Pour the sugar mixture carefully onto a silicone mat and allow to cool slightly so that you can work the mixture without burning your fingers. Using scissors, cut off pieces about 1" in size and shape them with your hands into small, not too regular balls. The candy mass will harden quickly, so work quickly!

6. Put the powdered sugar in a shallow bowl. Roll the vomit pastilles in it all around so they don't stick together when stored, and store in an airtight container. Keeps for several months.

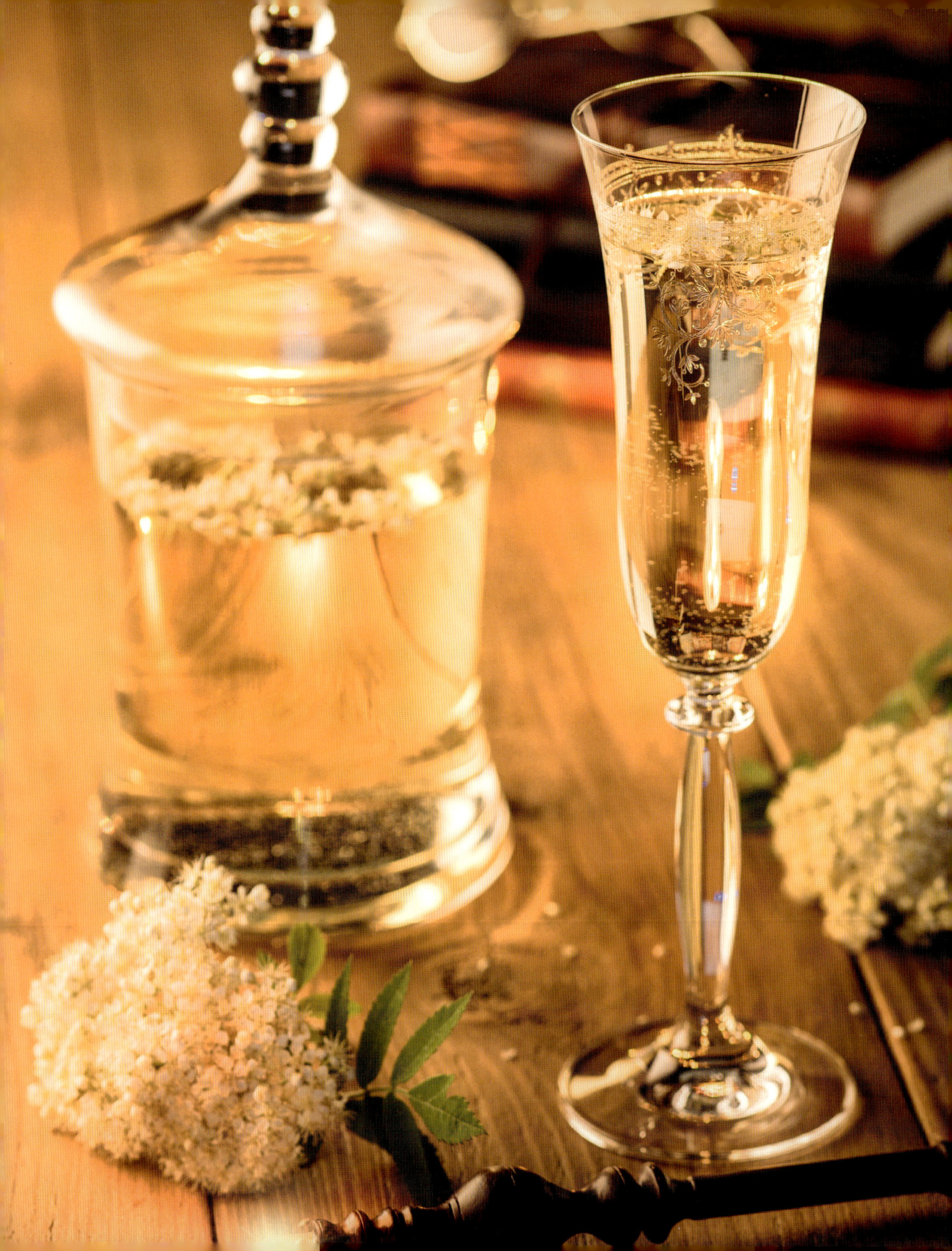

FELIX FELICIS

WITH ALCOHOL

INGREDIENTS FOR APPROX. 1 QT
18 oz blossom honey
25 fl. oz grain brandy
1 cinnamon stick
1 vanilla pod
1 cardamom pod
Some cinnamon blossom
1-2 cloves

Also required:
2-3 smaller or one large potion bottle,
edible glitter or gold leaf,
large canning jar.

1. Put the honey in the hot-rinsed preserving jar. Pour the grain over it and stir until the honey is completely dissolved. Then add all the spices, close the jar and store in a cool, dark place.

2. Leave to infuse for 3-4 weeks in a cool, dark place. Shake vigorously every few days.

3. Strain the finished liqueur through a fine sieve and pour it into the hot washed bottles. Add some edible glitter or small pieces of edible gold leaf to give it the most magical look possible. Cap the bottles tightly and shake well. Optionally add a pretty label.

The longer the honey liqueur infuses, the more delicious it tastes!

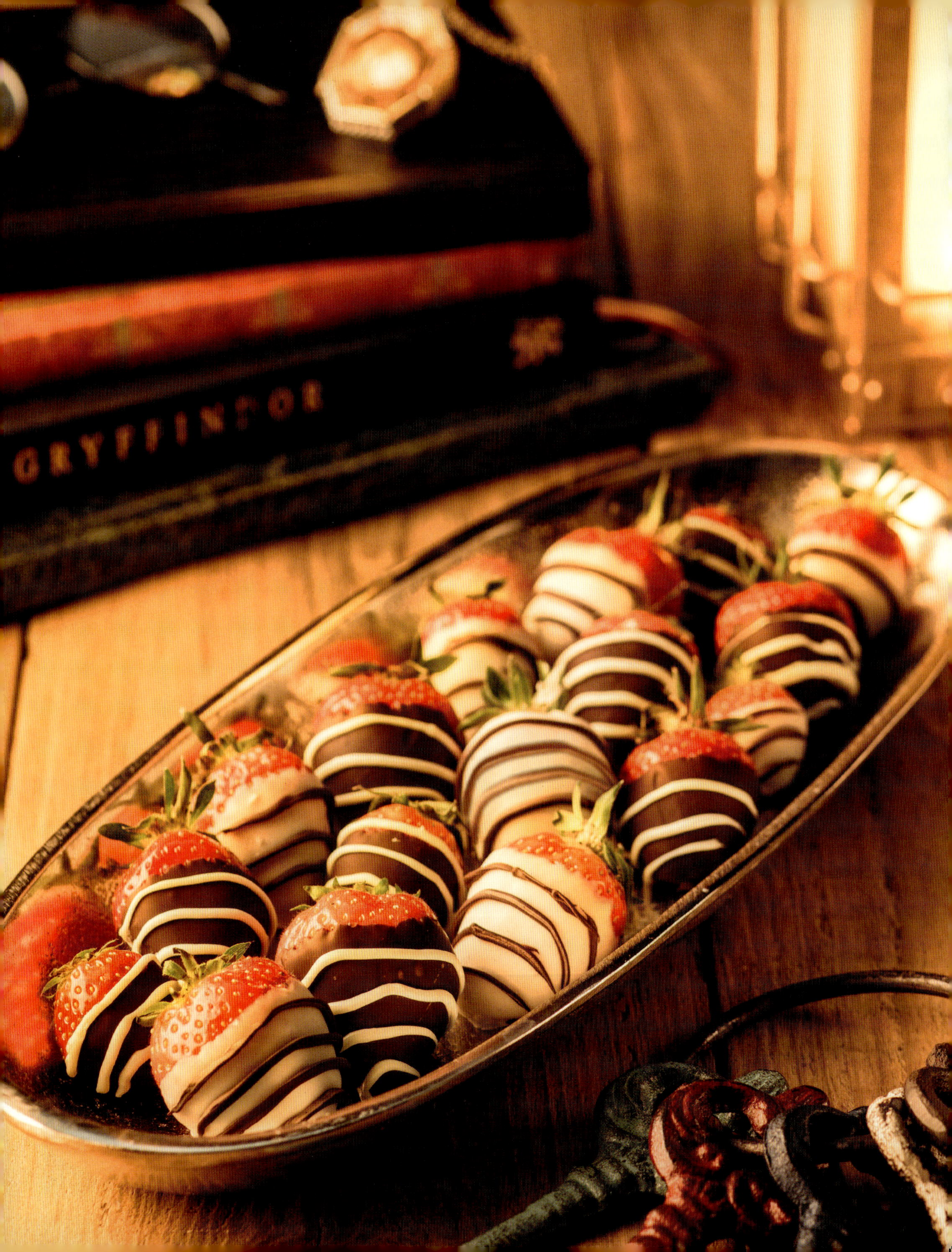
GRYFFINDOR

CHOCOLATE STRAWBERRIES

INGREDIENTS FOR 2 LB CHOCOLATE STRAWBERRIES

4 oz white chocolate, coarsely chopped
4 oz milk chocolate, coarsely chopped
4 oz dark chocolate, coarsely chopped
14 oz fresh strawberries

Also needed:
piping bag or freezer bag

1. Wash the strawberries and pat dry with kitchen paper.
2. Line a baking tray with baking paper.
3. In a bowl over a water bath, melt the chocolate, each kind separately. Make sure the bottom of the bowl does not touch the boiling water!
4. Stir the melted chocolate vigorously and pour each variety into a separate small bowl.
5. Holding the strawberries by their greens, dip them into the desired chocolate and let them drip a little. Then place the strawberries on the baking paper a little apart from each other and let them dry until the chocolate is set. Proceed in this way with all the strawberries.
6. Put the remaining liquid chocolate into piping bags or a freezer bag with the corner cut off and pipe streaks over the top of the strawberries. Allow the chocolate to dry. Then turn the strawberries over and add streaks to the other side, seamlessly following those on the other side. Again, allow to dry briefly and enjoy as soon as possible!

If the chocolate becomes too firm in the meantime, simply heat in 20-second bursts in the microwave to melt again!

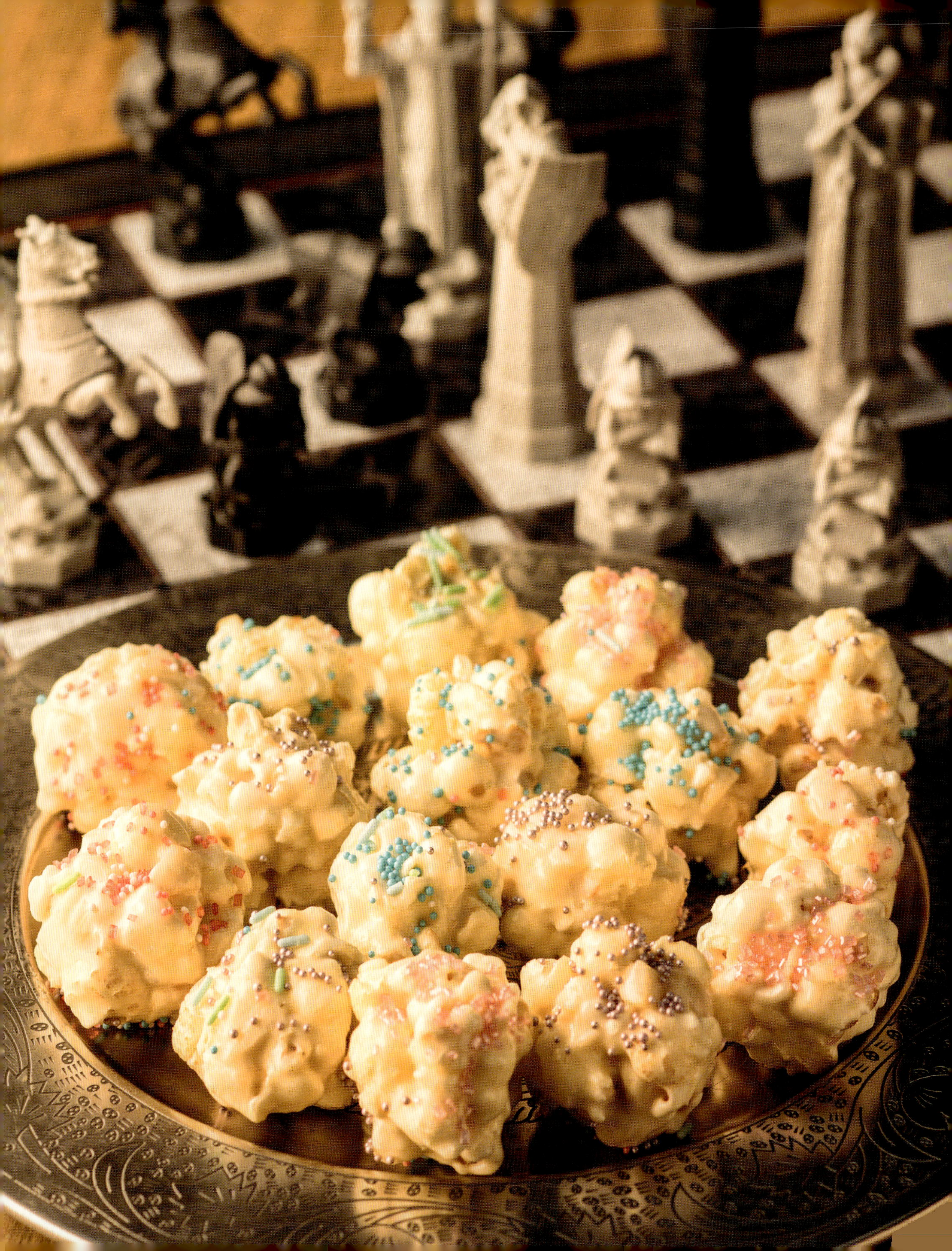

PROF. SLUGHORN'S POPCORN BALLS

INGREDIENTS FOR APPROX. 15 BALLS

3 oz microwave popcorn corn
1 oz butter
9 oz marshmallows
4 oz macadamia nuts, coarsely chopped
Colorful sugar sprinkles,
or
small sugar pearls
Some oil

1. Prepare the popcorn according to package directions.
2. In a small saucepan over low heat, melt the butter. Add the marshmallows and melt, stirring regularly with a heatproof, well-oiled cooking spatula.
3. Once the marshmallows are completely melted, remove the saucepan from the heat. Add in the coarsely chopped macadamia nuts and the finished popcorn and gently stir in. Be careful: it is very hot! Then allow the popcorn mixture to cool enough to work with without burning your fingers.
4. Meanwhile, line a baking tray with baking paper. Place the colored sugar sprinkles in a small bowl.
5. Grease your hands thoroughly with oil and quickly form the popcorn mixture into balls of as equal size as possible. Turn them over in the bowl with the sugar sprinkles so that they are coated all around. Then place the balls on the baking sheet, spacing them slightly apart, and let them dry completely.

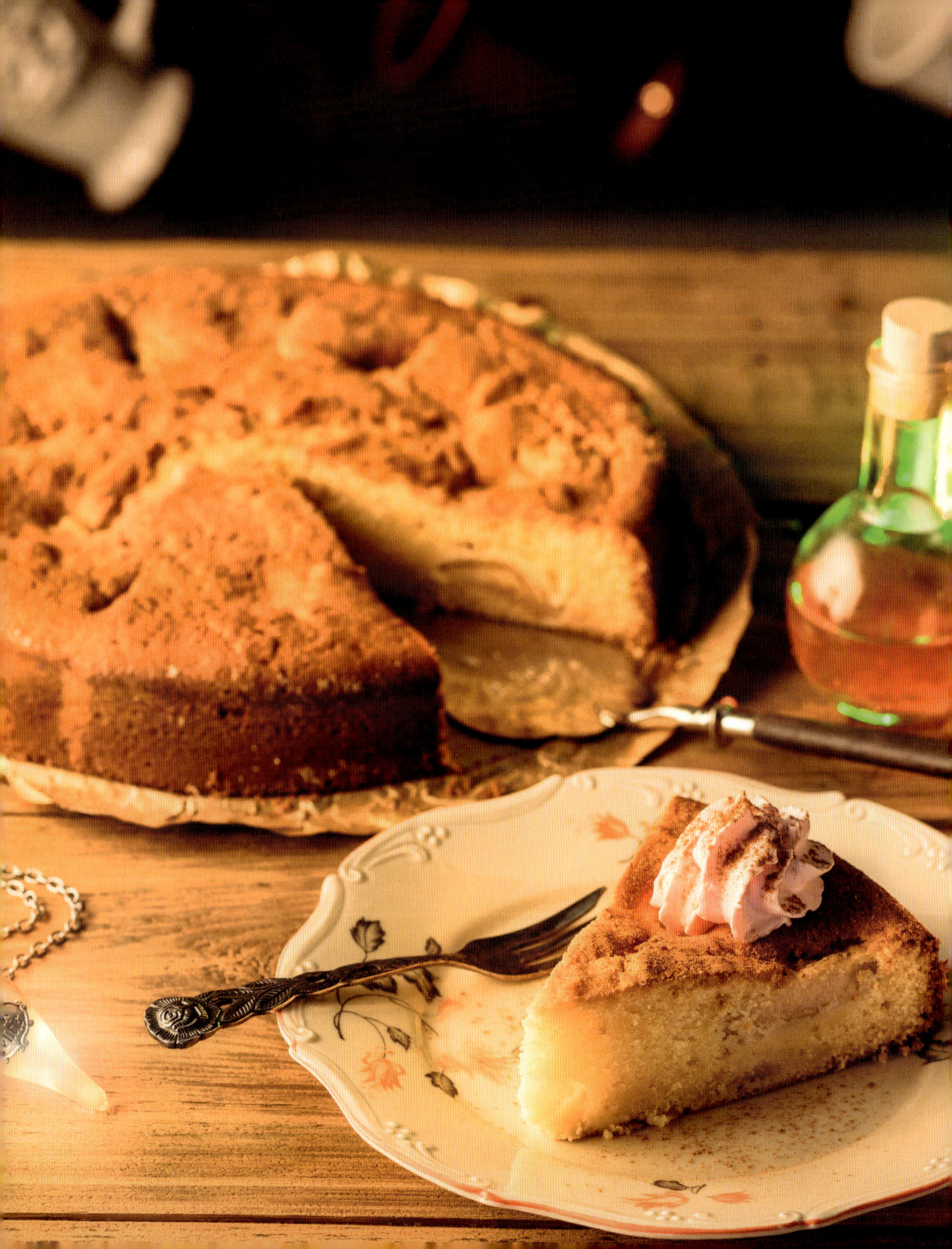

APPLE CAKE

INGREDIENTS FOR 1 CAKE
5 oz butter plus a little more, to grease the baking pan
5 oz sugar
2 eggs
Zest of ½ lemon
1 pinch of salt
7 oz wheat flour
2 tsp baking powder
2 tbsp milk
21 oz apples, peeled and quartered
Powdered sugar, to taste
Also needed: cake pan (approx. 10" diameter).

1. In a bowl, cream the butter and sugar with a hand mixer. Gradually add the eggs, lemon zest and salt.

2. In a separate bowl, mix the flour with the baking powder and sift into the butter and egg mixture. Mix everything together to form a dough and incorporate the milk.

3. Preheat the oven to 340 °F heat. Grease the cake tin with a little butter.

4. Slightly cut the tops of the apple quarters several times.

5. Pour the dough into the prepared baking pan, smooth the top and press the apple quarters lightly into the dough with a little space between them. Bake on middle rack in preheated oven for approx. 40-50 minutes or until the cake is golden brown and nothing sticks to a toothpick inserted in the center. Then remove from oven, let cool on a cooling rack and dust with powdered sugar to taste.

Harry Potter
The Cupboard Under the Stairs
4 Privet Drive
Little Whinging

PEPPER IMPS

**INGREDIENTS FOR APPROX.
14 OZ PEPPER IMPS**

11 oz sugar
5 oz white glucose syrup
4 fl. oz water
1 tbsp peppermint oil
1-2 drops of red food coloring
edible oil
5 oz powdered sugar

1. In a saucepan, heat the water over medium heat. Then stir in the glucose syrup and then the sugar. Cook, stirring constantly, until the sugar is completely dissolved and threads. Now remove the pot from the heat and mix the peppermint oil into the mixture. Pour half of the sugar mixture into a bowl and color it with red food coloring. Pour the remaining sugar mixture into a separate bowl. Let cool for a few minutes.

2. Once the two sugar mixtures have cooled a bit, but are not yet completely solid, so that they can be easily worked without burning your fingers, roll them into thin strings with fingers lightly greased with cooking oil. Then place one white and one red "candy cane" together and twist them together. Place on a baking sheet lined with parchment paper, spacing them slightly apart, and let dry for 10 minutes.

3. Put the powdered sugar in an airtight container.

4. Cut the candy canes with kitchen scissors into pieces about 1" long, put them into the container with the powdered sugar, close the container and toss everything gently.

5. Put the pepper imps into a sieve, tap off the excess powdered sugar and put the mints back into the container. Store tightly sealed for several weeks.

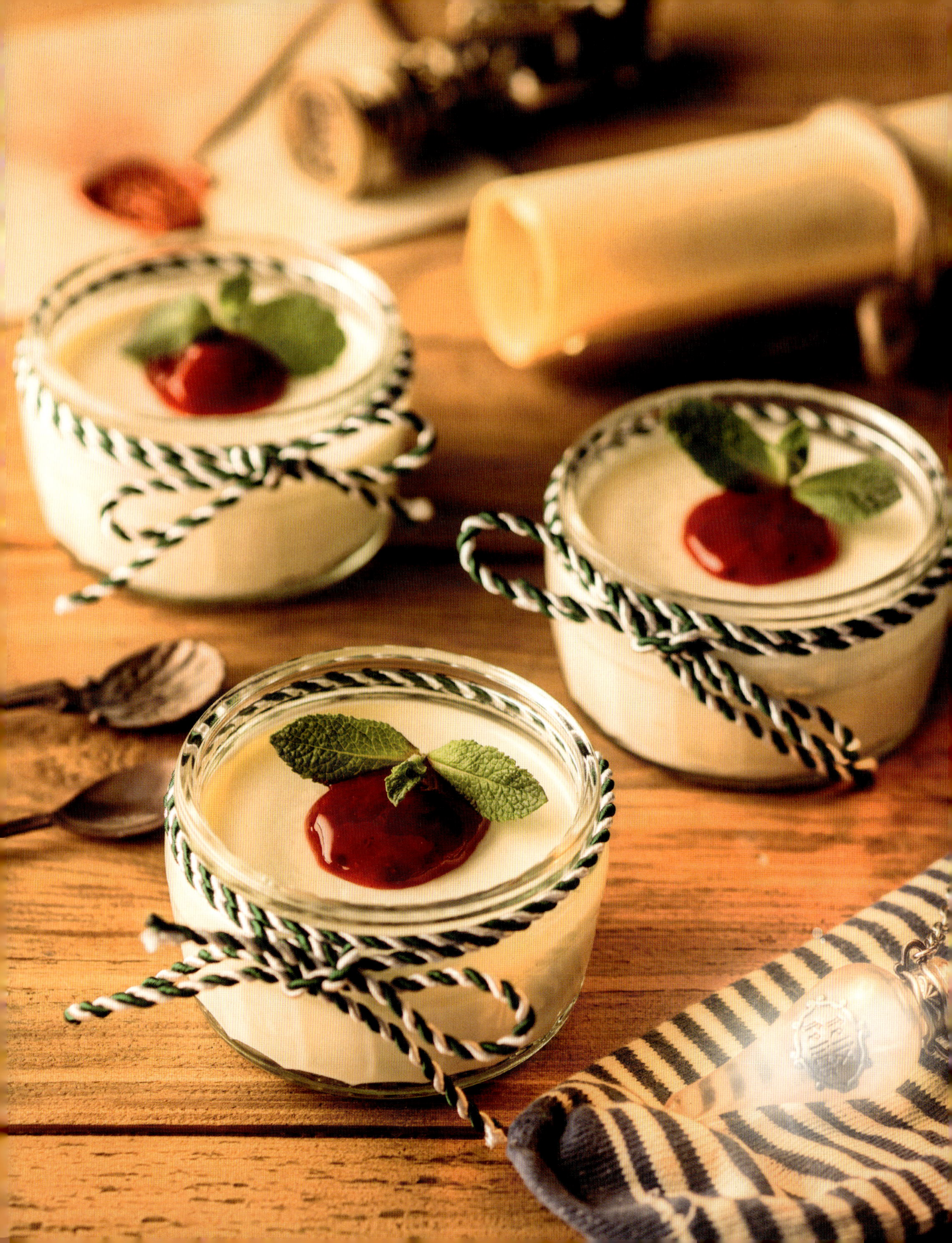

BLANCMANGE

INGREDIENTS FOR 4 PORTIONS

5 sheets white gelatin
9 fl. oz milk
2.3 oz ground almonds, without skin
1 oz sugar plus 5 tbsp
½ vanilla pod
9 oz whipped cream
2 drops of bitter almond flavoring
11 oz frozen raspberries, defrosted
1 tbsp lemon juice
Fresh mint leaves, as garnish

1. Soak the gelatin in cold water in a small bowl.
2. In a saucepan over medium heat, bring the milk, almonds, 5 tbsp sugar and vanilla bean to a boil, stirring constantly. Remove from heat and let steep for ten minutes. Then drain through a sieve and collect the vanilla almond milk. Add the whipped cream and bitter almond flavoring and stir well.
3. Gently squeeze the gelatin and add to the vanilla-almond milk. Stir until the gelatin is completely dissolved. Pour into desired serving glasses and chill in the refrigerator for at least three hours.
4. In the meantime, prepare the raspberry sauce. To do this, place the remaining 1 oz sugar in a small saucepan with the defrosted frozen raspberries and lemon juice and bring to a boil over medium heat, stirring constantly. Remove from heat, let cool slightly and strain through a kitchen sieve.
5. When the almond sauce has cooled, spread the sauce on top and serve garnished with mint leaves.

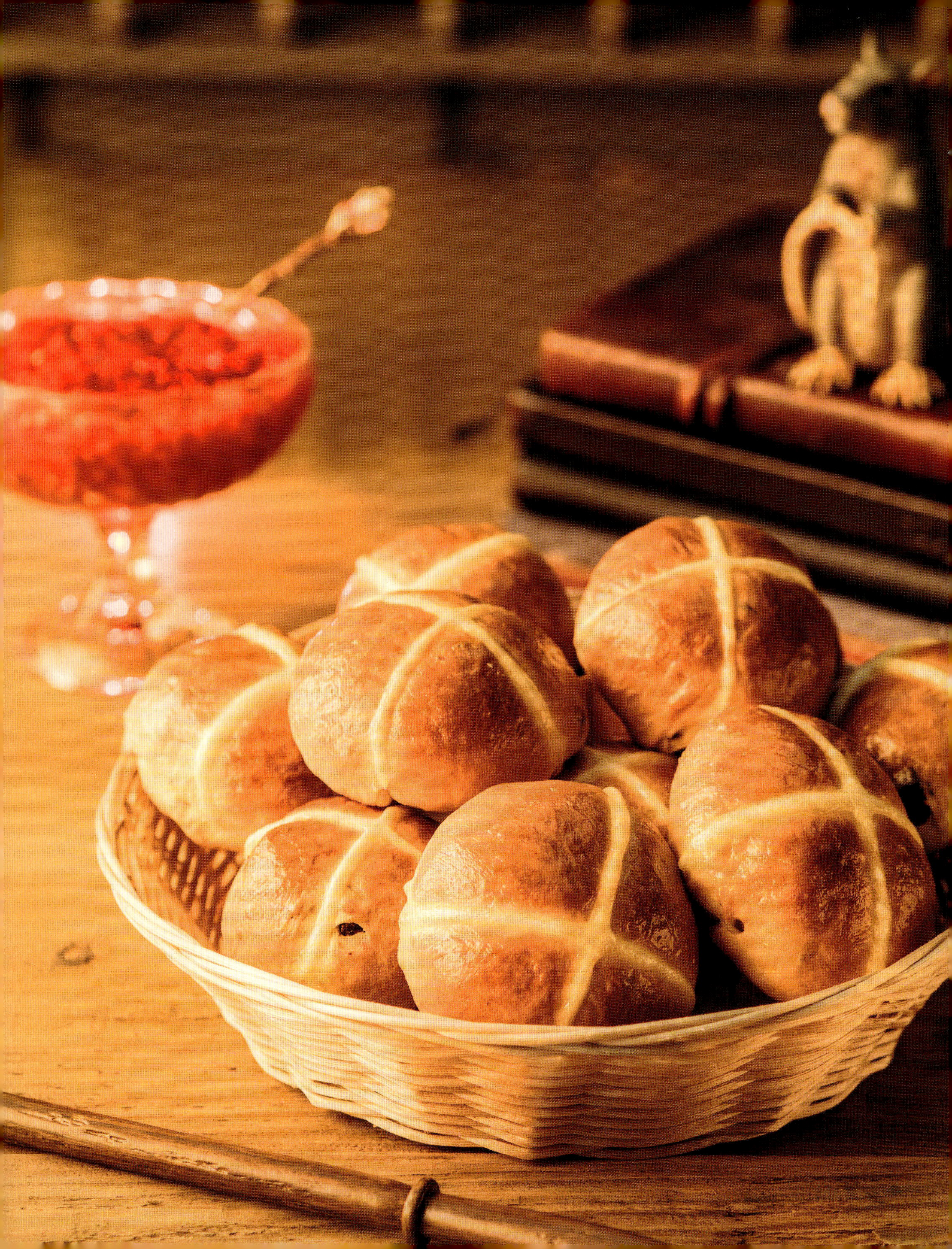

CROSS BUNS

INGREDIENTS FOR APPROX. 8-10 BUNS

For the rolls:
4 oz raisins
Some apple juice
10 fl. oz lukewarm milk
2 oz butter
18 oz flour, a little more if necessary
1 packet of dry yeast
1 pinch of salt
½ tsp cinnamon
3 oz sugar
1 egg

For decorating:
3 oz flour
1 tsp sugar
Approx. 3-5 tbsp water
2 tbsp apricot jam, strained

Also needed:
piping bag or freezer bag.

1. Put the raisins in a small bowl and pour enough apple juice that they are completely covered. Let soak for 1-2 hours.

2. In a saucepan over low heat, warm the milk and butter. Stir until the butter is completely melted. Remove from heat and let cool to room temperature.

3. Combine 18 oz flour, the dry yeast, the salt, the cinnamon and 3 oz sugar in a bowl. Then add the egg and the lukewarm milk. Knead everything well by hand or with a food processor fitted with a dough hook until the dough separates from the sides of the bowl by itself. If necessary, add a little more flour.

4. Form the dough into a ball and let it rise, covered with a clean tea towel, in a warm place for an hour or until it is almost twice as big as before.

5. Line two baking sheets with baking paper. Preheat the oven to 390 °F heat.

6. Drain the raisins. Knead the dough again vigorously and incorporate the raisins. Divide the dough into twelve equal pieces. Shape each of them into a ball with your hands and place them on the prepared baking sheets with enough space between them. Let rise for another twenty minutes.

7. Meanwhile, for the cross decoration, in a bowl, mix the flour and sugar with the water. Stir until you have a thick paste that is not too runny. Pour into a small piping bag or a freezer bag with the corner cut off and pipe each cross onto each bun. Bake the cross buns in preheated oven for about 20 minutes until golden brown.

8. Meanwhile, gently heat the apricot jam strained through a sieve in a small saucepan and brush the tops of the still hot buns generously with it immediately after heating. Let dry for a few minutes.

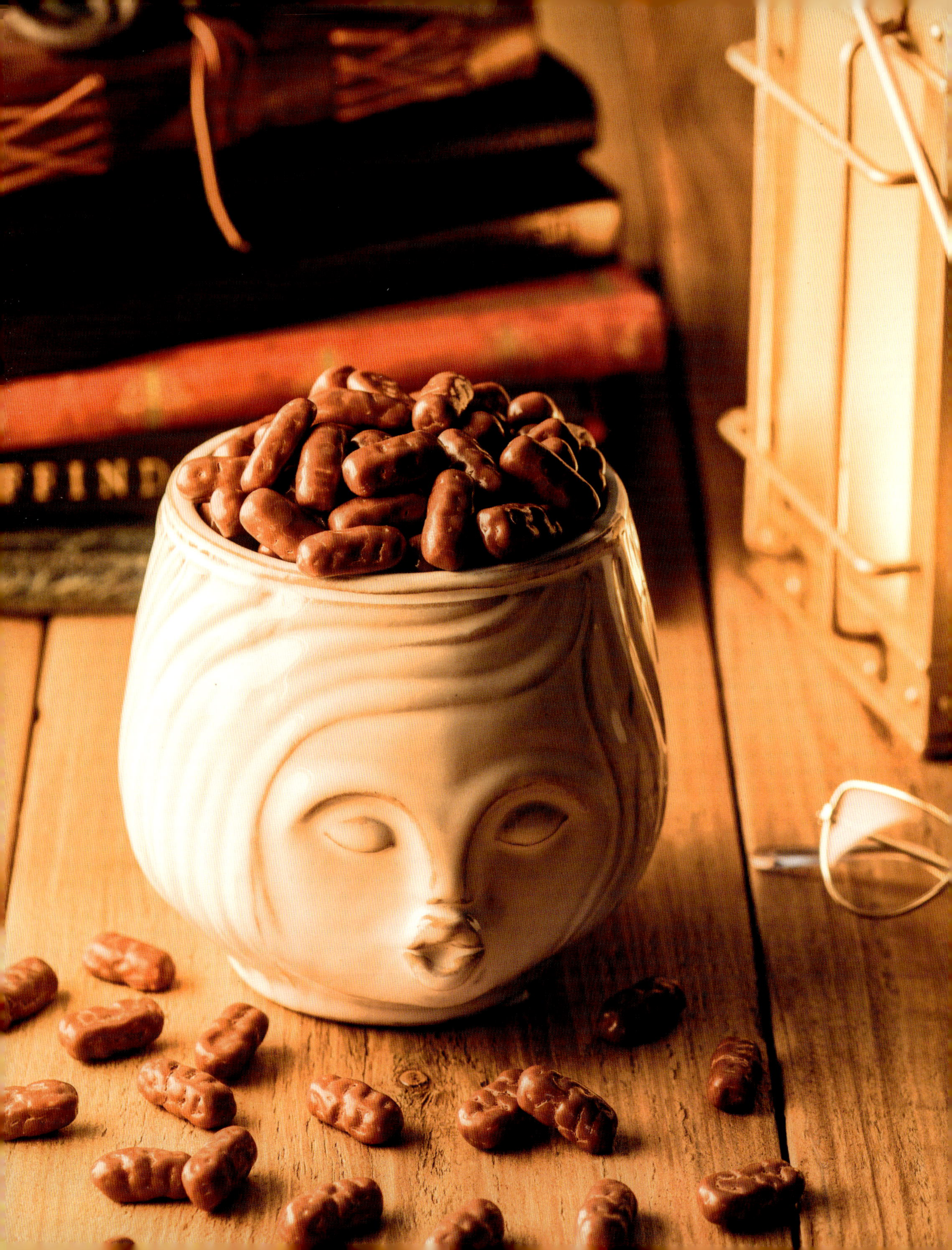

MAGIC BEANS

INGREDIENTS FOR APPROX. 14 OZ MAGIC BEANS

7 oz saltine crackers
7 oz milk couverture chocolate, coarsely chopped
½ tsp rum flavoring
½ tsp cinnamon

1. Put the saltine crackers in the freezer for 3-4 hours; this makes them easier to cut later without breaking.

2. Cut the frozen saltine crackers into small, oblong strips on a cutting board with a large, sharp knife.

3. Melt the coarsely chopped chocolate coating in a bowl over a water bath. Add the rum flavoring and cinnamon, stir in thoroughly, and add the saltine crackers. Gently toss so that the crackers are coated with chocolate all around.

4. Remove the individual "magic beans" from the chocolate, let them drip off and dry completely on a baking sheet lined with parchment paper, spacing them a bit apart.

5. Store in an airtight container.

Although you will need so-called rum flavoring for this recipe, these magic beans are non-alcoholic because the flavoring used, while reminiscent of rum in smell and taste, is a water-propylene glycol mixture. Rum without rum? Well, if that's not magic...

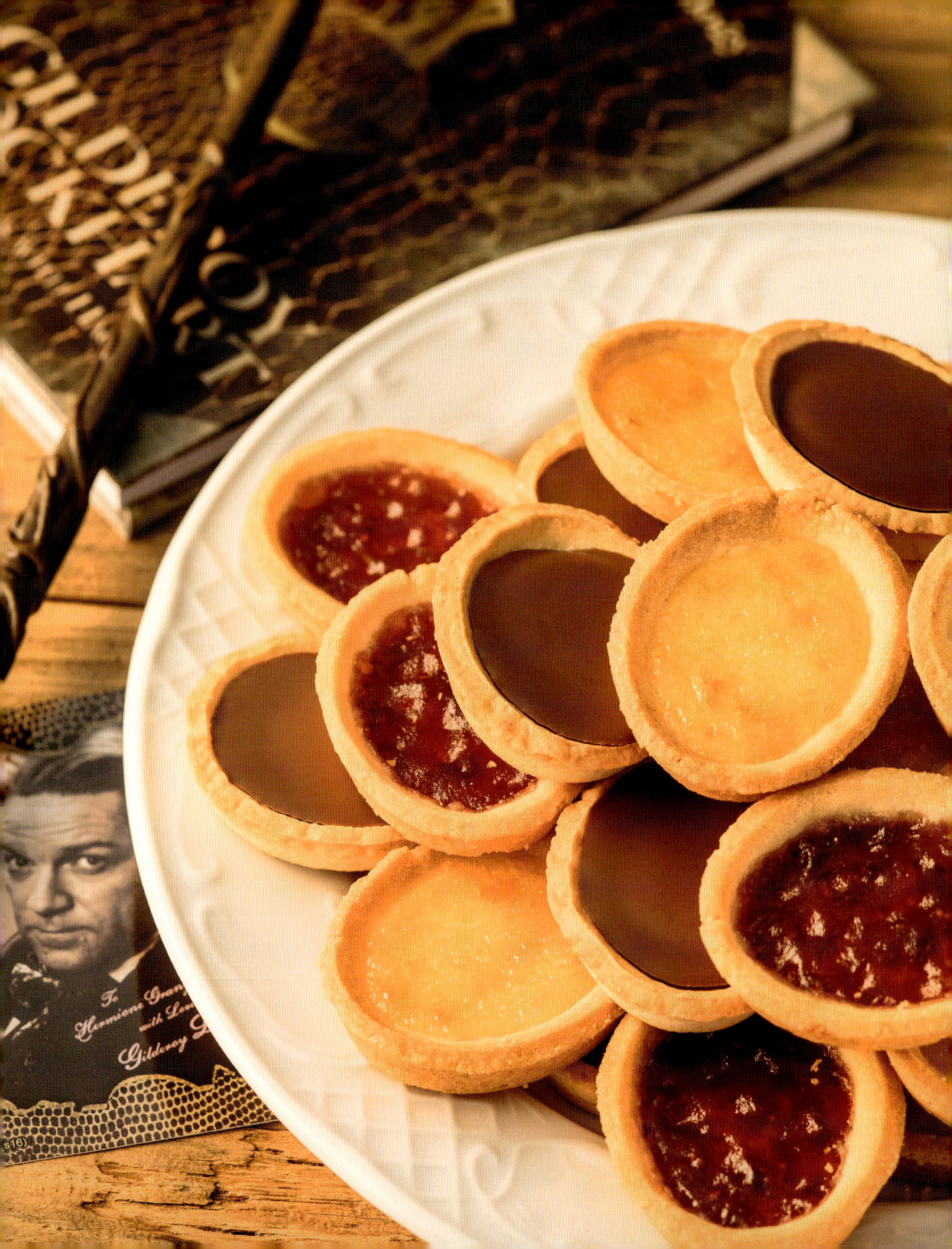

TRIPLE TARTLETS

INGREDIENTS FOR APPROX. 18 TARTLETS

For the tartlets:
5 oz room-warm butter plus a little more
5 oz powdered sugar
½ egg
1 tbsp cold water
9 oz flour plus a little more
0.5 oz baking powder
0.1 oz salt
Some lemon zest, to taste

For the chocolate filling:
3 oz white chocolate, coarsely chopped
3 oz dark chocolate, coarsely chopped
1.5 oz butter
5 tbsp cream

For the lemon curd:
Juice and zest of 5 lemons
5 eggs
5 oz sugar
125 cold butter Raspberry jam, as filling (see p. 180)

Also required: tartlet molds (approx. 4" diameter), round cookie cutter (approx. 5" diameter), piping bag, 1-2 screw-top glasses (depending on size) :

Prepare the tartlets:

1. In a bowl, using an electric hand mixer, thoroughly combine the butter and powdered sugar. Add half the egg and the cold water and knead well. Then add the flour, baking powder, salt and lemon zest and knead until a soft, homogeneous dough is formed. Chill in the refrigerator for 30 minutes.

2. Roll out the chilled dough on a lightly floured work surface to a thickness of about 0.5" and cut out circles with a cookie cutter that are a bit larger than the tartlet molds you are using.

3. Carefully place the dough circles in the greased tartlet cups, press down lightly on all sides and refrigerate for at least one hour.

4. Meanwhile, preheat the oven to 265 °F.

5. Bake the tartlets for about 50-60 minutes, until they are firm and crisp throughout. Remove from the oven and let cool completely. Then remove the tartlets and fill with chocolate (see below), raspberry jam (see p. 180), or lemon curd (see below) using a piping bag. Allow each filling to set for a few minutes before serving.

Prepare the chocolate filling:

6. Place the chopped chocolate in a bowl.

7. In a small saucepan, bring the butter and cream to a boil over medium heat, stirring constantly; add the chocolate and stir together until the chocolate is completely melted. Remove from the water bath, let cool briefly and fill the tartlets with it.

Continued on the next page...

Prepare the lemon curd:

8. Put the lemon juice and lemon zest in a saucepan and bring to a boil over medium heat.

9. In a bowl, beat the eggs and sugar with a handheld electric mixer until white and creamy. Add half of the boiled lemon juice. Keeping the other half of the juice in the saucepan, pour in the egg-sugar mixture and let it set over lowest heat, stirring constantly. Then immediately strain through a sieve into a clean container and let cool until the whole thing stops steaming. Finally, in small pieces, gradually stir in the cold butter. Leave to cool for a few minutes and use immediately to fill the tartlets.

10. Put the lemon curd that you don't need for filling the tartlets into hot rinsed screw top jars and store in a cool place.

LEMON-CURD ECLAIRS

INGREDIENTS FOR 10-12 ECLAIRS

For the dough:
4 fl. oz water
4 fl. oz milk
3.2 oz butter
1 oz sugar
1 packet vanilla sugar
1 pinch of salt
4 oz flour
3 eggs

For the filling:
1 packet vanilla pudding powder
12 fl. oz milk
2 oz sugar
Juice and zest of ½ lemon
4 tbsp lemon curd (see p. 163)

For decorating:
5 oz white chocolate, finely chopped
Freeze-dried strawberries, finely chopped
Fresh small mint leaves

Also required: piping bag with star-shaped nozzle and filling nozzle

1. Preheat the oven to 390 °F heat and line two baking trays with baking paper.

2. Place the water, milk, butter, sugar, vanilla sugar and salt in a saucepan and bring to a boil over medium heat, stirring constantly. Add the flour and stir in with a mixing spoon. Stir vigorously over low heat until the dough separates from the bottom of the saucepan on its own as a ball, leaving a white starchy layer there. This may take a few minutes. Then remove the pot from the heat and transfer to a mixing bowl. Allow to cool slightly.

3. Add the eggs, one at a time, to the bowl and beat with an electric mixer until the mixture is smooth and creamy. Pour into a piping bag fitted with a star nozzle.

4. Pipe the dough evenly onto the baking paper in strips about 4" long, with enough space between them, and bake in the preheated oven for about 30 minutes or until the eclairs are golden brown. Important: Do not open the oven during this time!

5. Meanwhile, prepare the lemon curd cream. To do this, prepare the custard powder according to package directions, but use only 12 fl. oz milk and 2 oz sugar. While stirring constantly, incorporate the lemon zest and lemon juice. Stir in the lemon curd and leave to cool for 15 minutes.

6. Put the lemon curd cream into a piping bag with a nozzle and carefully pipe it into the eclairs from both ends. If you don't have a nozzle, simply cut the éclairs open horizontally, fill them, and put the top half back on.

Continued on the next page...

7. Melt the white chocolate over a water bath, place in a piping bag or small freezer bag with the corner cut off, and pipe evenly over the eclairs. Sprinkle the finely chopped freeze-dried strawberries over the chocolate that has not yet set. Decorate with small mint leaves and let dry for a few minutes before serving.

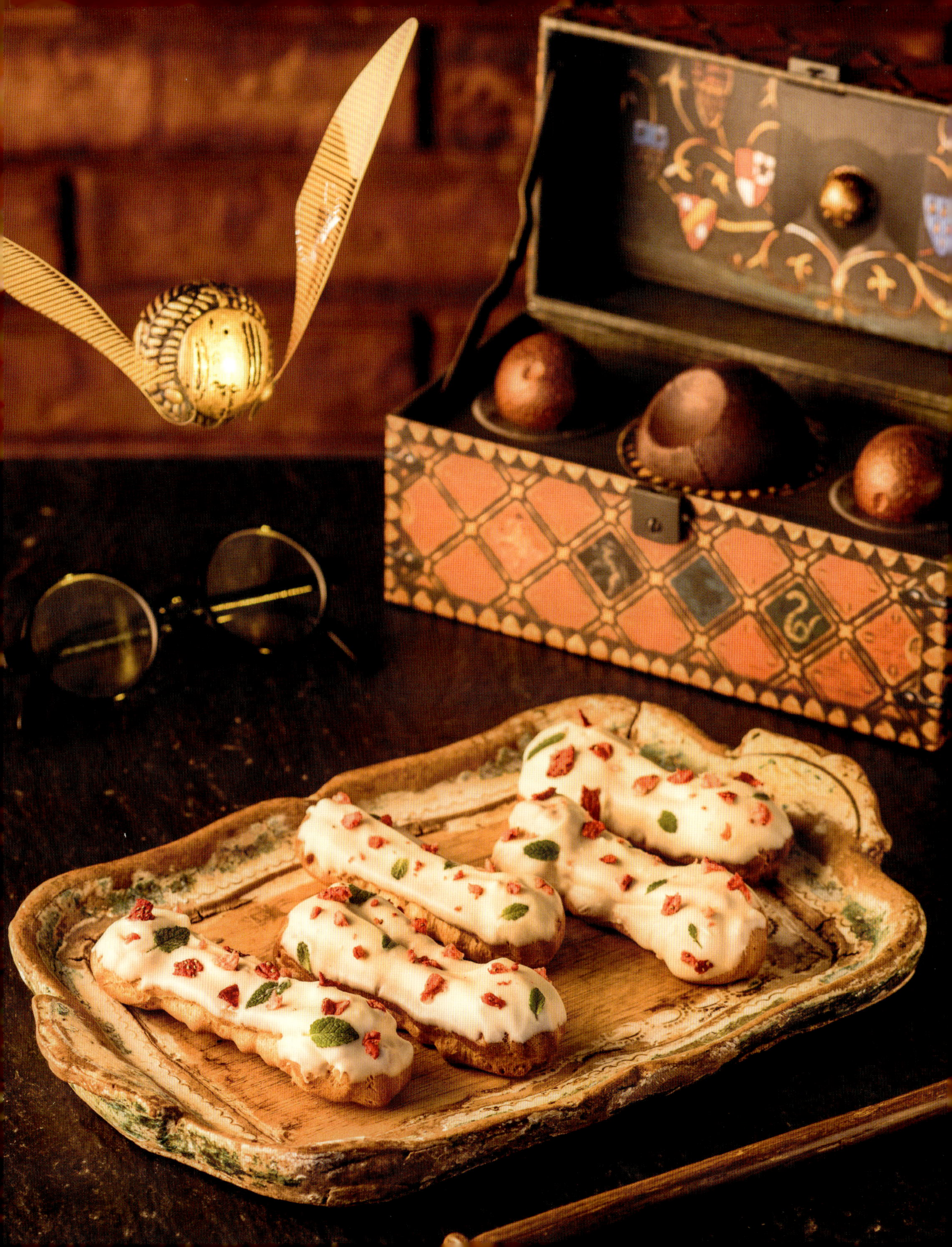

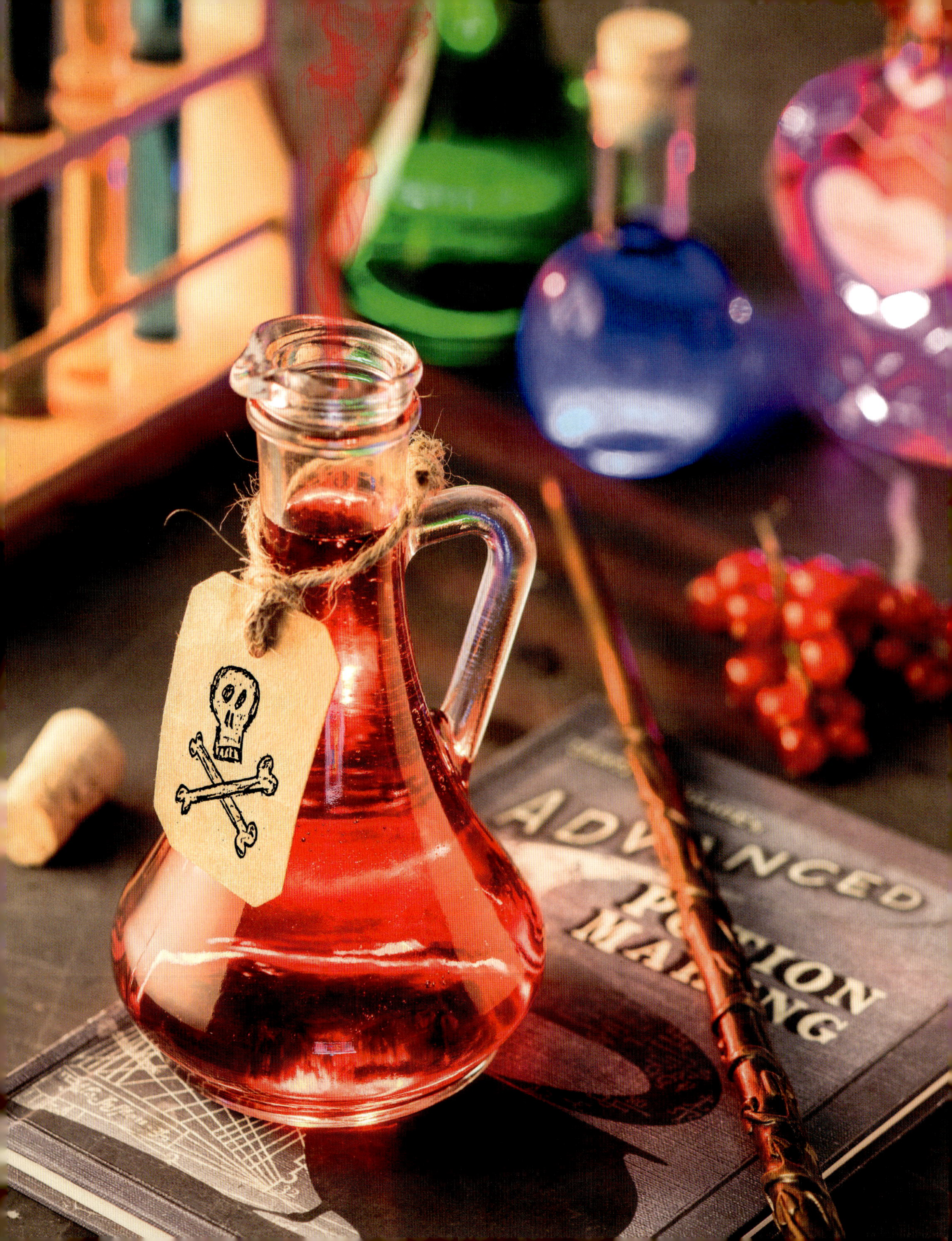

RED CURRANT SYRUP

INGREDIENTS FOR APPROX. 1-1½ QT SYRUP

5.5 lb red currants (fresh or frozen)
5 fl. oz water
18 oz sugar juice of one lime pulp of ½ vanilla pod

Also required:
straining cloth, sealable glass bottle of at least 1½ qt capacity.

1. Wash the currants and remove the stems.
2. Place the berries in a large saucepan, add the water and bring to a boil over medium heat, stirring occasionally. Simmer uncovered for about 10 minutes until all the currants have burst open. Stir vigorously several times. Remove from heat and let cool.
3. Drain through a straining cloth into a clean saucepan. Squeeze the berries in the cloth and add the sugar, lime juice, and scraped vanilla to the saucepan. Bring to a boil, stirring occasionally, and simmer for about 10 minutes or until the sugar is completely dissolved. Stir occasionally with a wooden spoon.
4. Pour the currant syrup into a hot-rinsed glass bottle and seal it. Leave to infuse for 2-3 days before use. Shake well a few times in between.

This currant syrup is extremely versatile. Apart from being the ideal base or addition to numerous drinks, it is also ideal for enhancing ice cream, desserts, and fruit salads, for example.

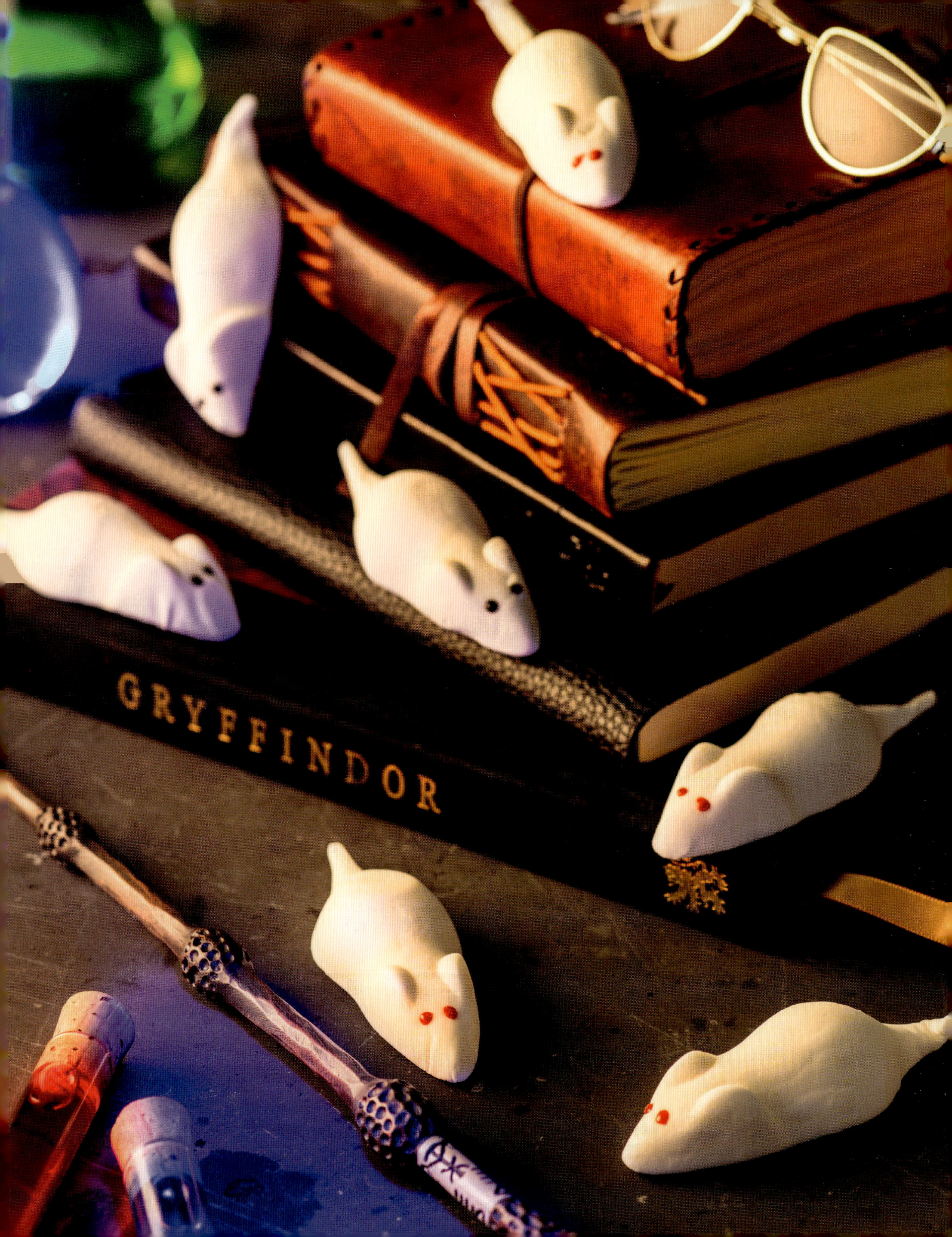
GRYFFINDOR

SQUEAKING SUGAR MICE

INGREDIENTS FOR APPROX. 20 SUGAR MICE

For the sugar mice:
2 tbsp cornstarch
9 oz powdered sugar plus 2 tbsp
1 tsp butter, for greasing the silicone mold
2 packets vanilla sugar
0.5 oz ground white gelatin
5 fl. oz water
2 drops of white food coloring

For the eyes:
2 tbsp powdered sugar
A few drops of water
2 drops of red or black food coloring, as desired

Also needed:
silicone mouse mold, piping bag with very fine nozzle

1. In a small bowl, mix the cornstarch and 2 tbsp powdered sugar.

2. Thinly butter the silicone mouse mold and dust with half of the starch mixture.

3. In a mixing bowl, mix the powdered sugar with the vanilla sugar.

4. Put the ground gelatin and the water in a small saucepan and bring to a boil over medium heat, stirring constantly, until the gelatin has completely dissolved.

5. Gradually add the hot gelatin to the mixing bowl with the powdered sugar and slowly stir in with a handheld electric mixer. Add the food coloring. Increase the speed steadily to the highest setting until you have a fluffy, but still runny mixture.

6. Pour the sugar mixture into the prepared silicone mold, smooth the tops of the wells and dust with some of the starch-powdered sugar mixture. Let sit for at least an hour. Then gently release from the mold and sprinkle again with the starch-powdered sugar mixture. Tap off the excess starch and add eyes to the mice.

7. To do this, mix the powdered sugar with just enough water in a small bowl to make a thick but still runny mixture. Color as desired with red or black food coloring, place in a piping bag with a very fine nozzle and pipe the eyes onto the sugar mice. Let dry for a few minutes. (If you want to use a second eye color, do the same with the other food coloring).

8. Store the sugar mice in an airtight container.

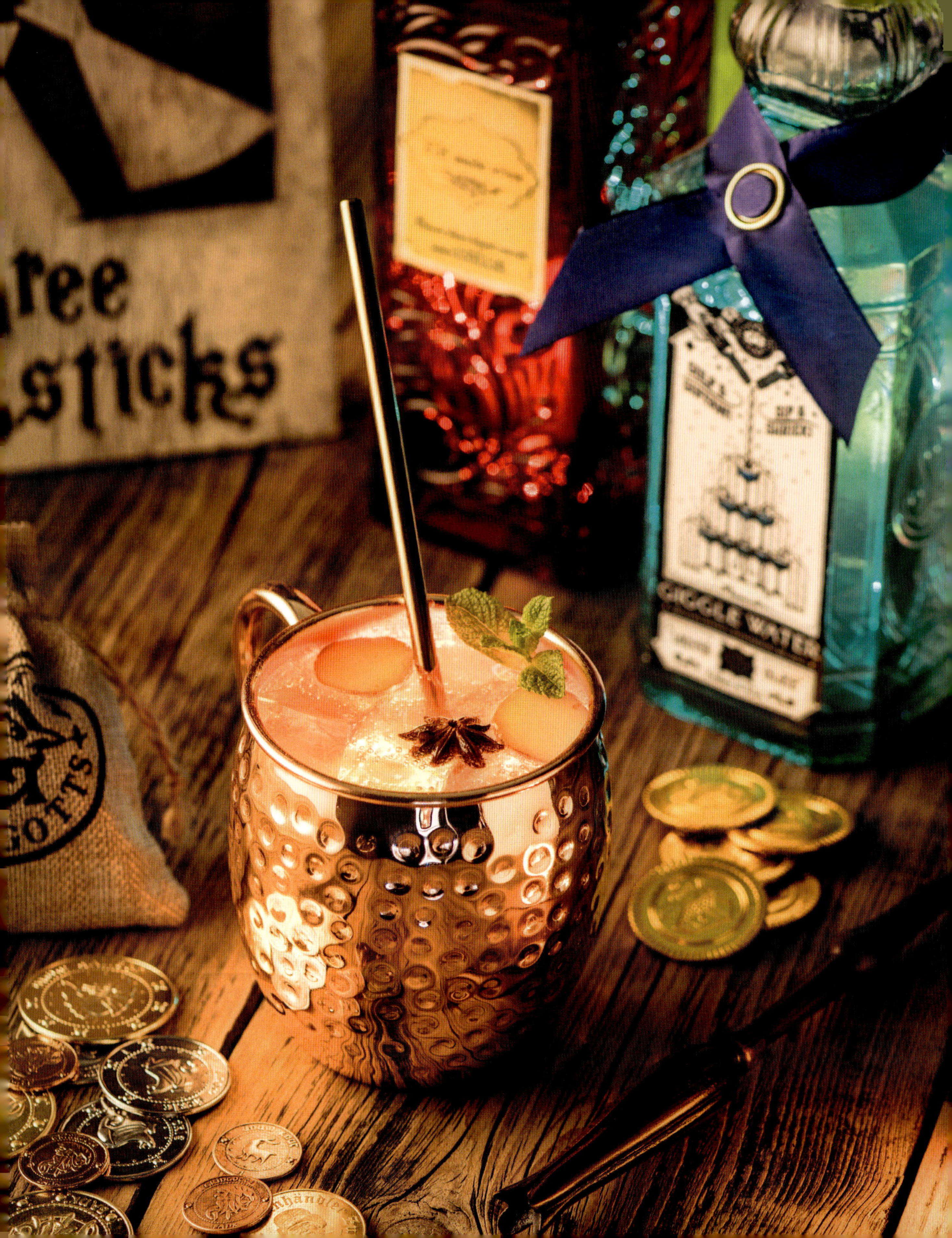
ree
sticks
GIGGLE WATER

MAGIC POTION

WITH ALCOHOL

INGREDIENTS FOR 1 DRINK
Crushed ice
1 fl. oz vodka
2 fl. oz ginger beer
2 fl. oz tamarind juice
2-3 slices of fresh ginger
1 star anise
Fresh mint, as garnish

1. Put some crushed ice in a small pitcher or copper mug.
2. Pour the vodka, ginger beer and tamarind juice over ice. Add the ginger slices and star anise, stir gently, and serve garnished with some fresh mint.

The best place to get tamarind juice is on the Internet. Alternatively, you can also use tamarind paste. In this case, dissolve 1 tbsp of the paste in 2 fl. oz water, stirring constantly, and add it to the potion instead of the juice.

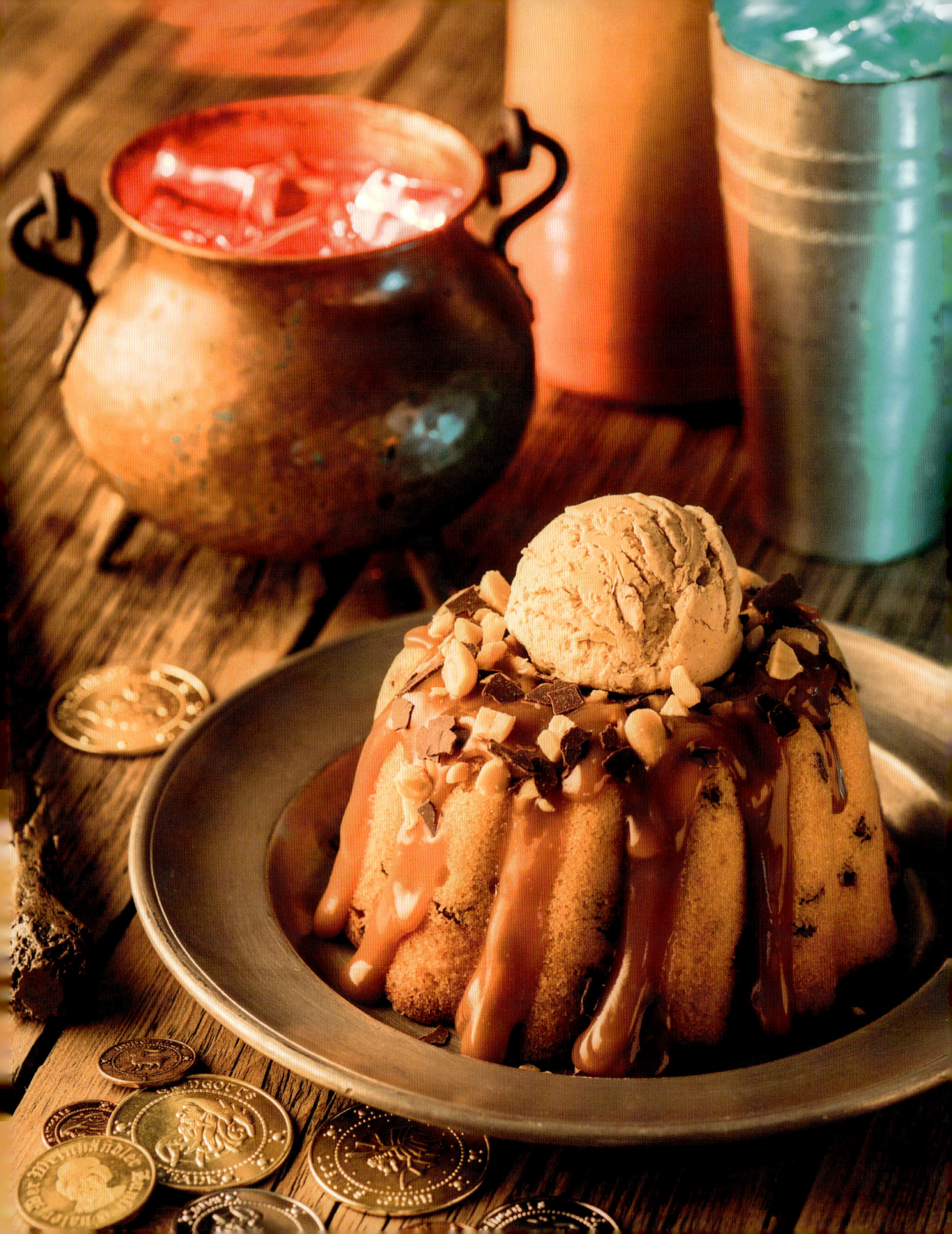

STICKY TOFFEE PUDDING

INGREDIENTS FOR 1 PUDDING

6.3 oz dates, dried, pitted and finely chopped
1½ tsp baking powder
7 oz butter plus a little more, for greasing the baking pan
7 oz sugar
1 tbsp vanilla sugar
1 egg
9 oz cake flour
1 tsp cinnamon
½ tsp ginger powder
3.2 oz cane sugar
4 fl. oz whipped cream
As garnish: chopped nuts, your choice of chocolate sprinkles
Butter beer ice cream (see p. 42) or other ice cream

Also required:
Bundt mold (approx. 7-8" diameter).

1. Put the finely chopped dates and 1 tsp of the baking powder in a bowl, mix and pour over so much hot water that the dates are completely covered with it. Leave to stand for about 5 minutes.

2. Meanwhile, preheat the oven to 390 °F heat.

3. Drain the soaked dates through a sieve, place in a tall container and puree finely with a hand blender.

4. In a bowl, cream 6.5 oz of the softened butter with the sugar and the vanilla sugar using a hand mixer with whisk attachment. Add the egg, the remaining baking powder, the flour, the cinnamon, and the ginger powder and stir until you have a smooth, supple dough. Finally, fold in the dates, pour into a buttered Bundt pan and bake in a preheated oven for about 50 minutes. Then remove and let cool completely in the mold.

5. In the meantime, in a small saucepan over medium heat, stirring constantly, mix the remaining butter with the cane sugar and cream and bring to the boil briefly. Then reduce the heat to low and simmer, stirring constantly, for about 3-4 minutes. Remove the toffee sauce from the heat and allow to cool for a few minutes.

6. Gently invert the cooled toffee pudding onto a serving platter, pour a generous amount of the toffee sauce over it and garnish with chopped nuts, chocolate chips and a scoop of ice cream.

7. Serve immediately.

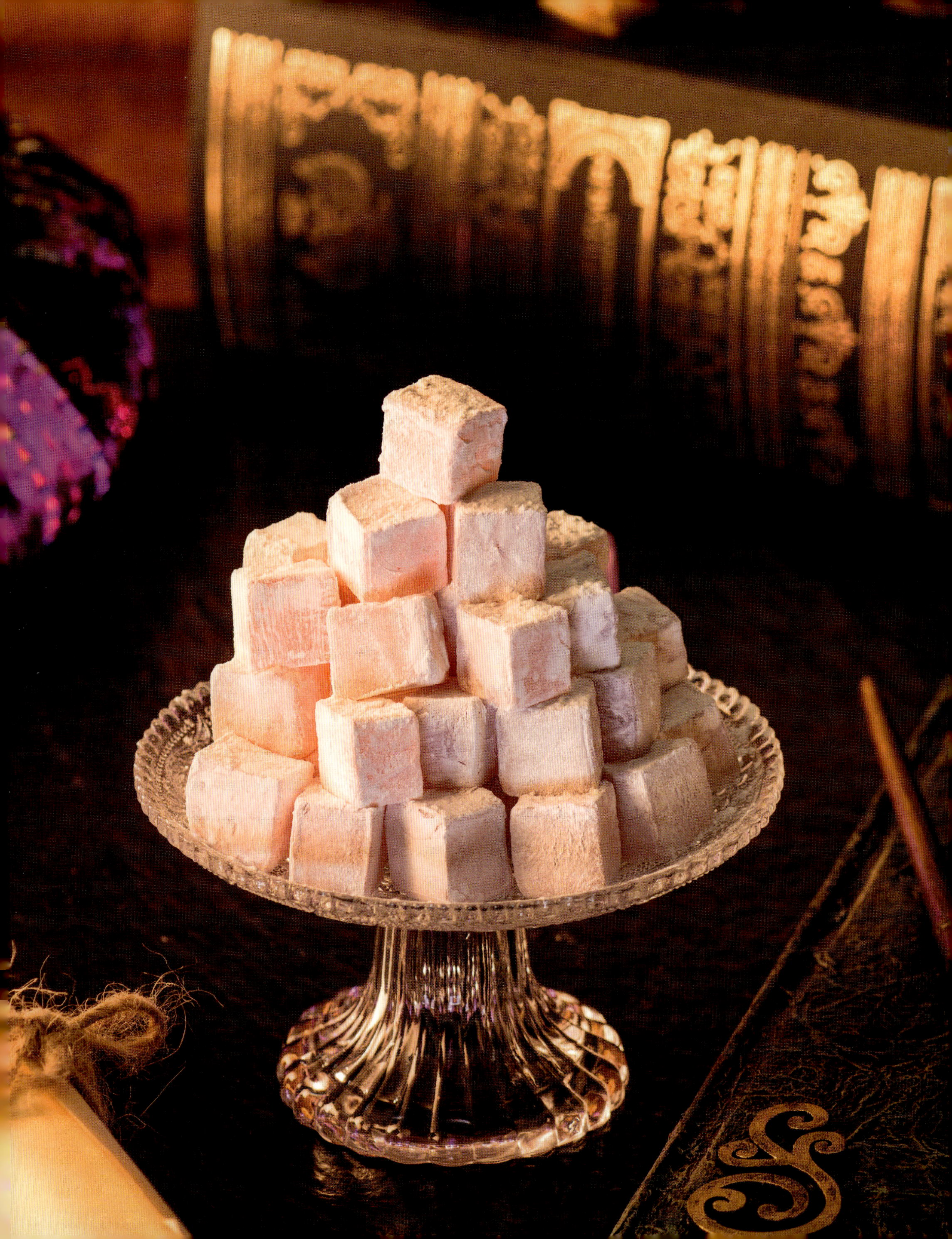

SKIVING SNACKS

INGREDIENTS FOR APPROX. 10 PORTIONS
2.2 lb sugar
1 qt cold water
1 tsp lemon juice
5 oz cornstarch
1 tsp cream of tartar baking powder
2 tbsp rose water
Red food coloring
Sunflower oil, for greasing
3.2 oz powdered sugar

Also required:
sugar thermometer, baking pan
(approx. 9" x 9")

1. Put the sugar, 13 fl. oz water, and the lemon juice in a pot. Stir over low heat until the sugar has completely dissolved. Then bring to a boil and continue to simmer until the mixture reaches a temperature of 240 °F. Remove from the heat.

2. Mix 4 oz of the cornstarch with the cream of tartar baking powder and 9 fl. oz of the water in a heatproof bowl until smooth.

3. Bring the remaining water to a boil in a saucepan and stir into the starch mixture. Add the lemon-sugar syrup and whisk over medium heat until the liquid thickens and bubbles. Then return to a boil and simmer, stirring regularly, for about 75 minutes or until light golden. Then stir in the rose water and add enough red food coloring to tint the liquid a pale pink. Pour into a baking dish lightly greased with sunflower oil and let sit for at least twelve hours.

4. Mix the powdered sugar with the remaining starch in a shallow bowl.

5. Carefully turn the treat out of the baking dish onto the work surface and cut into bite-sized cubes with a lightly oiled knife. Toss in the powdered sugar and starch mixture. Sprinkle generously with remaining sugar mixture. Stored in an airtight container in a cool, dry place, they will keep for about 3-4 weeks.

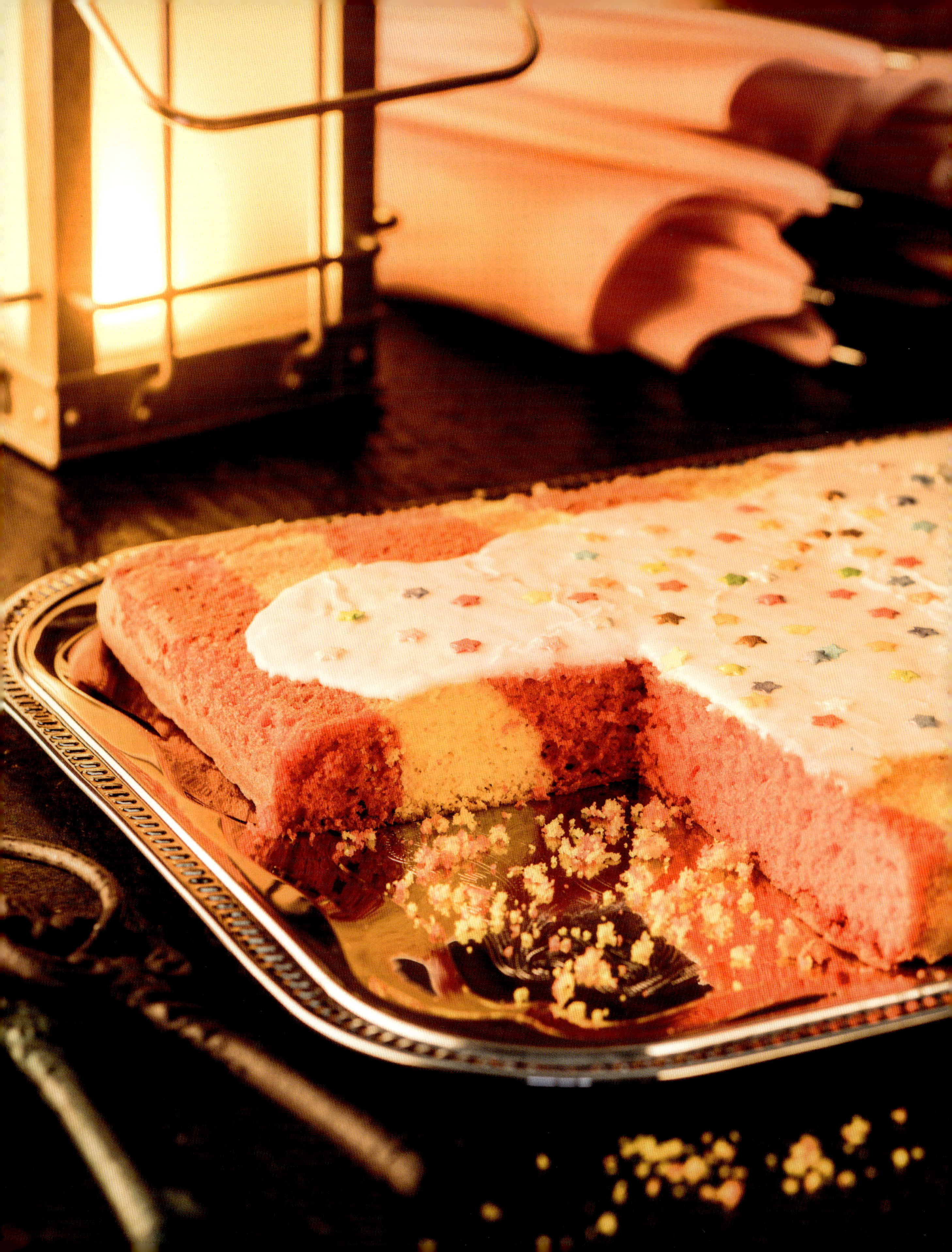

HAGRID'S GRYFFINDOR HOUSE CAKE

INGREDIENTS FOR 1 CAKE

For the dough:
9 oz room-temperature butter plus a little more, to grease the baking pan.
11 oz flour
1 packet of baking powder
1 pinch of salt
¼ tsp vanilla extract
9 oz sugar
4 eggs
5 tbsp milk
Red and green food coloring

For the frosting:
9 oz powdered sugar
5 tbsp lemon juice
Colored sugar sprinkles, for sprinkling

Also needed:
piping bag with large nozzle

1. Preheat the oven to 350 °F heat. Generously grease a small baking tray with butter and sprinkle with flour.

2. In a small bowl, mix the flour and baking powder with the salt.

3. Beat the butter, vanilla extract, and sugar with a hand mixer in a mixing bowl. Beat in the eggs one at a time, then add the milk and flour mixture alternately, incorporating each thoroughly. Divide the batter between two bowls and color each half of the batter with one of the two food colors.

4. Place each of the colored doughs in a piping bag fitted with a large nozzle, and pipe alternating, wide, lengthwise stripes onto the baking sheet until the entire sheet is covered. (If you don't have a piping bag, simply cut a corner off a freezer bag.)

5. Place the tray in the preheated oven for about 25-30 minutes. Near the end of the baking time, prick a toothpick into the center of the cake; if the toothpick stays clean when you pull it out, remove the cake from the oven. Otherwise, bake a little longer. Let cool completely.

6. Meanwhile, for the frosting, in a small bowl, carefully whisk together the powdered sugar and lemon juice and pour evenly over the cooled cake. Smooth with a spatula, sprinkle with colored sugar sprinkles, and let the frosting set before serving.

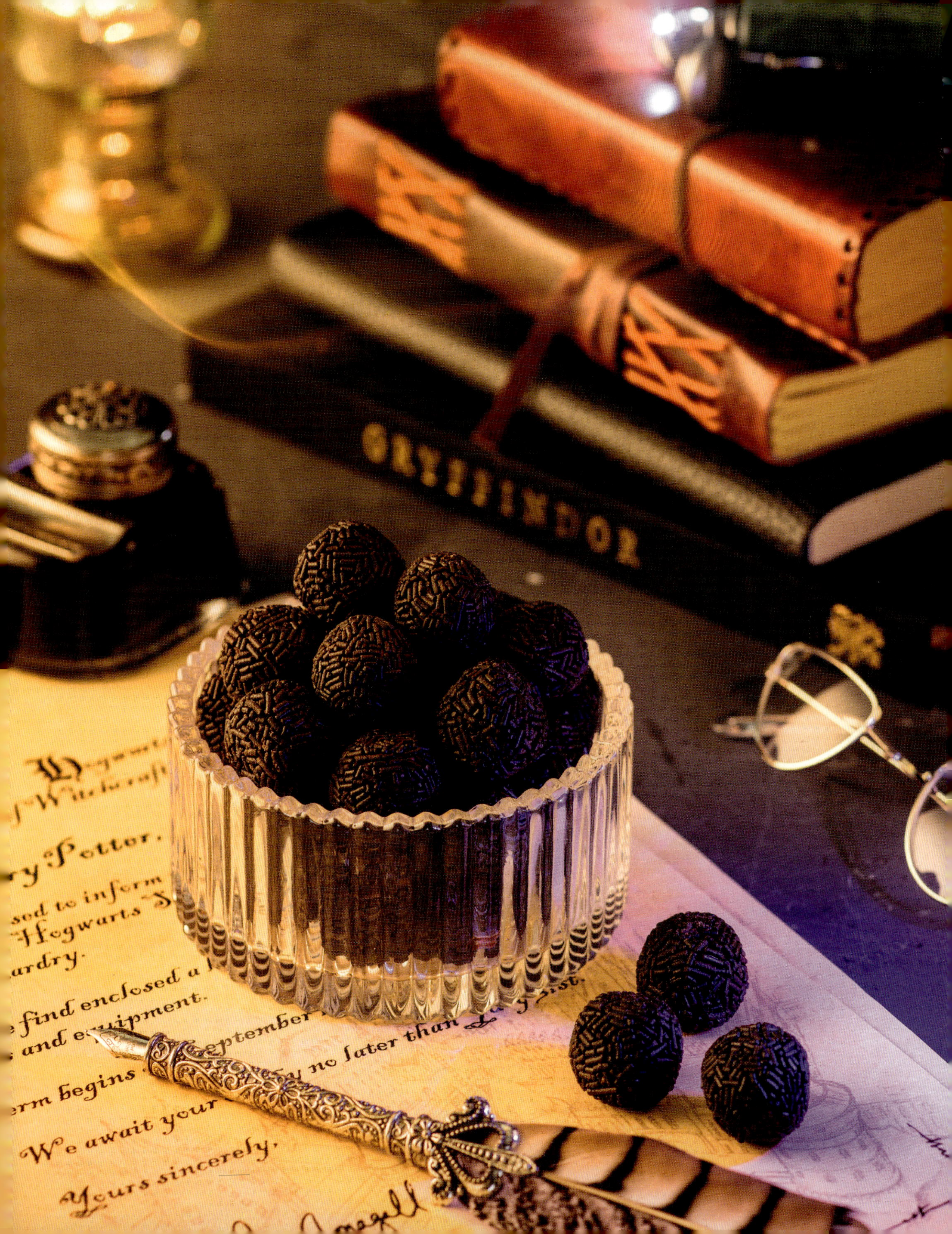
GRYFFINDOR
We await your
Yours sincerely,

BRANDY BALLS

WITH ALCOHOL

INGREDIENTS FOR APPROX. 50 BRANDY BALLS
4 fl. oz brandy
3 oz dried sour cherries
5.5 oz milk chocolate, coarsely chopped
5.5 oz dark chocolate, coarsely chopped
5 oz butter
7 oz tree nuts, finely chopped
21 oz honey cake
6.5 oz powdered sugar
1 tsp gingerbread spice
7 oz chocolate sprinkles

1. In a small saucepan over medium heat, bring 2 fl. oz brandy to a boil, add the dried sour cherries and soak for 2-3 hours. Place in a colander to drain.

2. In a bowl over a boiling water bath, melt the milk chocolate, dark chocolate, and butter, stirring constantly. Make sure that the bottom of the bowl does not touch the water!

3. Roast the walnuts without fat in a pan until golden brown. Remove from heat, let cool and finely grind half of the nuts with a blitz chopper.

4. Crumble the honey cake in a bowl and drizzle with the remaining brandy. Add the ground and the chopped tree nuts, the powdered sugar and the gingerbread spice and mix everything together. Then add the chocolate-butter mixture and mix thoroughly until a homogeneous mass.

5. This fine confection is wonderful as a dessert or - nicely packaged - as a gift for people to whom you would give a sock without hesitation! Shape into balls the size of grapes. Press a cherry into the center of each, seal the opening with the confectionery and shape into a nice round ball.

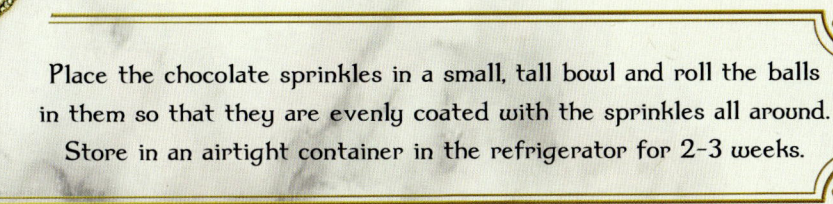

Place the chocolate sprinkles in a small, tall bowl and roll the balls in them so that they are evenly coated with the sprinkles all around. Store in an airtight container in the refrigerator for 2-3 weeks.

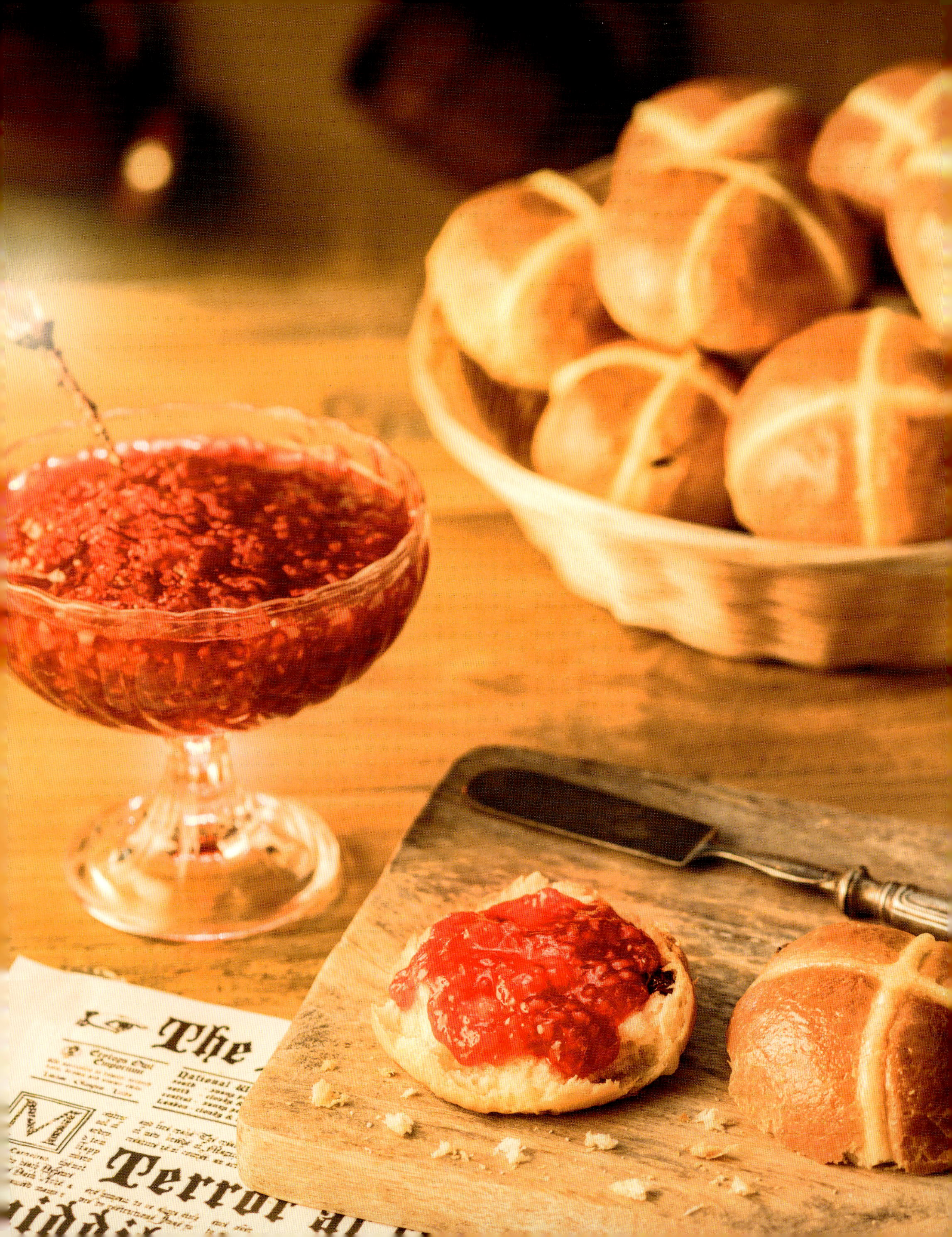
The
Terror

RASPBERRY JAM

INGREDIENTS FOR APPROX. 1 QT JAM
2.2 lb raspberries, fresh or frozen
18 oz gelling sugar
2 tbsp lemon juice, freshly squeezed
Pulp of ½ vanilla bean

Also required:
2-5 canning or screw-top jars
(depending on size).

1. If you are using fresh raspberries, sort the berries, wash, and drain.

2. Put the berries in a large pot and mash them to a pulpy mass, e.g. with a potato masher. Then add the gelling sugar, lemon juice, and vanilla pulp; bring to a boil over high heat and simmer for at least three minutes until bubbling. Stir all the time with a wooden spoon with as long a handle as possible, as the hot jam tends to splash.

3. Remove the pot from the stove. If you wish, you can now use a slotted spoon or a small sieve to remove the foam that has formed on the surface. This is just a matter of appearance.

4. Pour the jam into clean, hot-rinsed preserving jars or screw top jars. Leave roughly ¼ inch of space to the top of the jar.

5. Turn the filled jam jars upside down for about 5-10 minutes to create a vacuum. But be careful: the jars are very hot! Then leave to cool for 3-4 hours. Store in a cool, dark place.

WIZARDING WHEEZES

FAINTING FANCIES

INGREDIENTS FOR APPROX. 35 FAINTING FANCIES
21 oz powdered sugar plus a little more, for sprinkling on the work surface
2 egg whites
2 tsp lemon juice
10 drops of flavoring, your choice (e.g. raspberry, bubble gum, peppermint)
2-3 drops of red food coloring

1. In a mixing bowl, using the dough hooks of an electric hand mixer, roughly knead the powdered sugar, egg whites, lemon juice and desired flavoring. Then continue kneading with your hands until you have a slightly shiny, firm, but easy to roll out mass.

2. Divide the mixture into two equal halves. Put one half in a bowl and color it pink with the red food coloring.

3. Roll out the two sugar masses on a smooth work surface generously sprinkled with powdered sugar to the same size and thickness. Smooth the tops. Place the two sugar sheets on top of each other as flush as possible and gently roll over once more with a rolling pin.

4. With a large, sharp knife, straighten the edges and cut bite-sized rectangles from the dough sheet. Place side by side on a baking sheet lined with parchment paper and let dry for at least 12 hours. Turn over regularly during this process.

5. Keeps for several weeks in an airtight container.

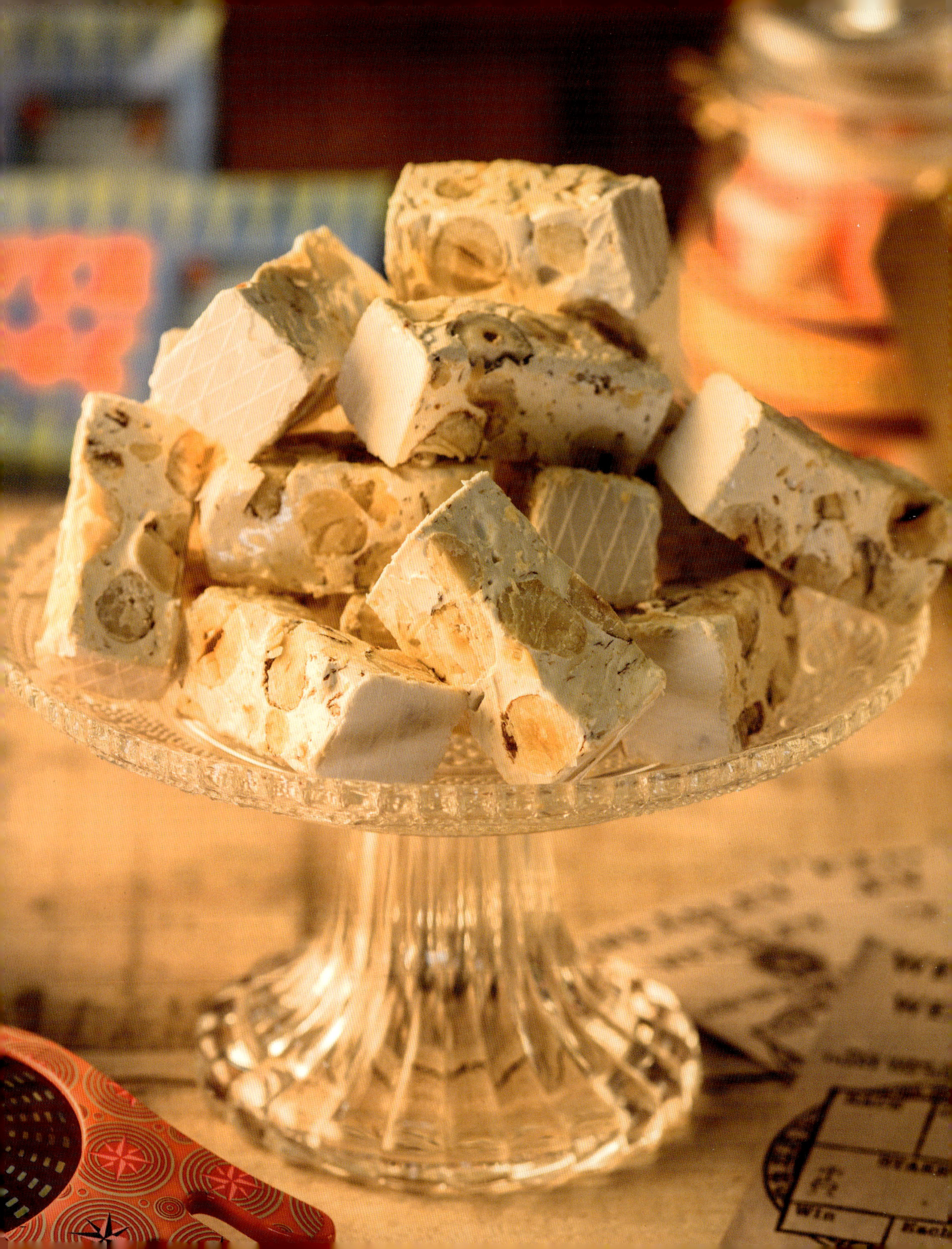

NOSEBLEED NOUGAT

INGREDIENTS FOR APPROX. 1 LB NOUGAT

4 egg whites
1 pinch of salt
11 oz sugar
2 packets vanilla sugar
4 tbsp honey
1 dash of lemon juice
4 oz whole hazelnuts
4 oz peeled almonds
4 oz pistachios
4 rectangular wafers

1. In a glass bowl, beat the egg whites with the salt using an electric hand mixer until stiff. Gradually add the sugar and vanilla sugar and continue beating until the egg whites become threadbare. Then stir in the honey and lemon juice.

2. Heat the bowl with the honey and egg white mixture over a bain-marie and stir until the mixture gradually becomes thick and firm. Now add the hazelnuts, the almonds, and the pistachios and stir them in.

3. Place two of the wafers seamlessly on a baking sheet lined with parchment paper, spread the honey mixture evenly on top to the thickness of a finger and cover with the remaining two wafers to fit snugly. Let rest for a few minutes.

4. As soon as the mixture begins to set, cover with a piece of baking paper and weigh down with books or similar. Allow to dry for at least 12 hours.

5. Transfer the completely dried nougat to a cutting board and cut into bite-sized cubes with a large, sharp knife. Store in an airtight container.

Instead of hazelnuts, you can use coarsely chopped walnuts if desired.

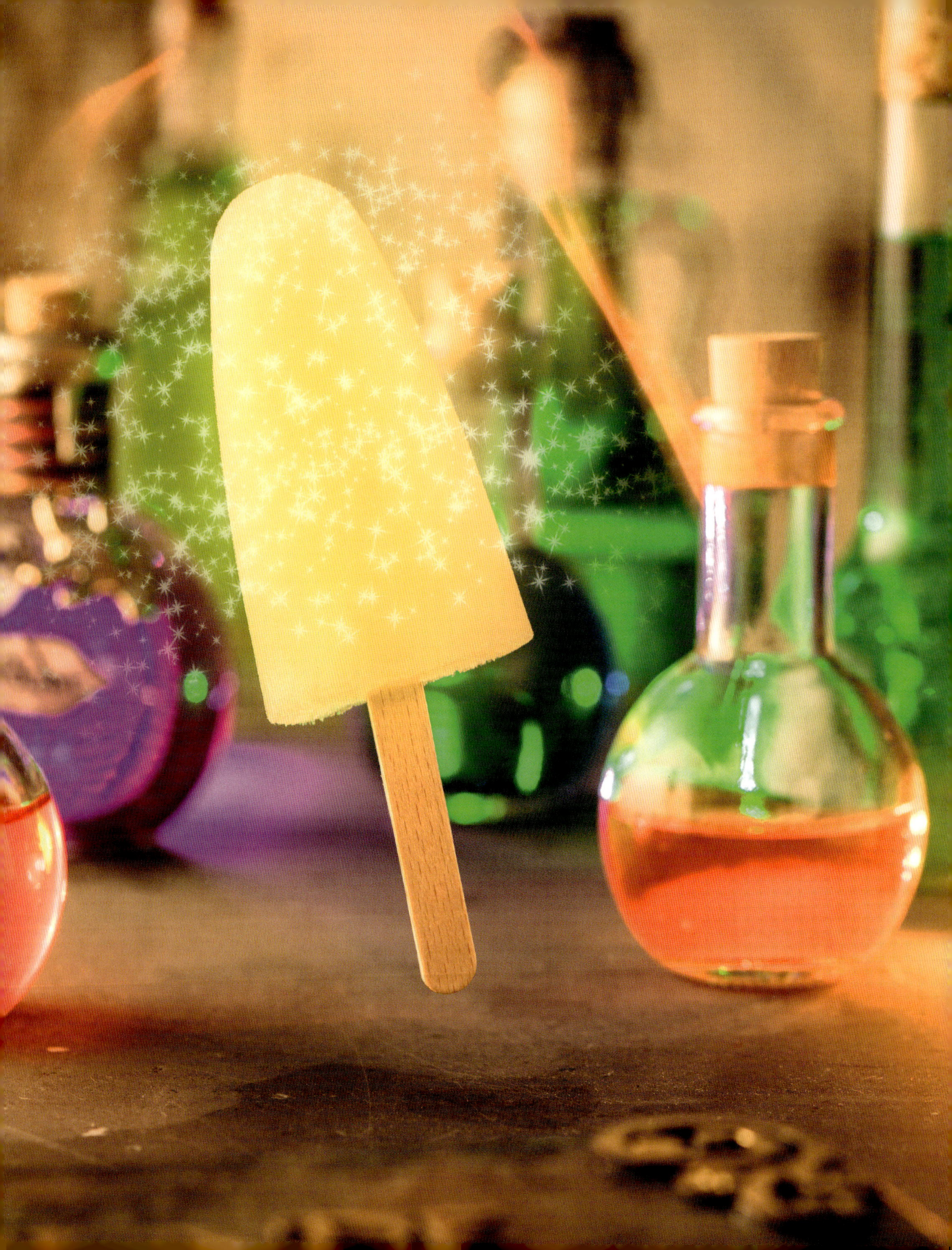

LEMON ICE POP

INGREDIENTS FOR 4 ICE POPS
2 lemons
9 fl. oz water
1 oz sugar
3 tbsp elderflower syrup

Also required:
4 popsicle molds

1. Wash the lemons thoroughly, cut them in half and use a spoon to extract the pulp from them. Discard the peel.
2. Put the lemon pulp, water, sugar, and elderflower syrup in a tall container and puree as finely as possible with a hand blender.
3. Pour evenly into the popsicle molds and place in the freezer overnight.

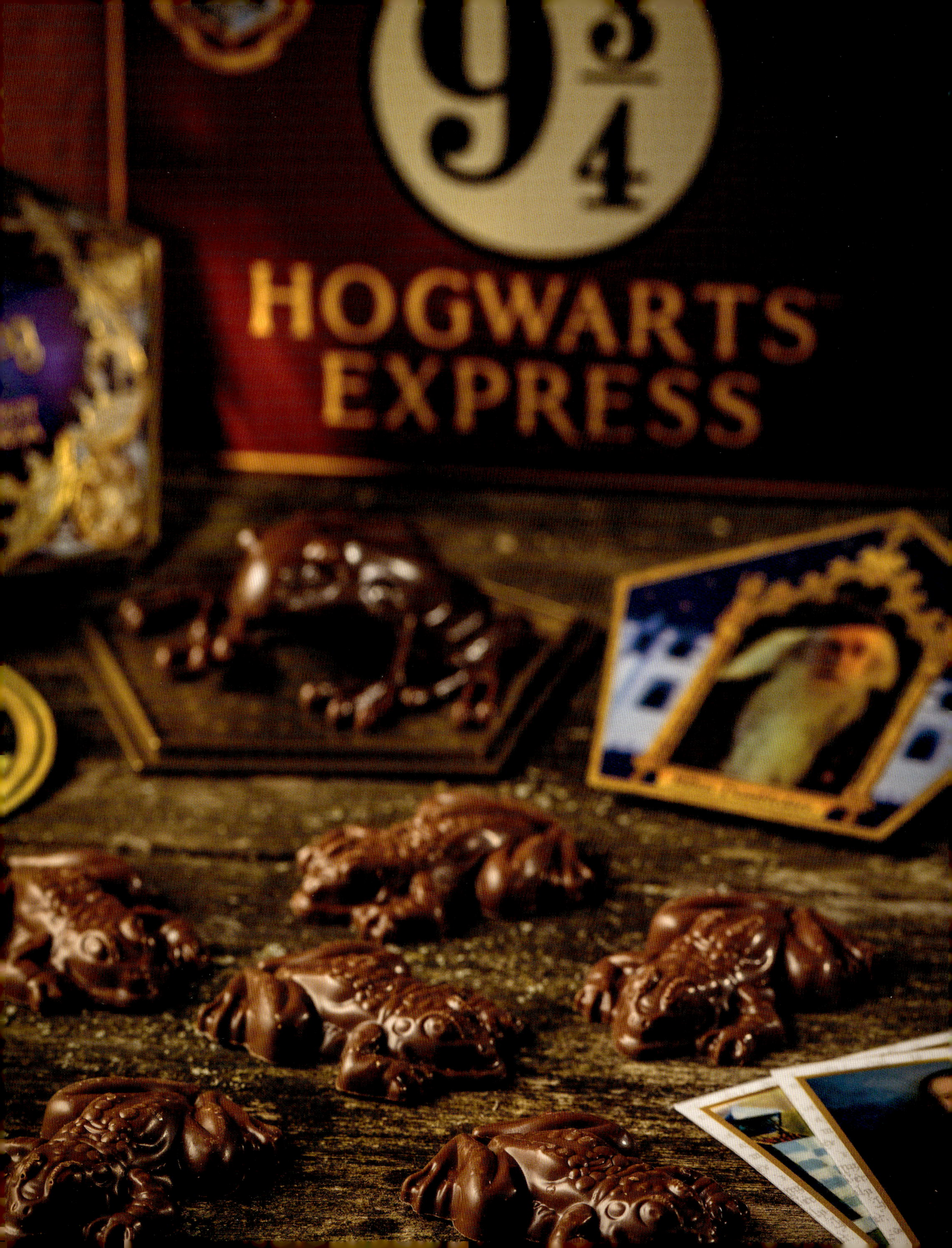
9¾
HOGWARTS
EXPRESS

CHOCOLATE FROGS

**INGREDIENTS FOR
6 CHOCOLATE FROGS**
9 oz dark couverture chocolate,
finely chopped
2-3 drops of peppermint oil
2-3 drops vanilla extract

Also needed: frog chocolate mold.

1. Place ⅔ of the chocolate in a metal bowl and melt gently over a water bath, stirring regularly. Important: the bowl must not touch the water! Once the couverture melts, remove from heat and stir in the remaining chocolate until completely dissolved. Add 2-3 drops of peppermint oil if desired and 2-3 drops of vanilla extract if desired and stir thoroughly.

2. Now carefully pour the chocolate into the cavities of the chocolate mold. Gently tap the mold several times with a spoon to allow any air bubbles to escape. Cover loosely with cling film, place in the refrigerator, and allow to set.

3. Gently remove the chocolate frogs from the mold and eat them before Ron beats you and your loved ones to it! Because as we all know, Harry's best friend loves chocolate frogs more than anything!

Authentic Harry Potter chocolate frog molds can be found online. Some even come with wizard trading cards and folding boxes as seen in the movies!

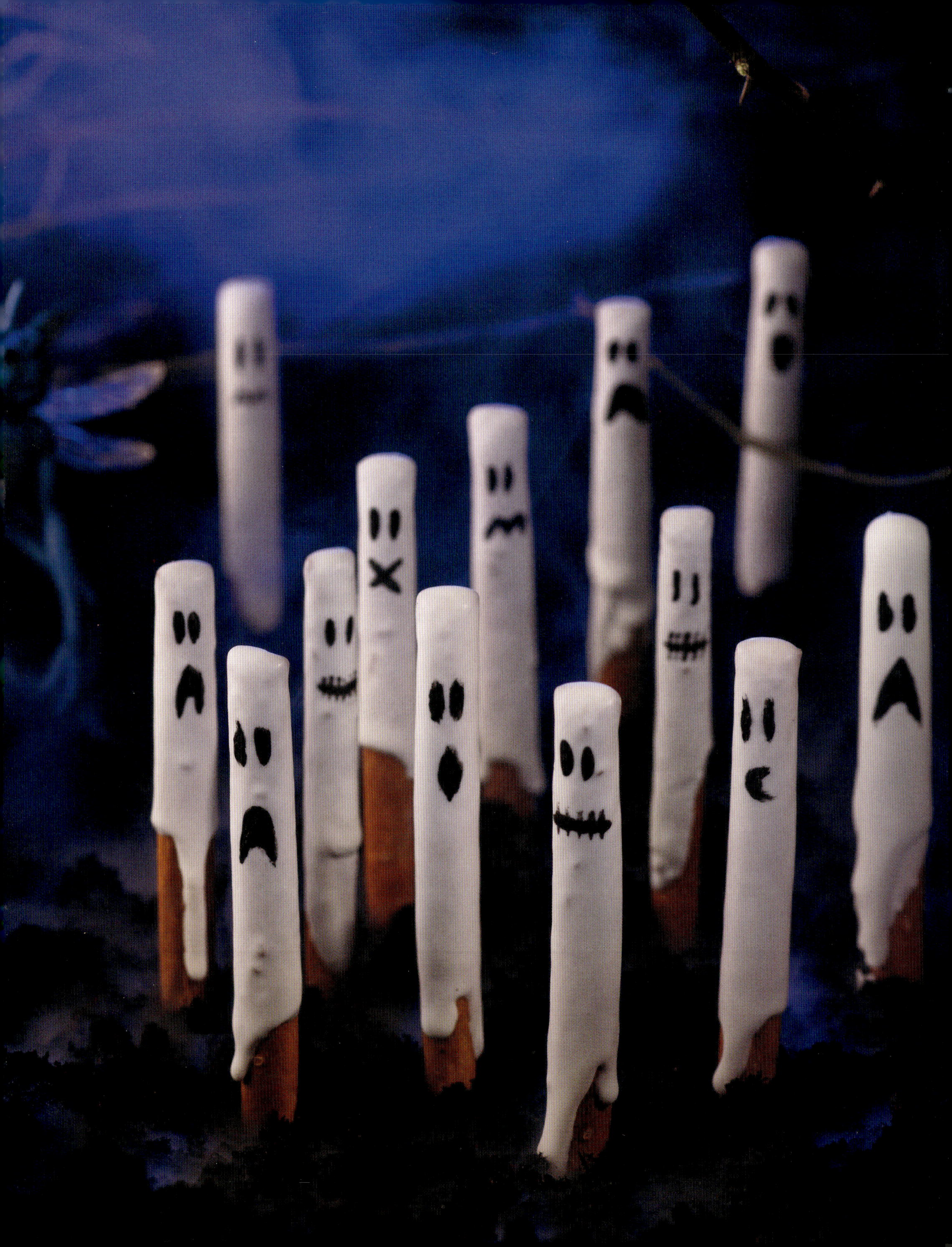

GHOST PRETZELS

INGREDIENTS FOR APPROX. 20 PRETZELS
5 oz white couverture chocolate, coarsely chopped
5 oz thick pretzel sticks

Also needed:
black food pen, sugar thermometer

1. Set up a water bath. To do this, put water in a saucepan, place a smaller metal ladle in it and warm it on the stove over low heat. Then melt ⅔ of the coarsely chopped couverture in it; make sure that the underside of the bowl does not touch the water, and that the water does not boil! Once the couverture has completely melted, add the remaining chocolate and allow to cool slightly. Then gently heat the chocolate mixture back up to 90 °F (check with a sugar thermometer) and remove the chocolate from the water bath.

2. Dip the pretzel sticks into the flowing chocolate, as the couverture quickly solidifies again when it cools down. Cover the salt sticks with ⅔ of the white chocolate and then place them upright in a glass, with the chocolate side up and a little distance between them so that they do not stick together.

3. Let the pretzels dry for about 15 minutes. Once the chocolate is dry, use a black food pen to draw spooky ghost shapes on the couverture.

Special thanks

Just as you can't conjure up good food and drink out of nothing according to "Gamp's Law of Elemental Transfiguration," no one - Muggle or wizard - produces a book like this all by themselves. (Quite possibly, this is another "Major Exception" to "Gamp's Law"). In fact, numerous talented people have worked wonders over a period of months, even without magical powers, to ensure that you now have this work in your hands. They are: Jo Löffler & Holger Jo Löffler & Holger "Holle" Wiest, my "dinos", without whom nothing would be the way it is; Roberts "Rob" Urlovskis, who uses a PC instead of a magic wand to work his magic; Angelos Tsirigotis, my Swabian Greek, for his terrific contributions to this book; Oskar "Ossi" Böhm & Annelies Haubold; the K-Clan with Tobi, Andrea, Finja & Lea; Katharina "the only true cat" Böhm; my "brother from another mother" Thomas B. together with his appendix, for many unforgettable moments in the past, present and future; Ulrich "The Pest" Peste, for the same reasons; Dimitrie Harder, my "partner in crime" in all things cooking and baking books, and the only person on earth who ever called me a "bully" with impunity; Thomas Stamm and his wife Alexandra, for appreciation and friendship; and last but not least Karin Michelberger, Franz-Christoph Heel, as well as the always-patient Hannah Kwella, for many great projects. For everything you like about this book, thanks go to these wonderful people. On the other hand, the author is responsible for any shortcomings in content, questionable wording, incorrect quantities, and too much butter-vanilla flavoring. In any case, we are always happy to receive praise, suggestions and criticism, preferably via the following social media channels:

Tom Grimm

- @tom.grimm.autor
- @tom.grimm.autor
- www.grinningcat.de

over	follow	know	again
change	same	turn	after

Bonus Words

eyes
funny

Name_____

Name_____

around   because   need   land
try   off   different   big

Bonus Words

together
under

little	back	very	came
need	also	new	must

Bonus Words

laugh
feet

Name

Name

read picture does say
page show great should

Bonus Words

write
hear

where	through	went	away
air	high	world	home

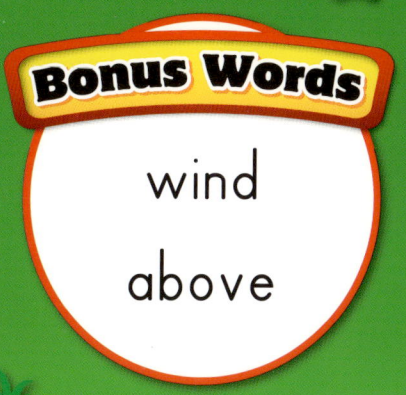

Bonus Words

wind

above

Name_____

CD-140084 © Carson-Dellosa

Name_____

| animal | play | think | why |
| take | point | put | kind |

Bonus Words

happy
watch

mother	ask	only	another
answer	place	old	good

Bonus Words

who

night

Name_____

CD-140084 © Carson-Dellosa

Name

live	much	name	large
such	found	still	another

Bonus Words

family
sleep

large	years	because	old
live	end	us	tell

Bonus Words

plant

earth

Name_____

© Carson-Dellosa

CD-140084

Name_____

animal	house	want	work
help	small	here	things

Bonus Words

country

river